JUSTICE, DISCRETION AND POVERTY

Supplementary Benefit Appeal Tribunals in Britain

Edited by

Michael Adler and Anthony Bradley

Reprint 1982

PROFESSIONAL BOOKS LIMITED
Milton Trading Estate
Abingdon, Oxon OX14 4SY
England

Printed and published
in Great Britain in 1982 by
Professional Books Ltd.
Milton Trading Estate, Abingdon
Oxfordshire

ISBN 0 903486 08 3 (Paperback)
      0 903486 09 1

This book has been typeset in 11pt Times by Inforum Limited of
Portsmouth and printed by Professional Books Limited.

CONTENTS
Abbreviations and acknowledgments

ABBREVIATIONS

The 1943 Act:	Unemployment Assistance Act 1934.
The 1948 Act:	National Assistance Act 1948.
The 1966 Act:	Ministry of Social Security Act 1966; by section 99(18) of the Social Security Act 1973, this Act is now to be cited as the Supplementary Benefit Act 1966.
CPAG:	Child Poverty Action Group
DHSS:	Department of Health and Social Security.
ECA:	exceptional circumstance addition, being a regular addition to weekly benefit payable under the 1966 Act, Schedule 2, para. 4(1)(a).
ENP:	exceptional needs payment, being a lump sum payment to meet exceptional needs, payable under the 1966 Act, section 7.
FIS:	family income supplement, payable under the Family Income Supplements Act 1970.
Handbook:	Supplementary Benefits Handbook, 2nd. edn., 1974.
IO:	(Local) Insurance Officer, who decides claims for national insurance benefit at first instance, and appears before national insurance local tribunals in the case of appeals.

LTA:	long term addition to the normal rates of benefit, formerly payable to supplementary pensioners and certain other recipients of supplementary benefit under the 1966 Act, Schedule 2, paras. 11 and 12. The LTA was superseded in 1975 when new long-term scale rates were introduced.
MAT:	medical appeal tribunal, which hears appeals from medical boards under the National Insurance (Industrial Injuries) Act 1965.
NAB:	National Assistance Board, established by the 1948 Act.
NAT:	National Assistance Appeal Tribunal, established by the 1948 Act.
NI:	National Insurance.
NILT:	National Insurance Local Tribunal appointed to hear appeals under the National Insurance Act 1965 and the National Insurance (Industrial Injuries) Act 1965.
PAC:	public assistance committee (through which local authorities exercised their public assistance functions before the 1948 Act).
PO:	Prescribing Officer, a specialist officer who represents the Commission at supplementary benefit appeal tribunals.
RT:	rent tribunal appointed under the Rent Act 1968.
SB:	Supplementary Benefit.
SBAT:	Supplementary Benefit Appeal Tribunal, established by the 1966 Act.
SBC:	Supplementary Benefits Commission, established by the 1966 Act.
UAB:	Unemployment Assistance Board, established by the 1934 Act.

ACKNOWLEDGMENTS

The editors wish to express their thanks to the Nuffield Foundation for financing the conference held at Edinburgh University in December 1974 which has given rise to this book and for meeting the cost of retyping the conference papers. They also wish to thank Miss Helen Dignan for her help with the conference arrangements and, together with Mrs. Sheila Smith, for the excellent way in which they have helped to prepare the papers for publication.

I INTRODUCTION
Michael Adler and Anthony Bradley

The problem of poverty in Britain today is a very considerable one. The major statutory means of dealing with the financial aspects of poverty is the Supplementary Benefits Act 1966 which, for the first time, gave households whose resources are less than their requirements as laid down by Parliament a right to benefit. At the same time, the 1966 Act gave the Supplementary Benefits Commission, which administers the supplementary benefits scheme, very considerable discretionary powers to ensure that the payment of benefit corresponds to the individual needs of claimants and their dependants. This book is primarily concerned with the standards of justice which characterise the administration of discretion towards poor people.

Since the Second World War, the number of individuals in Britain who have been wholly or partly dependent first on means-tested national assistance and then on its successor supplementary benefits has not declined, as Beveridge hoped, but has instead increased threefold. In December 1973, supplementary benefit was being paid to 2,675,000 people to meet their own needs and those of 1,347,000 dependants, altogether to 4,022,000 people. With the prospect of unemployment running at an even higher level in 1976 than in 1975, the numbers dependent on supplementary benefit are likely to increase still further.

The scale of the administrative machinery required to conduct this operation is immense, not only because of the numbers involved but also because of the difficulties involved in administering a complex means-test and in exercising the very wide discretionary powers of the Supplementary Benefits Commission to respond to the financial needs of individuals and families. The task of deciding which of these needs should be met from public funds is often one of great difficulty requiring sensitive administration, and disputes inevitably will arise between claimants and officials whose perceptions of need may differ considerably.

I

Since 1934, there has been provision for such disputes to be settled, not in Parliament or through the courts, but in special tribunals established for the purpose. These tribunals, which are now called Supplementary Benefit Appeal Tribunals, have a very important role to play in dispensing justice and in ensuring that the supplementary benefits scheme functions properly according to the legislation and the principles which underlie it.

In recent years there has been mounting criticism — from academic observers, rights organisations and other pressure groups — of the work of SBATs. Although some relevant aspects of these tribunals (notably the extension of legal aid and the promotion of wider lay representation) have quite recently been actively considered by official committees, the structure of supplementary benefit tribunals has not received similar consideration. We therefore decided in 1974 that it would be appropriate to convene a conference to discuss deficiencies in the Supplementary Benefit Appeal Tribunal system and ways in which these could be overcome. With the financial support of the Nuffield Foundation, we organised a two-day conference on Supplementary Benefit Appeal Tribunals which was held at Edinburgh University on 13th and 14th December 1974. This book is one result of that conference.

The conference was sponsored by the Socio-Legal Studies Committee of the University. Its aim was to consider the historical development, functions and operation of the system of supplementary benefits appeal tribunals; their place within the administration of the supplementary benefits scheme; and possible improvements to the system. It was attended by 40 people drawn from university departments of law and social administration; welfare rights organisations; and welfare rights workers from local government, the trade unions and other voluntary organisations. There were also present two chairmen and one member of SBATs, as well as observers from the Department of Health and Social Security, the Lord Chancellor's Office and the Council on Tribunals.

Eleven papers were presented to the conference, all of which have been reproduced — some after substantial revision — in this book. The book also contains two papers (by Richard Wilding and Hilary Rose) which were not presented to the conference. Both these papers had previously been published in *Social Work Today* and are included in the book both because they represent perspectives which were absent from the conference and because they are not as well known as they deserve to be.

The chapters of this book are grouped into four sections concerned respectively with the historical background to the present system of supplementary benefit adjudication, with the concept of discretion and its place in the scheme, with the actual functioning of tribunals, and with proposals for reforming the system. The origins of the SBAT system can be traced directly back to the Unemployment Assistance Act 1934 and the Appeal Tribunals set up under that Act. In chapter 2, Tony Lynes discusses some of the arguments surrounding the establishment of Unemployment Assistance Tribunals and describes some of their main characteristics as they existed in the 1930s, when they were solely concerned with the unemployed and their right to assistance. In chapter 3, Anthony Bradley describes the role which National Assistance Tribunals played in the national assistance scheme from 1948 until they and the scheme were superseded by the 1966 Act. He reviews the evidence given to the Franks Committee and the Committee's findings, as these related to NATs, and considers those improvements in NATs which flowed directly from the Franks Report. These two chapters demonstrate the very strong element of administrative continuity in the structure of tribunals between 1934 and the present day and make it very clear that the characteristics of SBATs today can only be understood in historical perspective.

In chapter 4, Richard Wilding gives an account of the ways in which the Supplementary Benefits Commission has sought to exercise the wide discretionary powers given to it under the 1966 Act, in an attempt to resolve the conflicts of opposing principle implicit in the notion of rules governing the exercise of discretion. In the following chapter, Henry Hodge argues that discretion is effectively exercised only by those administrators who lay down the rules which govern the granting of benefit, since front-line staff are not free to depart from the rules and tribunals are equally reluctant to do so; he criticises SBATs for failing to exercise individual discretion and rubber-stamping the application of Commission policy. In chapter 6, Norman Lewis examines some of the legal problems associated with the exercise of discretion by tribunals and with judicial control over its exercise, distinguishing between full rights of appeal and judicial review on such grounds as abuse of discretion and improper considerations. He concludes that SBATs should be required to operate more closely within the legal framework set up for them. These three chapters together demonstrate that the role and functions of SBATs must be considered in the context of the supplementary benefits scheme as a whole.

Five of the six chapters in the third section consider the way in which the tribunals presently function. In chapter 7, Steve Burkeman illustrates some of the tribunals' present shortcomings on the basis of his considerable experience of tribunal advocacy in Liverpool. The following chapters are based on current or recent empirical research: by Ross Flockhart into the membership of tribunals (chapter 8); by Michael Adler, Elizabeth Burns and Rosemary Johnson into the conduct of tribunal hearings (chapter 9); by Coral Milton into the claimants' perceptions of the tribunal process (chapter 10) and by Hilary Rose into styles of representation (chapter 11). From their different perspectives, these chapters contribute towards our detailed understanding of the workings of the present system. Also in this section Martin Partington examines the work of the Parliamentary Commissioner for Administration in investigating complaints of injustice caused by maladministration within the supplementary benefits scheme (chapter 12).

The final section is devoted to proposals for reform. In chapter 13, after summarising some of the present shortcomings of SBATs, Ruth Lister puts forward proposals dealing with membership, the hearings themselves and the general structure and organisation of the appeals system. These reforms are within the context of the existing supplementary benefit scheme. Harry Calvert's proposals (in chapter 14) are far more sweeping in that he advocates the creation of a Social Security Commission with responsibility for overseeing adjudication throughout the entire social security system. The final chapter, by the editors, draws very considerably on the discussion which took place at the Edinburgh conference. We would like to thank all those who took part for the stimulating and constructive exchange of views which took place, without of course seeking to associate them in any way with the views we express. In this chapter we put gorward a set of principles upon which appeal tribunals should be based and proposals which would give effect to them.

As the statistics in Appendix A show, the number of cases handled by SBATs trebled between their introduction in 1966 and 1973. The decisions which these tribunals make in individual cases are of immense significance to the many poor people who are dependent, wholly or in part, on supplementary benefit for their livelihood. Yet there is much evidence to suggest that the standards of justice which are administered by these tribunals are both lower than they should be and also lower than those achieved in other tribunals. The case for reform is a very strong one. But, as with many other problems affecting poor people, the cause of tribunal reform suffers from a lack of powerful support e.g. from the political parties, the trade unions, the legal and other professions. One of our reasons for producing this book is the hope that it will influence public opinion and official thinking and thereby contribute in some way towards raising the standards of justice for poor people in this country. At the same time we hope that the book will be seen as a contribution to the developing field of socio-legal studies in Britain.

II UNEMPLOYMENT ASSISTANCE TRIBUNALS IN THE 1930s*
Tony Lynes

The origins of the Supplementary Benefit Appeal Tribunal system can be traced directly back to the Unemployment Assistance Act 1934, one of the most important pieces of social legislation of this century, which created a national assistance scheme for the unemployed. The appeal tribunals set up under that Act have undergone many changes in the past 40 years but their essential nature remains much the same. This chapter describes some of the main characteristics of the tribunals as they existed in the 1930s, when they were solely concerned with the unemployed and their right to assistance.

The political case for appeal tribunals

The existence of appeals machinery in the supplementary benefit scheme is now taken for granted, but it was not self-evident to the Ministers and officials concerned with the creation of the Unemployment Assistance Board (UAB) that applicants should have a right of appeal against its decisions. In a perceptive survey of the origins of the National Assistance Tribunals which replaced the Unemployment Assistance Tribunals in 1948, George Lach has argued that appeal tribunals under the unemployment assistance scheme were historically inevitable, since the unemployed had been accustomed to Courts of Referees deciding doubtful claims to benefit and, since 1931, had become accustomed to making representations to the local Public Assistance Committees (PACs) about the refusal

* This chapter is based on research on the policies and administrative practices of the Unemployment Assistance Board carried out by the author while employed as a research officer at the Centre for Environmental Studies and financed by a grant from the Social Science Research Council. Most of the material quoted is to be found in the files of the UAB deposited in the Public Record Office and catalogued in two classes: AST 7 (general correspondence) and AST 13 (codes of instructions and circulars). The author will be glad to supply references to individual files on request. Unpublished material in the Public Record Office, for which Crown Copyright is reserved, is reproduced by permission of the Controller of H.M.S.O.

or the amount of transitional payments (the locally administered means-tested benefit which unemployment assistance was to replace).[1] But there was no formal right of appeal against the decisions of the PACs and the proposal which Neville Chamberlain (then Chancellor of the Exchequer) put to his Cabinet colleagues in the early months of 1933 for a national Commission, to take over from the PACs not just the relief of the unemployed but the whole field of public assistance other than institutional care, similarly did not envisage any appeal machinery external to the Commission itself. Chamberlain and Hilton Young (Minister of Health) explained that the Commission would have "a semi-judicial character" and could itself hear appeals from the decisions of its local officials. An outside appeal body would weaken the Commission's independence and powers of control and would probably result in a large number of appeals. At most, Chamberlain thought, the right of appeal to a tribunal might be conceded in cases where the division of responsibility between the Commission and the local authority was at issue.[2]

Against this view, the Minister of Labour, Sir Henry Betterton (later to become the first Chairman of the UAB and to be elevated to the peerage as Lord Rushcliffe), who wanted the Commission to deal only with the unemployed, argued strongly that they should have the right of appeal to an outside body, both on the amount of relief granted and on the Commission's interpretation of the regulations governing the scheme. Neither Parliament nor public opinion would tolerate a situation in which the only appeal possible was from one official to another.[3] The result, he feared, would be that the Minister would be held responsible for decisions on individual cases,[4] which was precisely what the Government was trying to avoid by appointing a Commission.

Chamberlain agreed that appeals to a tribunal might be allowed where it was alleged that the Commission had not complied with the regulations, but not where there was disagreement about the use of discretion by the Commission, since this would not only weaken the Commission but would mean that there would be a number of tribunals all over the country each giving different decisions.[5] In other words, there should be a right of appeal to a local tribunal only on a point of law (the possibility of different tribunals making conflicting decisions on questions of law does not seem to have caused any serious misgiving). In the end a compromise was arrived at. Section 39(5) of the 1934 Act provided that an appeal against the determination of an allowance should not go before the full tribunal without the leave of the chairman, which could only be given if it appeared to him that there was reason to doubt whether the regulations had been properly applied or that there were other special circumstances affecting the case. This solution was, in fact, proposed by Betterton himself. He argued that it was essential to ensure that the appeal machinery kept to its "proper job" and did not attempt to alter the general standards laid down in the statutory scales and rules. The kinds of special circumstances in which, he suggested, appeals should be heard by the tribunals would include mortgages, hire purchase debts, the cost of maintaining the higher personal standards expected of teachers, clerks, shop assistants, etc., convalescence, voluntary insurance premiums, and the maintenance of children at fee-paying institutions.[6]

Underlying Betterton's insistence on the need for appeal tribunals was the fact that the first task of the Unemployment Assistance Board (as the Commission was called) was that of establishing a national scale of relief for the unemployed, based on the principle of a household means test, to replace the payments being made by the PACs under the "transitional payments" scheme. Transitional payments were a form of means-tested unemployment benefit—the latest in a series of expedients to help those whose normal unemployment insurance benefit entitlement had expired. In theory they were based on the standards applied locally to unemployed people receiving public assistance but, in practice, transitional payments were often administered more generously, with little regard for the earnings of other members of the household which, according to the rules, should have been treated as available for the maintenance of the unemployed person. It was both expected and intended that the application of the UAB's uniform scale in place of the varied practices of the PACs would lead to large numbers of cuts. The appeal tribunals offered one means of countering the dissatisfaction which the cuts were bound to produce. They were also one of the features of unemployment assistance which would differentiate it from public assistance under the Poor Law, an objective to which Betterton attached great political importance.

The creation of the unemployment assistance tribunals was thus a deliberate political act, aimed at making an inherently unpopular reform more acceptable and at the same time protecting the Minister of Labour from the impact of parliamentary and public criticism of the actions of the Board and its officials. It had little to do with any abstract ideas of justice or legal rights. The judicial role of the tribunals was from the start played down.

A circular issued by the Board to its officers in December 1934 on the subject of appeal tribunals stressed that, while some of their functions were judicial in nature, involving issues of law or the imposition of "disciplinary and deterrent conditions" on applicants who refused work or failed to maintain themselves or their dependants, their main function was administrative rather than judicial:

> "The Tribunal acting as a Tribunal on ordinary appeals against determinations of need will be acting in an administrative capacity exercising the same discretion upon the facts before it as the officers of the Board might exercise, but no more. It will really be expressing a second (and final) opinion on the case in its own right as a competent administrative body and will not be sitting in judgment upon the officer's determination or deciding an issue between the Area Officer and the applicant. In this connexion it must be remembered that the issues arising on such determinations will frequently be a matter of opinion and it cannot be too clearly realised that a successful appeal does not necessarily connote a careless or unsound first decision."

There is a remarkable similarity between this view and the comparison which the Franks Committee was to draw 23 years later between a National Assistance Tribunal and "an assessment or case committee, taking a further look at the facts and in some cases arriving at a fresh decision on the extent of need".[7]

· The Board's first annual report, for the period to 31 December 1935, stated that the statutory rules of procedure (the Unemployment Assistance (Appeal Tribunals) Provisional Rules, 1934) "were designed to reduce formality of procedure to a minimum, the aim being to allow chairmen to conduct proceedings as easy, friendly examinations of facts, bound as little as possible by formal rules".[8] Summing up its account of the tribunals' first year of operation, the report said, "There is little doubt that they play a real part in spreading confidence in the Board's administration among applicants. Many District Officers report that while relatively small use may be in fact made of the tribunal system, the knowledge that it is available is widespread, and this knowledge acts as a safety valve among aggrieved applicants."[9] A safety valve, however, is an integral part of the machine.

Constitution of tribunals and appointment of members

If the tribunal was to be an "outside" body, decisions had to be made as to its composition. A number of possibilities were considered. Finally, it was decided that each tribunal should consist of a chairman appointed by the Minister of Labour, a workpeople's representative appointed by the UAB from a panel drawn up by the Minister, and a representative of the UAB. Thus two members of this supposedly impartial body were appointed by the UAB, one of whom was appointed specifically to represent its interests, while the third was appointed by the Minister answerable to Parliament for the operation of the scheme. The proposal to constitute the tribunals in this way was commended to the Cabinet Committee by Betterton, in a memorandum dated June 28 1933, as being "designed to give as much protection to the general standards of the Commission as is practicable".[10] As an additional precaution, the rules provided that a member's appointment should be terminated if he or a member of his household applied for an unemployment assistance allowance.

There were initially 138 local tribunals, each with a chairman and one or more reserve chairmen — 353 in all, 22 of whom were women. The Courts of Referees which adjudicated on unemployment insurance questions provided an obvious source of recruitment for the unemployment assistance tribunals, but they had legally qualified chairmen and legal knowledge was felt to be of less importance in unemployment assistance appeals. Moreover, as Wilfred Eady, the official appointed as the first Secretary of the UAB, observed, if the same person was to hold both offices (a possibility which was not at first excluded, though the Board later decided that it was undesirable), he would have to be "competent to understand that he will be working under two different codes". Although the Minister of Labour was responsible for appointing the chairmen, it was accepted that the Board had an interest in the matter and its officials did not hesitate to express their views to the Ministry (the fact that most of these officials, including Eady, had come to the Board from the Ministry made the relationship a particularly close one, though it was to become strained at times, usually when the Ministry sought to exert what the UAB officials considered undue influence in the Board's affairs). The Ministry's Divisional Controllers were asked to recommend suitable persons for appointment as chairmen. A memorandum of guidance issued to them stated:

"Apart from members of the legal profession, the field should be regarded as including other persons of standing in the locality with experience, either official or unofficial, of dealing with administration whether in central or local government, or in the running of important voluntary organisations, or possessing experience as a magistrate. Due weight should be given to experience in all branches of public administration, including public assistance, education, housing and health. Persons to be selected should of course have a general knowledge of industrial and working class conditions in the areas for which they are to sit."

Persons active in party politics were generally to be excluded, as were "employers or directors of companies employing a considerable number of workpeople, and persons actively connected with organisations of employers or employed persons", since they would not be regarded as possessing the necessary impartiality. Such persons might, however, be included "provided that their personal qualifications are satisfactory and that the regard in which they are held in the locality would outweigh considerations adverse to their selection".

In addition to the considerations mentioned above, there was a further reason for steering clear of chairmen of Courts of Referees, cogently expressed by one of the UAB officials, A.P. Hughes-Gibb: "Chairmen of Courts of Referees would be convenient and no doubt quite suitable candidates. But I am rather anxious about the effect on the minds of our clients of a large number of such appointments. 'Turned down by the Court of Referees' has rather unpleasant associations in the (transitional payments) world: and I think the Courts are quite unreasonably regarded with some suspicion in these quarters as part of a convenient administrative arrangement for getting rid of tiresome claimants. We want to establish from the first a reputation for impartiality." That the fear of the tribunals' reputation being tarnished by association with the Courts of Referees was not wholly unfounded is borne out by two comments by the Board's District Officers in its first annual report. C.G. Ward (London II District) wrote: " . . . more than one Area Officer reports that applicants are slow to use their right of appeal and regard the Tribunals with some suspicion as being only Courts of Referees under another name";[11] while J. Emrys Thomas (Wrexham) reported: "At the outset applicants were inclined to look upon the Appeal Tribunals as similar to the Courts of Referees", but added: "This misconception has since been dispelled".[12]

The selection of the Board's representatives on the tribunals raised questions of a rather different kind. A degree of impartiality might be desirable but was not the only consideration. George Reid, later to succeed Wilfred Eady as Secretary of the Board, argued strongly for the appointment of officials: "I do not see how a person can by virtue merely of being a respectable citizen be said in any real sense to 'represent' the Board. It seems to me that the only person who can 'represent the Board' is one who enjoys the Board's confidence and is amenable to its instructions. The obvious person who satisfies these conditions is an officer of the Board." Eady, however, was equally strongly opposed to this suggestion and it was decided that, as a general rule, suitable non-official persons should be appointed, although the District Officer was to be a reserve member of each tribunal in his district. The Board's instructions to officers stressed the importance of the District Officer's role:

"He will have to keep in close touch with the working of the

Tribunals in his District. He may attend sittings as an observer with the leave of the Chairman. On occasion, he may have to sit on a Tribunal itself as a representative of the Board, but this is only contemplated where suitable non-official representation of the Board is unobtainable or there are very special reasons for ensuring that the Board's point of view in a particular case shall be put and maintained with the greatest possible official authority available."

It was in areas such as Durham and South Wales that difficulty was expected in finding reliable non-official representatives of the Board but, so far as is known, even in these areas District Officers did not in fact have to serve as regular members of the tribunals.

Once again, as in the selection of chairmen, the Ministry's Divisional Controllers were asked to suggest candidates. The Board explained to them the kind of people it had in mind: "In view of the direct representation of workpeople on the Tribunals it is clearly desirable to have a balancing factor. The Board's representative should therefore be a person of standing and personality who could be relied upon to appreciate and state the point of view of the Board as the trustee of the Unemployment Assistance Fund, the preponderant share of which . . . .is contributed by the general body of taxpayers." Accordingly, while employers and company directors were acceptable, "workpeople, persons connected with organisations of employed persons and others whose qualifications would fit them to sit as representatives of workpeople" were not. Retired civil servants were regarded as a hopeful source of recruits and the Establishments Officers of all Government departments were asked for suggestions. The outcome of all this activity was a list of over 5,000 people, out of whom 138 were appointed as substantive representatives and 589 as reserves (including the 28 District Officers). Ninety-five were women. "A large majority", the Board's annual report stated, "had their main contact with social conditions in commercial or professional work, combined in most cases with experience in Local Government administration or voluntary welfare work of one kind or another".[13] It is not difficult to discern a broad similarity between this group of people and those who now act as "other" members of Supplementary Benefit Appeal Tribunals, though the latter are not appointed as representatives of the Supplementary Benefits Commission.

Finally, the Minister of Labour, acting through the Local Employment Committees, nominated about 7,500 persons as panels of workpeople's representatives — an average of about 54 for each tribunal. There is no evidence that, in nominating panels of this size, the Minister sought to reduce the effectiveness of the workpeople's representatives by ensuring that each of them was called upon to act only at rare intervals, but this was inevitably the result. It was the Board itself which eventually took the initiative in asking the Minister to reduce the size of the panels, and this was done in 1937. The scale of the reduction is not known but it may be assumed that any individual workpeople's representative still appeared on the tribunal far less frequently than the other two members.

The Board's representatives on the tribunals were appointed initially for what may perhaps have been regarded as a probationary period of six months, after which they were reappointed annually (it is not known whether any of them proved unsatisfactory and were not reappointed). The chairmen were appointed annually from the start. Prior to their reappointment for 1936, the Board's District Officers were asked for a report on the performance of each chairman. The following year, it was decided that individual reports could be dispensed with, the District Officers being asked merely for general observations on the work of the chairmen. At the same time, Eady suggested to J.S. Nicholson, Principal Assistant Secretary at the Ministry of Labour, that it might save trouble if the appointments were now made for a period of three years. Nicholson's reply to this suggestion is revealing:". . . . we feel that until the Appeal Tribunals have been in existence for some time, it is desirable that the appointments should be reviewed annually. Apart from this and the probable repercussions of your proposal in connection with Courts of Referees, we feel that it is desirable that chairmen should not be encouraged to regard these appointments in any way as 'freeholds' and that it is wholesome for them to know that they are — or may be — considered on their merits every year."

The tribunal clerk

The Unemployment Assistance Act placed upon the UAB the duty of assigning a clerk to each appeal tribunal. In each of the 28 districts into which the Board's administrative structure was divided, an Assistant District Officer was appointed as clerk of the tribunals in the district. Great importance was attached to the clerk's role, since it was only through him that the Board could exert any direct control over the activities of the tribunals.

The Tribunal Rules required the clerk to be present "at all sittings of the chairman or the tribunal for the consideration of any matter under the Act".[14] This rule was not included in the preliminary draft prepared by the Solicitor's Department of the Ministry of Labour and must have been added in order to ensure that, at all relevant times, the clerk's restraining influence would be available to counteract any tendency for the tribunal or its chairman to stray from the path of virtue. This assumption is borne out by the instructions issued by the Board in 1934, in which no attempt was made to conceal the fact that, even while acting as clerk to the tribunal, he was regarded as answerable to the Board for the satisfactory performance of his duties as Assistant District Officer:

"Great importance is attached by the Board to the position and functions of the Clerk of the Tribunal. There is no superior Court above the Tribunals; their decisions are final. Upon the Clerk, therefore, falls a real responsibility for securing a measure of administrative co-ordination, particularly in the work of Chairmen when sitting without the other members of Tribunals to consider scope appeals and application for leave to appeal, but also in the work of the Tribunals sitting as such — though here the Clerk should be able to look to the member directly representing the Board for assistance. In view of these considerations it has been decided to provide by Statutory Rules under the Seventh Schedule that the Clerk or his deputy shall be present at all sittings at which any matter coming before a Chairman or a Tribunal is considered. This is designed to give to the Clerk a special standing and it is hoped that the Chairman and the Tribunal will look to him for guidance in consistent practice and in the avoidance of arbitrary findings unrelated to the broad practice of Tribunals and as an officer of the Board in constant touch with the Board's work, the Assistant District Officer should be in a specially favourable position to give counsel and advice where they are needed."

What dissatisfied applicants appealing to the tribunals against the Board's decisions thought about the fact that the clerk was a senior officer of the Board is not known. Probably most of them had no idea by whom the clerk was appointed or paid and, if they had known, would have been neither surprised nor shocked. One body which did question the propriety of officers of the Board acting as tribunal clerks was the Association of Municipal Corporations. The Association's interest in the matter derived from the fact that one of the functions of the tribunals was to decide in case of dispute whether a particular person came within the scope of the Unemployment Assistance scheme or remained the responsibility of the Public Assistance Committee of the local authority. Appeals of this kind were to be decided by the chairman sitting alone, not by the full tribunal, but the clerk was still required by the rules to be present and was expected to play an active part in the decision-making process. The memorandum of guidance on "question of scope" issued by the Board to its officers was also supplied to the tribunal chairmen and the clerks were urged to "make themselves fully acquainted with the contents of this document so that they may be in a position to help their chairmen both before and during sittings to understand any points on which they are not quite clear as to the views of the Board". They were encouraged, when necessary, to consult a senior officer of the Board before the hearing in order to clear up any difficulties.

Local authority officials attending "scope" hearings to put their case to the chairman may not have been aware of the extent to which the clerk was encouraged to influence the proceedings. Nevertheless, it is hardly surprising that they were sometimes critical of the fact that the clerk was an official of the body against whose decision they were appealing (appeals on scope could be brought by the local authority as well as by the applicant himself). In April 1937, on the "second appointed day" under the 1934 Act, the UAB took over responsibility for most of the able-bodied unemployed still in receipt of public assistance, but the Public Assistance Committees remained responsible for those who did not have a "normal occupation" insurable under the Contributory Pensions Acts, unless their failure to acquire such an occupation was due to the industrial circumstances of the district in which they lived. A large number of scope appeals resulted and there were complaints about the role of the clerks. At a meeting with local authority representatives in October 1937, Eady, assured them that "steps were being taken to bring to the notice of Clerks of Tribunals the importance of making it clear that they appeared at Tribunals in their capacity of officer of the Tribunal and not as officers of the Board". Whether they were entirely placated by this assurance is not known. At all events, the practice of officials of the Board acting as tribunal clerks and remaining with the tribunal throughout its deliberations continued without serious challenge and was in due course to be perpetuated in the procedure of the Supplementary Benefit Appeal Tribunals, whose clerks are officers of the Department of Health and Social Security.

The Presenting Officer

The Tribunal Rules permitted the officer of the Board concerned, or any other officer of the Board on his behalf, to attend and be heard at an oral appeal hearing.[15] The instructions issued by the Board specified that this task should normally be carried out by the Area Officer (i.e. the manager of the local office) but could be delegated to an Assistance Officer working in the area office. Cases of particular importance could be taken by an officer from the district office. The function of the Board's officer at the hearing was defined in the instructions as "merely to elucidate before the Tribunal the facts of the case presented in the submission papers". He must not present at the hearing any new points which were not set out in the papers sent out to the tribunal members and to the appellant before the hearing. The instructions reminded him that he had no right to cross-examine the appellant or the friend who was allowed to accompany him. He should not ask leading questions or attempt to confuse or trip up the appellant or his friend. If he thought it important to contest any statement but could not do so by a direct statement which he was in a position to prove, he was instructed that the proper course was to ask for an adjournment so that the matter could be investigated; and he was reminded that, if the tribunal went ahead and made a decision on a basis that was afterwards shown to be false, that decision could be put aside by the issue of a new determination by an officer of the Board.

In short, while it was clearly envisaged that the officer of the Board at the hearing would act as an advocate for the Board's point of view, he was not expected to behave in a way that would introduce an unduly adversarial atmosphere into the proceedings.

Representation

Strictly speaking, the Tribunal Rules did not allow representation of appellants at appeal hearings. The preliminary draft of the rules envisaged that representation by "a person approved by the Chairman" would be permitted, but the final version provided that "the person concerned may be accompanied by a friend(not being of counsel or a solicitor and appearing as such) for the purpose of assisting the chairman or the tribunal (as the case may be) in the elucidation of the facts .... "[16]

On average, about one appellant in six was accompanied by a friend, the proportion remaining fairly constant between 1935 and 1938. Then as now, those performing this role included friends, relatives, trade union representatives, "welfare" workers, and members of political bodies and pressure groups. The National Unemployed Workers' Movement, a communist-dominated body with some similarities to present-day claimants' unions, was particularly active in both encouraging appeals and accompanying applicants at tribunal hearings. Some of its members made regular appearances as the "friend" of numerous appellants. Inevitably it is only where their behaviour gave grounds for complaint that a record of their activities has survived. In October 1935, for example, the clerk of the Walsall tribunal reported that Councillor G.W. Newman, alleged to be a communist (according to the Walsall Area Officer the local colliery companies refused to employ him because of his political activities), had appeared as an appellant's friend and "proceeded to address the tribunal and generally conduct the case, without reference to the appellant, who made no remarks". When the clerk suggested that "the question of advocacy arose", Newman had insisted on his right to present the case; he "became rather excited and accused the tribunal of wishing to starve the applicants". Eventually the chairman asked him to withdraw, which he did, saying that "he should bring some 200 men to the Area Office — obviously with the idea of making a demonstration".

Some confusion was caused by the fact that another gentleman named Newman was active in the Hanley District and was at first thought to be the same man. He was a prominent NUWM member, himself one of the Board's applicants, and had appeared as "friend" before the Potteries tribunal on at least six occasions between March and October 1935. The District Officer reported that his case was being "closely watched" with a view to the possibility of cutting off his allowance on the grounds that, as a result of his NUWM activities, he was not "available for work" as required by section 36(1) of the 1934 Act.

These examples, however, are clearly atypical, and there is no evidence that either the Board or the tribunals were in any way opposed to appellants being accompanied by "friends", provided that the friends' activities were limited to helping to present the facts. The Board's officers were instructed that they must not regard the appellant's friend as a "hostile witness", and the annual report for 1936 commented: "A number of appellants have brought 'friends' with them to attend the hearing of their appeals and the attendance of the 'friend' has frequently been of material assistance to the tribunal in elucidating the facts of the case."[17]

There was no serious pressure for the admission of legal representatives to tribunal hearings during the 1930s, but this question was raised by the Secretary of the Law Society in a letter to Sir Walter Womersley, Minister of Pensions, in September 1940. It is perhaps significant that the Law Society's knowledge of the subject was so deficient that its approach was made to the wrong Minister! The letter pointed out that under the Supplementary Pensions (Appeal Tribunals) Rules, 1940 (the Assistance Board's main function now having changed to that of paying means-tested supplementary pensions) appellants could not be represented by counsel or solicitor, and referred to the advantages which tribunals would derive if legal representation were permitted "since there would be some certainty that the case would be properly presented without irrelevancies and consequent waste of time." It also pointed out that it was not in the public interest that members of the public should be deprived of the normal right of legal representation and urged that the matter should be reconsidered with a view to the amendment of the regulations. The letter was passed on to the Board, which sent a courteous but discouraging reply.

Tribunal decisions and the Board's policies

Some of the ways in which the Board sought to ensure that the tribunals would not step too far out of line with its policies have been mentioned above. To a considerable extent, however, the Board's policies were embodied in instructions to its officers, which were not generally available to the public. Although Oliver Stanley, who had succeeded Betterton as Minister of Labour in 1934, urged that the Board should be prepared at least to place a copy of these instructions in the Library of the House of Commons, the Board consistently maintained that confidential instructions to its officers on the use of their discretionary powers could not be made public, even in this limited way. Absolute refusal to publish the instructions, however, was not only likely to cause political difficulties but also conflicted with the Board's wish to acquaint the tribunals with the lines along which its officers were working and to which it hoped the tribunals would conform. As Eady explained in a letter to Sir Thomas Phillips, Permanent Secretary to the Ministry of Labour, on January 22, 1935, two weeks after the Board commenced payment of allowances to the unemployed, it had been decided that "a memorandum on the interpretation of the Regulations" should be issued to the Board's representatives on the tribunals. "If it is issued to the Board's representatives it will clearly have to be issued to the Chairman, and I think inevitably also to the workpeople's representative. It will thus become a public document." The solution adopted was to publish the initial instructions to the Board's officers in the form of a white paper, edited so that it no longer read as a series of direct instructions.[18]

It is ironic that, throughout the debate on the non-publication of the Board's (and the Commission's) instructions that has now continued intermittently for 40 years, it has never been generally realized that the UAB's original instructions on the calculation of allowances and the exercise of discretion actually *were* published. Subsequently the practice was adopted of issuing to tribunal members copies of circulars dealing with particular aspects of policy, such as adjustment of allowances in special circumstances and winter additions, so that they were kept informed of the main lines of the Board's policies, though they did not receive the detailed and increasingly voluminous instructions issued to the Board's officers. It is doubtful whether they would have made much of these instructions even if they had received them. As early as April 1936, the Board's Director of Finance and Establishments, A.E. Watson, was complaining to Eady: "For anybody not closely in touch with the day to day administration of the regulations it is already impossible without a great expenditure of time to find instructions on any given point of policy or procedure, and even after an instruction .... is found there is nothing to show whether it is the complete instruction on any given matter." He suggested that a real attempt should be made to codify the instructions with a view to preparing memoranda for the guidance of local advisory committees and MPs (and, presumably, for the appeal tribunals): " ... if we were able to produce a fair number of leaflets of this kind we should probably meet every reasonable demand of Members for information as to the Board's work. They would be corrected and republished from time to time." Codification, however, was not achieved until 1940, and another 30 years elapsed before a comprehensive memorandum on the use of discretion, the Supplementary Benefits Handbook, was published — though not everybody would agree that the Handbook meets "every reasonable demand for information".

The statement in the Board's first annual report that "The circular instructions issued to officers to guide them in dealing with cases have been made accessible to the Tribunals and a considerable number of memoranda explaining the Board's policy and practice in matters on which Tribunals have asked for special information have been prepared from time to time"[19] should not, therefore, be taken to mean that tribunal members were supplied with the 1935 equivalent of the "A Code". What they did receive were detailed explanations of some of the policies underlying the Board's treatment of the individual cases coming before the tribunal. There is no evidence that the Board or its officials felt that there was any impropriety in briefing the tribunals in this way. Nor does there seem to have been much complaint on this score from other quarters. Indeed, in March 1938, when a minor change of policy had occurred following representations by the TUC, a letter to the UAB from the General Secretary of the TUC suggested that chairmen and members of tribunals should be notified, "as reports have been received to the effect that these persons are not always aware of the instructions issued to the Board's officers."

As in the matter of the Board's officials acting as tribunal clerks, the sole dissenting voice seems to have been that of the Association of Municipal Corporations, one of whose representatives at the meeting in October 1937, mentioned above, referred to "the system under which Chairmen of Tribunals had received copies of the Board's Instructions". Eady replied that differences of opinion between local authorities and the Board regarding the scope of the 1934 Act turned less on the contents of the instructions than on the application to particular cases. "If the instructions had not been put in the hands of the Chairmen," he added, "the alternative would have been for the Board's officer to expound the relevant parts of the instruction as occasion arose." At the same meeting, other local authority representatives complained of variation between the decisions of different chairmen on similar cases and it may be supposed that such variations would have been considerably greater if the chairmen had been left wholly without guidance. It was undoubtedly true, moreover, that whenever a chairman was considering a scope appeal the Board would quite legitimately have wanted to ensure that he was aware of their interpretation of the Act, and a good deal of time and trouble was saved by simply providing him with a copy of the instructions. Yet the fact remains that, however pure the Board's motives might have been, its actions invited the accusation that it was trying to exert improper influence on chairmen. This dilemma has never been fully resolved, and the present-day practice of supplying all SBAT members with the Supplementary Benefits Handbook, whatever its practical justification, is open to precisely the same criticism.

Sometimes the Board's officers intervened more directly to bring the tribunals into line with the policies of the Board. One issue on which tribunals tended to take an independent view was that of families breaking up in order to minimize the effects of the household means test. In calculating the amount of assistance payable to an applicant, the Board was required to take into account (subject to certain disregards) the resources of all members of the household. A young unemployed man living with his parents could thus be denied assistance on the grounds that his father's wages were sufficient to maintain him; or, if he were working and his father unemployed, he might find that his presence in the household was preventing his father from receiving assistance from the Board. In either situation, the obvious solution was for the son to move out into lodgings, so that he would no longer be a member of the same household as his father. In addition to the many cases where this actually happened, there were undoubtedly others where the applicant claimed to have left home though he had not in fact done so. The Board was concerned both about the possibility of fraud and about the consequences, for the families involved and for its own reputation, of cases where the move was genuine. Even in the genuine cases, there was a fundamental difference between those where the unemployed man had been compelled to leave home because the family refused to support him and those where "collusion" had occurred and he had left of his own accord, though possibly claiming to have been thrown out.

To cope with this problem, the Board adopted the principle of the "constructive household". Unless it was clear that the applicant had been compelled to leave home, he was treated as if he were still a member of the household and his allowance (if any) assessed accordingly. Towards the end of 1935, District Officers in both Liverpool and Manchester reported that special measures had been necessary to persuade local appeal tribunals to follow this principle. In Manchester, there had been a difference of opinion between the District Officer, F.W. Fletcher, and the Manchester South and East Tribunal on the question of the onus of proof. The Tribunal Chairman, Mr. J.C. Jolly, took the view that "it was the responsibility of the Board's officers to satisfy the Tribunal that the applicant's removal was voluntary, or made in collusion with his family, in cases where it was not possible to reach this conclusion by examination of the applicant at the hearing". Fletcher was concerned that, if tribunals accepted too readily that a change of residence justified the grant of an allowance, the practice of leaving home for this purpose would become more prevalent. He doubted, therefore, whether Jolly's view was "in accordance with sound public policy" (there was no suggestion that the tribunal's decisions were wrong in law; if anything, it was the "constructive household" principle that was of doubtful legality). Fletcher's report continues:

"In view of the considerations mentioned, it has been thought to be desirable to stress the seriousness of the position which might arise in the absence of effective check, and it was decided to invite the consideration of the Tribunal to the question on broad lines. Accordingly, Mr. Harvie, Assistant District Officer, attended the Tribunal sitting at Openshaw on the 10th October, at which two appeals of this type were to be heard, and with the Chairman's consent discussed the matter from the points of view outlined above. The Tribunal appreciated very keenly the force of the submissions made, and recognised the undesirability of the creation in the minds of applicants of erroneous impressions as a result of their decision in these cases."

Of the two cases referred to, one appellant had already found work and did not attend the hearing, while the other was closely questioned by the tribunal which decided that "the removal could not be regarded as compulsory". The Board's decision was confirmed in both cases.

From Liverpool, the District Officer, C. Marshall, reported:

"Tribunals were inclined to the view that if an applicant was living in lodgings and not as a member of a household, he was legally entitled to an allowance . . ., and in order to secure a different and broader outlook on this question so far as it applied to doubtful cases, the Clerk explained the District Office policy and pointed out the social inequalities that must inevitably arise from a general acceptance of the above view."

This blatant attempt by the clerk to persuade the tribunal to adopt the Board's policy seems to have been successful, temporarily at least. On the next two occasions when appeals of this sort were being heard, the Board's case was presented by an Assistant District Officer and the tribunal confirmed both determinations. Marshall reported that the tribunals had also "readily accepted the principle of interviewing the parent (if his attendance can be secured) before granting an increased allowance to an applicant who states that he has been evicted from home."

It should not be assumed, however, that the tribunals were always as compliant as these examples suggest, even when the Board's policy and the reasons for it had been explained to them. A year later, in November 1936, a summary of the situation regarding "leaving home" cases in the districts mainly concerned showed that a substantial proportion of them were the subject of appeals and that the success rate in these appeals was, if anything, higher than the average for all appeals in 1936 (the success rate for all appeals was about one in four). From Liverpool it was reported that there had been 270 cases during the year where applicants had "purported to leave home in circumstances leaving little doubt that the sole object was to circumvent the law and the Regulations." The appeal tribunals had considered 228 such cases and upheld the Board's determination in 140, leaving 88 or 39% of appeals which were successful (though some of these may have had their allowances increased for other reasons than the fact that they had left home). In the Durham District, where the problem was said to be the most acute, in the six months from May to October there had been 58 cases in which it was felt that the applicant's leaving home was "not bona fide", producing 28 appeals (six successful), and 98 in which a wage-earner had left home apparently so that the applicant's allowance would be increased, producing another 28 appeals (8 successful). Glasgow II District reported 153 appeals involving applicants or wage-earners claiming to have left home, 41 of which were successful. In the Hanley District there had been 34 cases and 19 appeals, in only seven of which the Board's decision had been upheld by the tribunal. These were undoubtedly among the most difficult types of case with which the tribunals had to deal, involving questions of fact on which the evidence must often have been very thin and the balancing of moral judgements against a strict interpretation of the Act. Rather similar problems are posed for Supplementary Benefit Appeal Tribunals by the cohabitation rule.

The relatively uninhibited relationship between officials and tribunals, while clearly not conducive to the independent functioning of the appeals machinery, nevertheless did have its advantages. The co-ordinating function of the tribunal clerks has already been mentioned. Another type of co-ordinating activity was the conferences of tribunal chairmen which the Board arranged on a regional basis in March 1935. The tribunal chairmen had been held partly to blame for the political difficulties following the introduction of the unemployment assistance scheme in January 1935, since it was felt that they had been unduly restrictive in considering applications for leave to appeal. In inviting them to the conferences, however, the Board was careful to avoid any suggestion of criticism of or interference with the performance of their judicial functions. Instead, they were invited to give the Board the benefit of their experience in the task of reviewing the regulations following the "standstill" that had been imposed in February in order to contain the political situation. The particular points mentioned in the letter of invitation were the scale rates of assistance, the "rent rule" (under which allowances had been reduced in many cases to take account of low rent), the treatment of earnings in the means test, and the exercise of discretion in special circumstances. There were six regional conferences, at each of which one of the six members of the Board took the chair. Inevitably, the discussion was not limited to the regulations but covered also the working of the appeals machinery.

From the viewpoint of the officials, these conferences were probably more useful for the insight they gave into the opinions and feelings of the chairmen than for any new information or ideas that emerged from them. Their main value was almost certainly for the chairmen themselves, who must have welcomed the opportunity to learn from each other's experiences without having to use their clerk as an intermediary. That the Board should have had to take the initiative in bringing them together was no doubt regrettable and, to the extent that the conferences were used as a means of influencing the chairmen's conduct, even reprehensible; but if the Board had not done it, it is fairly certain that nobody else would. It can at least be said in the Board's defence that, at that particular moment in its history, it was anxious for political reasons to encourage both a more liberal use of the chairmen's power to grant leave to appeal and a more flexible approach by the tribunals to the use of their discretionary powers in favour of appellants.

The last resort

One of the questions discussed at the Chairmen's conference held at the Board's headquarters in March 1935 was reported by one of the officials present as follows:

"There was clearly a cleavage of opinion as to whether an Appeal Tribunal should be (i) the normal place of recourse for the applicant (like the Court of Referees); or (ii) the last resort after all other means of adjustment have been exhausted. The Act and the Board's instructions are based on the latter conception — the Act giving only a restricted right of appeal to the full Tribunal, and the Board's officers being instructed to interview claimants and, where necessary, to revise their determinations so as to avoid in suitable cases the need for recourse to the Tribunal procedure. Very few Chairmen seemed to have grasped the distinction between the two conceptions . . . "[20]

The distinction was both real and fundamental. The restriction placed on the right of appeal to the full tribunal is discussed below, but first we must consider the administrative processes which took place before the case went to the chairman for a decision on leave to appeal.

The preliminary draft of the tribunal rules prepared by the Solicitor's Department of the Ministry provided for notice of appeal to be sent by the applicant to the chairman or clerk of the tribunal, who would forward a copy to the officer concerned. In the final version of the rules, this procedure was dropped. Instead, notice of appeal was to be lodged in the prescribed form at the office designated by the Board.[21] The alteration was an extremely important one. It meant that the Board's local office would see the appeal form and have an opportunity of intercepting it and taking appropriate action to satisfy the applicant that there was no need for his appeal to go to the tribunal. The formal machinery of the tribunal was indeed intended to be "the last resort after all other means of adjustment have been exhausted".

The steps taken to avoid recourse to the tribunal were not limited to reviewing the determination before forwarding the appeal form to the clerk. A note attached to each appeal form issued at the Employment Exchange to a dissatisfied applicant reminded him that officers of the Board were always available to explain the grounds upon which their decisions had been reached and invited him, if he did not understand the grounds of the decision or thought there were facts which might not have been known to the officer, to ask for an interview at the Board's local office. The Board's instructions (not published in the White Paper on the regulations) set out in detail the procedure to be followed by officers. They were told that, even if an appeal form was received without a request for an interview, it was still open to the Area Office to arrange an interview either at the applicant's home or elsewhere. In the course of the interview the officer was to explain that, while it was always open to an applicant to put a case forward for consideration by the chairman of the tribunal, the chairman could only give leave for a hearing by the full tribunal if he saw reason for doubting whether the assessment was in accordance with the regulations or decided that there were special circumstances. If the interviewing officer decided that there were grounds for looking at the case again, he was to tell the applicant that this would be done, which would generally lead to the applicant withdrawing the appeal or agreeing that action on it could be held up pending investigation. The applicant was to be told that he would have a right of appeal against a new determination but warned that, if he withdrew his appeal and no new determination was made, he would have to relodge it within 14 days of the original decision (the time limit allowed by the rules): but it was also to be made clear to him that, if he did not withdraw the appeal and a new determination was made, "the fact will be made known to the chairman whose attitude towards the application for leave to appeal will no doubt be influenced by the new determination". The instructions stressed, however, that it must be made clear to the applicant that the purpose of the interview was to help him understand the Board's decision, and that "nothing should be said to him which could reasonably be interpreted as pressure on him to withdraw his appeal."

In the post-mortem following the "standstill" on the operation of the Board's regulations, the Ministry of Labour officials looked closely into the appeals machinery and did not like what they saw. R.M. Gould who, before the Board's senior staff were hived off from the Ministry, had worked under Eady and Reid on the transitional payments scheme and might have been expected to have some sympathy for their point of view, wrote in a minute dated February 27, 1935:

"It is questionable whether, as a matter of policy, the Board's officers should be enjoined to have a second shot at a case if there is any question of appeal. When appeal machinery is provided, it is more usually held that once an appeal is lodged, any attempt to intervene is regarded as an attempt to interfere with the appeal machinery. It is apparently contemplated quite freely that the Board's officer, on learning of an appeal, shall consider whether he should give a new determination, and that the giving of the new determination will render the appeal unnecessary. It may or it may not, but there is no guarantee that even under the new determination, the man would get as much as the Tribunal would have determined if the case had gone before them."

After quoting cases which had come to the notice of the Ministry in which one applicant stated that he had been asked whether, if he received an extra 2s.6d. for boots and clothing for the children, he would be satisfied, another stated that he had been told there was no ground on which he could appeal, and yet another objected to the tribunal clerk's assumption that, having received a new determination, he no longer wished to appeal, Gould concluded:

> "I should think there is little doubt that this practice of interviewing all applicants who wish to appeal, has the effect of stifling appeals; but the withdrawal of the appeal does not necessarily signify that the applicant is satisfied that he has no longer any ground for complaint."[22]

Despite the Ministry's doubts, the Board continued to encourage its officers not only to forestall appeals by interviewing dissatisfied claimants but to seek interviews with those who had already lodged appeals in the hope that they would withdraw them. In March 1936, some embarrassment was caused by a case taken up by the Communist M.P., William Gallacher, in which four applicants in similar circumstances lodged appeals which three of them later withdrew after an interview with the Board's officer. The fourth persisted and won his appeal. Although the Board maintained that its actions in this case were above reproach, new instructions were drafted making it clear that once a notice of appeal had been received at the local office, unless an interview was requested at the same time by the appellant and resulted in a decision not to pursue the appeal, it was to be regarded as formally lodged. In other words, if an officer took the initiative in seeking an interview with an applicant who had already sent in an appeal form, the appeal must go forward to the chairman of the tribunal even if the appellant wished to withdraw it.

Before issuing the instruction, Eady sent a copy to Sir Thomas Phillips at the Ministry of Labour for his observations. In his reply dated November 3, 1936, Phillips made two criticisms. The first, which he described as "a point of detail", was that it would be better to say without qualification that every appeal sent or handed in must go the tribunal, rather than excluding those where an interview was requested at the same time. The second criticism concerned the interviewing of appellants and prospective appellants.

"We do not ourselves like the suggestion of an interview which accompanies the blank appeal form", Phillips wrote, "but I regard it as a matter which the Minister could if necessary defend as carrying out the deliberate policy of the Board in the way of helping the applicant to understand the circumstances fully before he appeals". To seek an interview after receiving an appeal. however, was open to much more serious objection and would not be endorsed by the Minister. "You had better cut it out altogether". Phillips peremptorily urged, "and lay it down that once an appeal has been sent or handed in, the matter is out of the hands of your officers except when the applicant on his own initiative wishes to have an interview with regard to it."

Eady referred this "vexatious correspondence" to the Chairman of the Board, Lord Rushcliffe, who agreed that the Board should stand firm:

"To accept the view that when an appeal is once lodged the matter is out of our hands and our officers can take no further action by way of explanation or otherwise, would be a fundamental departure from the policy which the Board has hitherto followed on the relations of an aggrieved applicant to its officers."

In his reply to Phillips. Eady rejected the suggestion that every appeal should go forward even if the appellant had withdrawn it before the papers were sent to the tribunal chairman. "The Chairman can do nothing with it", he wrote; "it has been removed from his jurisdiction and he may well wonder why he has been troubled. It looks simply like slovenly administration." Turning to the "more serious issue" of the action to be taken, or not to be taken, by officers after an appeal had been lodged, he wrote: "I suggest that your view must be based on a misunderstanding of the nature of appeals and the place of the appeal machinery, and also of the considered policy of the Board." He did not accept the analogy with Courts of Referees, whose function in the unemployment insurance scheme was to interpret the facts of the case in the light of a legal title to a fixed sum and on the basis of previous decisions by the Umpire. Unemployment assistance appeals were concerned with variable sums of money and the appeal form often disclosed facts whose existence or significance had not previously been apparent. "It would be foolish", Eady argued, "to say that the officer should be precluded from revising his determination merely because an appeal form had been lodged. Indeed it is his duty to revise it, whether the appeal eventually goes forward or not. The tangled facts and considerations out of which a determination is evolved can, in very many cases, more easily be resolved by a talk between the applicant and the Board's officer than by the procedure of an Appeal Tribunal."

It could hardly be denied that, if an officer knew that an applicant's allowance ought to be increased, it was his duty to increase it as soon as possible, whether an appeal had been lodged or not; and it was no less reasonable to say that, if there was reason to think that the allowance ought to be increased, it was the officer's duty to investigate the facts at once, without waiting for the appeal hearing. The more difficult question was how this could be done without the Board being suspected, whether justly or unjustly, of trying to stifle legitimate appeals. In a slightly more conciliatory reply dated December 7, 1936, Phillips suggested a possible solution. He would not press his objection to the interviewing of appellants if the procedure could be amended to ensure "(1) that every appeal made would, in fact, go to the Chairman of the Tribunal . . . and would never be withdrawn without the Chairman's consent, and (2) that every application for withdrawal was entirely spontaneous". The difference in the nature of the questions under consideration in assistance and insurance appeals did not seem to him to affect the general principle laid down by the unemployment insurance Umpire, that "when once an appeal has been submitted to a statutory authority it cannot be withdrawn in any circumstances without the consent of the authority to whom the appeal was addressed".

Eady, however, was not prepared to compromise. The Board's instruction went out without further amendment and he wrote to Phillips on December 14: ". . . . you may of course proceed on the assumption that if an appellant withdraws his appeal it is because he wishes to do so, and not because he has been improperly cajoled or coerced by an officer of the Board. This being so, it is not easy to understand why his action should be subject to the consent of the Chairman of the Appeal Tribunal, who will not have had the appeal, at that stage, brought within his jurisdiction at all". He still refused to recognize the analogy with unemployment insurance appeals.

The rights and wrongs of this Olympian controversy remain far from clear. At what point is an appeal so irrevocably lodged that it cannot be withdrawn? What is the effect of a new determination on an appeal that has already been lodged? If an applicant (or "claimant" in modern terminology) has expressed his dissatisfaction by appealing, are officials acting improperly if they review the disputed decision without waiting for the tribunal to do so? And in what ways are appeals in connection with variable and partly discretionary means-tested benefits different in kind from those concerned with legal rights to insurance benefits? These questions are as relevant, and nearly as difficult to answer, now as they were in

1936.[23] So far as the UAB was concerned, however, they do not seem to have been major issues after 1936. By 1939, it was no longer the normal practice to invite appellants to the Board's offices for interview, although those who lodged their appeals in person were still sometimes interviewed and either withdrew their appeals or disclosed facts on the basis of which a new determination was made.

Leave to appeal

Betterton's proposal that appeals relating to the determination of allowances should be heard by the tribunal only with the leave of the chairman quickly proved to have been a serious blunder. The chairman could grant leave to appeal, under section 39(5) of the Act of 1934, only if it appeared to him that there was reason to doubt whether the regulations had been correctly applied or that there were other special circumstances. In the crucial period January-February 1935, leading up to the "standstill", leave to appeal was refused in the majority of cases, some chairmen allowing few appeals, if any, to go forward to the full tribunal. Reports given by District Officers at a conference held on February 2 showed that the proportion varied considerably from one tribunal to another. Glasgow I District had 70 appeals in the first week, a third of which went to the tribunal, while in Glasgow II District the chairmen had considered 227 cases and granted leave to appeal in only 16 of them. In the Sheffield District only seven out of 200 appellants had been granted leave, though the District Officer reported, "I can honestly say that the Chairmen . . . are definitely looking for cases where they can send them . . . " Others were more critical of the chairmen. The Birmingham District Officer, whose chairmen had granted leave to appeal in 16 cases out of 78, commented, ". . . quite frankly, I think not enough cases are being sent by the Chairmen to Tribunal". For the country as a whole, up to the end of February, leave to appeal was refused in 66% of cases. As a Ministry of Labour memorandum, commenting on the Board's account of events leading up to the standstill, put it, "The appeal system was meant to be the safety valve of the whole procedure and it was not permitted to work freely."

The tribunal chairmen had been placed in an intolerable position. It was most unlikely that they would find more than a handful of cases in which there was doubt as to the correct application of the regulations. If "other special circumstances" were apparent from the papers submitted to the chairman, they were likely to have been taken into account by the Board's officers before the appeal reached him. The chairman of the Canning Town Tribunal (covering large parts of East London), Sir Edmund Phipps, described his experience so far in a letter to Eady dated February 24, 1935. Up to the announcement of the standstill on February 5, he had considered 75 applications for leave to appeal and had granted leave in six cases, five of which involved questions as to whether the applicant should be treated as a lodger rather than as part of the household—for instance, the case of a man aged 62 living with his dead brother's widow who was herself mainly supported by her son.

"All the others appeared to be protests—either virtually or in their actual expression—against the principles of the Regulations or the Act itself. So far as I could see, the Officers who had dealt with these cases had exercised their discretion, as they understood it, to the full: and I could not see that they possessed any more discretion than they believed. They had, e.g., evidently been on the look-out for cases in which it was fair to make allowance for cost of travelling or for special clothing or for extra nourishment, and in the cases that came to me (and which therefore they had not been able to regard as 'special' in other ways than those) I could not find other kinds of 'special circumstances' existing or alleged. A large proportion of the whole number of cases turned on the inclusion of the earnings of members of the family, which, apparently, had not been included formerly." .

The object of restricting access to the tribunal by requiring the chairman's leave to appeal had been to prevent the tribunals from trying to alter the general standards laid down in the regulations. If the tribunals were to act as an effective "safety valve", however, it was essential that they should be able to look carefully into the circumstances of applicants for whom a strict application of the regulations produced unreasonably harsh results and use their discretionary powers imaginatively and generously to mitigate any hardship that might otherwise be caused. Given the degree of control exercised by the Board and the Ministry of Labour over the selection of tribunal members and chairmen and the fact that the tribunals were bound by the regulations just as much as the Board's officers, there was no real danger of any widespread attempt by them to flout the rules and give more generous allowances without the justification of "special circumstances". As Melvin Herman has shown, tribunals find no difficulty in producing special circumstances when it suits them to do so, and may on occasion use this as a way of bending the rules.[24] But it was precisely this power of bending the rules without actually breaking them that was needed to prevent the introduction of the unemployment assistance scheme from causing a political explosion. Without this element of flexibility, the regulations proved unworkable.

Under the standstill, which lasted from February 1935 until November 1936, although the chairman's leave to appeal was still required, he could not refuse it if the amount of a supplementary allowance granted under the "Standstill Act" (the Unemployment Assistance (Temporary Provisions) Act 1935) was in question. Even in cases which did not involve standstill payments, chairmen gradually became more liberal in the use of their powers. In 1938, the first (and only) normal year after the liquidation of the standstill, leave to appeal was granted in 96% of cases.[25] The requirement was finally abolished by the National Assistance Act 1948.

Conclusions

In the light of the evidence now available in the UAB files, there is no reason to dissent from the conclusion reached by Lach 25 years ago without access to this evidence, that "in 1934 there was manifestly no inclination to create independent appeal machinery". Nor is there much than can usefully be added to Lach's summary of the ways in which the tribunals were weighted in favour of the Board:

· "This was achieved by having one member of the tribunal 'appointed by the Board to represent the Board'; by appointing this member to serve regularly and frequently, while the other member was drawn in rotation from a panel of workpeople and served infrequently; thirdly, by appointing a clerk 'of the senior rank of Assistant District Officer', who assumed a dominant position in relation to the tribunal; and fourthly, by requiring the clerk to be present when decisions of the tribunal were being discussed. The proceedings also were such as would dispose toward decisions acceptable to the Board. Firstly, the Board organised regional conferences of chairmen which were addressed by members of the Board and senior officers; secondly, all members of tribunals were on appointment given facilities for early consultation with the Board's senior officer; thirdly, unpublished memoranda prepared by the Board were issued to tribunals; fourthly, the Board's instructions to its officers were made available to the tribunals; fifthly, the tribunals met in the offices of the Board and consequently a number of informal contacts took place between officers and members of the tribunals."[26]

With all these safeguards, the Board still felt it necessary to take elaborate steps to reduce to a minimum the number of cases actually reaching the stage of a tribunal hearing, though this policy was modified as it became clear that the tribunals were not performing their intended role as a safety valve through which dissatisfaction with an inevitably unpopular system could be channelled.

NOTES

1. George Lach. "Appeal Tribunals under the National Assistance Act, 1948" in *Administrative Tribunals at Work*. ed. Pollard, 1950, p. 54.

2. P.R.O., CAB 27/501.

3. Ibid.

4. Ibid.

5. P.R.O., CAB 23/75, 25(33)2.

6. P.R.O., CAB 27/552

7. Report of the Committee on Administrative Tribunals and Inquiries, Cmnd. 218, 1957, para. 182. See also chapter 3 below.

8. UAB Annual Report 1935, Cmd. 5177, 1936, p. 51.

9. Ibid., p. 56.

10. P.R.O., CAB 27/552.

11. Cmd. 5177, 1936, p. 95.

12. Ibid., p. 256.

13. Ibid., p. 49.

14. Unemployment Assistance (Appeal Tribunals) Provisional Rules, 1934, Rule 8(4).

15. Ibid., Rule 8(2).

16. Ibid., Rule 8(2).

17. UAB Annual Report 1936, Cmd. 5526, p. 43.

18. Memorandum on the Unemployment Assistance (Determination of Need and Assessment of Needs) Regulations, 1934, Cmd. 4791, 1935.

19. Cmd. 5177, 1936, p. 52.

20. P.R.O. PIN 7/156.

21. Unemployment Assistance (Appeal Tribunals) Provisional Rules, 1934, Rule 4(1).

22. P.R.O., PIN 7/156.

23. R.J. Coleman. *Supplementary Benefits and the Administrative Review of Administrative Action*, CPAG Poverty Pamphlet No. 7, 1971.

24. Melvin Herman, *Administrative Justice and Supplementary Benefits*, 1972.

25. UAB Annual Report 1938, Cmd. 6021, 1939, p. 42.

26. Lach, pp. 56-7.

III NATIONAL ASSISTANCE APPEAL TRIBUNALS AND THE FRANKS REPORT
Anthony Bradley

If the Unemployment Assistence Tribunals were the grandparents of the present Supplementary Benefit Appeal Tribunals, the National Assistance Appeal Tribunals (NATs) which functioned between 1948 and 1966 were the parents. In 1957, midway through this period, the Franks Committee on Administrative Tribunals and Enquiries published its report after a two-year examination of (inter alia) the constitution and working of tribunals "other than the ordinary courts of law". The aim of this chapter is three-fold: (1) to outline the role which the NATs played in the national assistance scheme until they and the scheme itself were superseded by SBATs and the supplementary benefits scheme under the Act of 1966; (2) to examine the evidence given to the Franks Committee and the findings of the Franks Committee which related to NATs; and (3) to consider certain improvements made to these tribunals which directly flowed from the Franks Report.

The historical material in this chapter is included because the main argument is that supplementary benefit adjudication today is essentially part of a system of administering social security benefits on the basis of need which owes more to the continuing survival of certain deeply engrained official policies and attitudes than to any other cause. These policies like the tribunal system itself can be traced back to the unemployment assistance tribunals in the 1930s; they were, and have continued to be, influential both under the national assistance and supplementary benefit schemes.

Adjudication under the National Assistance Act 1948

The unemployment assistance scheme which operated from 1934

was administered by a national agency specialising in providing financial assistance to those whose need arose because of unemployment and who had exhausted their insurance entitlement. Wide administrative discretion was exercised within a skeletonic framework of statutory rules. So that decisions could be made in local offices of the national agency, powers were delegated by means of unpublished administrative directions. The dissatisfied claimant's sole remedy, apart from requesting the local office to reconsider his case, was to appeal to a local tribunal, beyond which no further appeal lay. The whole scheme expressed a strong determination to resist the creation of a centralised judicial agency, on the lines of the present National Insurance Commissioners (or the former Umpire in unemployment insurance cases), which might rival the national administrative agency as a source of decisions, rules and standards. As Tony Lynes has shown in chapter 2, care was taken to ensure that tribunals were fully conversant with the Unemployment Assistance Board's policies, which had to be taken into account by the tribunals. To our eyes today, these tribunals in the 1930s were too closely identified with the administrative agency itself to be able to exercise an independent appellate function.[1]

In 1940, the work of the Unemployment Assistance Board was extended to include the granting of supplementary pensions to those receiving old age pensions,[2] but the arrangements for deciding individual claims submitted to the Board continued unchanged. Because of war-time conditions, supplementary pensions soon became the main work of the Assistance Board, which in 1940 shed 'Unemployment' from its title. When the Poor Law was abolished by the Act of 1948, the word 'National' was added to the Assistance Board's title. The Board itself was placed under a general duty to offer assistance to those in need and to exercise its powers so as to promote the welfare of those seeking assistance.[3] Thus the NAB grew from a specialised agency concerned only with unemployment relief into a general agency responsible for assistance to all in financial need; and the appeal machinery under the 1948 Act perpetuated much of that first set up in 1934.

One important assumption on which the post-war welfare state was built was that the introduction of universal social insurance, providing flat-rate benefits in return for contributions, would reduce the numbers claiming national assistance to a small range of residual and difficult cases. As Aneurin Bevan said when introducing the National Assistance Bill, "I have spent many years of my life in fighting the means test. Now we have practically ended it . . . (The) amount left to the NAB after the whole of the needs have been met by all the other measures will be very small indeed.

Only the residual categories will be left."[4] This may be one reason why the adjudication arrangements made by the 1948 Act were so much less elaborate than the National Insurance scheme of adjudication. Another reason is the very sharp distinction which Beveridge himself drew between the legal character of an insurance scheme and the provision of means-tested assistance which in his view necessarily involved the exercise of official discretion. In Beveridge's view, a scheme ceased to rank as social insurance when the receipt of benefit depended in any way upon the discretion of some authority. It was the large element of discretion in the national assistance scheme which had such a large influence on the adjudication structure.

Many M.P.s who took part in the Parliamentary debates on the National Assistance Bill had had experience of the work of public assistance committees of local authorities and they emphasised the need to make discretion a reality. Thus Sir Harold Webbe stressed the need to ensure humane and not automatic administration of money grants. "However much one instructs one's officers to use their discretion, their common sense and the powers that are given to them, there is a fatal tendency for a printed scale to become a fixed scale. Only by the wisest administration will the Minister be able to make the discretionary powers given to these officers a reality and not merely a sham."[5] He feared that appeal tribunals would soon be hide-bound by "hosts of precedents." Mr. Hutchison said, "Need is not a precise term which can be solved in terms of simple arithmetic by considering the resources of some individual applicant for assistance, and calculating what one might say are his theoretical requirements."[6] Clearly the record of the Unemployment Assistance Board, despite its best endeavours[7], had given rise to the fear that administration by a national agency would leave little room for local discretion, compared with administration of the poor law by local government. For this reason the contribution that local advisory committees could make was stressed, both on general questions and for assisting local officials in case-work with difficult claimants.[8] But the Minister, James Griffiths, stressed the judicial work and character of the appeal tribunals which distinguished them from the local advisory committees.[9] Several M.P.s had reservations about the tribunals themselves, fearing that a tribunal would be too inclined to take the official point of view[10] and that the presence of the Board's officer at appeals would over-influence the tribunal.[11]

Despite the Minister's emphasis on the judicial character of the appeal tribunals, he was not willing to see a further right of appeal provided, although an amendment to this effect was proposed in committee. In the national insurance scheme, "where the right to a benefit is statutory", he considered it essential to have a system of case-law binding throughout the country.[12] But in national assistance, disputes would be almost entirely about the allowances to be made (a reference to the discretionary power of the Board to adjust the scale-rates of assistance either upwards or downwards to suit special circumstances[13]) and it would be both impossible and undesirable for an umpire to be asked to make general rules about the exercise of discretion. "When the umpire makes a decision, his ruling applies not only to the case before him, but to all other cases in similar circumstances. When an appeal tribunal comes to a decision, it only applies to the case in question and not to other cases."[14] "We ought to think twice before we decide in this scheme to make decisions subject to a final decision by an umpire who will then build up a lot of case-law which may be far more rigid than we want. Let us keep the discretion as wide as possible."[15] Although this argument came close to maintaining that like cases need not be decided alike, the dominant emphasis was the desire to avoid rigidity.

So tribunals needed to exercise a wise and unrestricted discretion: what of the Board's own staff? The debates recognised that administratively there would be a need to give guidance and direction to officials in local offices as to the use of discretion. It was pointed out that so long as Poor Law had been a matter for local government, the elected representatives on the Public Assistance Committees knew what instructions had been given to their officials. Would the same apply in future, so that M.P.s could expect to be informed of the Board's administrative instructions? The Minister rejected this suggestion. To make these circulars available to M.P.s would be to make them open to the public and that might destroy the confidential relationship between the Board and its officers; but he would consider whether some information could be given in general terms "in a kind of White Paper".[16] But apart from the annual reports of the NAB, it was not until the late 1960s that "a kind of White Paper" began to be published, by the Supplementary Benefits Commission.

While several M.P.s shared the Minister's distrust of a system of precedent, they regarded the tribunals' function as important. Support was given to the desirability of ensuring that all claimants knew of their right of appeal[17] and the Minister agreed to an amendment providing for the display of a conspicuous notice of the right to appeal in every assistance office.[18] A Scottish M.P. doubted whether the appeal tribunals would be as unbiassed of the official point of view as the sheriff had been in Scotland on appeals against the refusal of poor relief.[19] The practical value of representation was stressed[20] provided that the representative was not a lawyer. A few M.P.s regretted that there would be no criminal sanction available against officers of the Board (as there had been against relieving officers under the Poor Law) who failed to perform their statutory duty of giving assistance to those in need.[21] On the legal nature of the duty to be imposed upon the Board, Niall Macpherson commented, "One of the interesting features of this Bill from a rather theoretical point of view is that it places on the Board a duty to assist, and yet in a sense there is no correlative individual right." But he did not pursue this criticism, suggesting that "the right is the right of the community to ensure that it shall free itself from the moral blight and the practical scourge of want."[22] In fact the lack of a correlative right was later to be made good in the 1966 Act, which introduced the statutory right to supplementary benefit.

To illustrate the continuity which was maintained between the former tribunals and the NATs, transitional provisions of the 1948 Act enabled all members and chairmen of the former tribunals 'without further appointment' to serve on the new tribunals.[23] But certain changes in composition were made for future appointments.[24] The chairmen continued to be appointed by the Minister (by then the Minister of National Insurance) and the workpeople's representatives continued to be 'appointed' by the Board from a panel nominated by the Minister (on the nomination of trades councils). The member appointed by the Board to represent the Board's interests disappeared; in his place was put a second member appointed by the Minister. (The distinction between Board and Minister, always somewhat shadowy, was probably more important under the national assistance scheme, when the NAB had a greater degree of formal independence of the Ministry, than today, when the SBC and its staff are much more closely integrated with the Department of Health and Social Security). Some procedural changes were made.[25] A general right of appeal to the full tribunal was introduced. Previously, a representative could be appointed only by supplementary pensioners who because of infirmity or other good reason were unable to attend the hearing; other appellants could be 'accompanied' but not represented. Under the rules introduced in 1948, every appellant could be "represented or accompanied by any person not being a barrister, advocate or solicitor and appearing as such."[26] In all cases the right of oral hearing was established. The rules continued to provide that the clerk should be present when the tribunal was considering its decision. A late amendment to the National Assistance Bill permitted the remuneration of clerks to be by fees or salary: this would have enabled the appointment of a clerk from outside the service of the NAB (e.g. a local solicitor to act part-time, as in the case of the General Commissioners of Income Tax) but it is not known whether this power was ever exercised.[27]

Evidence given by the National Assistance Board to the Franks Committee

In the years immediately following 1948, it seemed that the NAB was coping adequately with the relief of poverty. Until the rediscovery of poverty in the early 1960s, remarkably little interest was shown in the Board's work or in the tribunals. A variety of general discontents about the nature of government gave rise to the appointment of the Franks Committee in 1955: Conservative disillusionment with post-war Government had been highlighted by the Crichel Down revelations in 1954; there was widespread dissatisfaction over procedures for compulsory purchase of land and town planning; and some tribunals, notably the rent tribunals, were attracting criticism. But discontent with the national assistance tribunals, if it existed, was not expressed. Apart from a passing reference in the evidence given by the National Committee of Citizens' Advice Bureaux, and the criticisms made by the Society of Labour Lawyers, the sole evidence given to the Franks Committee came from the NAB itself. This evidence expressed complete satisfaction with existing tribunal arrangements, and sought to justify three features of the system which came under scrutiny from the Committee, namely the ban on legal representation, the rule that hearings were in private and the fact that tribunals did not give reasons for their decisions. In so far as the Franks Report is considered by some to have engineered a "lawyers' revolution", applying legal values to areas previously left to the administrative process, this development seems to have been anticipated by the NAB, whose evidence sought to protect national assistance appeals from the effect of alien values which would have conflicted with the social purposes of the system.

The Franks Committee were told[28] that 95% of NAT appeals were against the refusal of assistance and against the amount of assistance grants. For the years 1950-1954 inclusive, a total of just on 48,000 appeals were heard under the 1948 Act and just on 3,000 appeals under the Old Age Pensions Act 1936, making a total annual average of approximately 10,200 appeals decided by 152 tribunals in Britain. Of the 151 chairmen 37 had legal qualifications.[29] The chairmen and the Minister's members of the tribunals were drawn "from men and women of standing in the area of the tribunal who have, for example, administrative experience in local government . . . or in the running of important voluntary organisations, or who have experience as justices of the peace, or are clergy-men". This description corresponded closely with the criteria for appointment first laid down by the Unemployment Assistance Board.[30] Under the rules for the appointment of chairmen,[31] the Minister reserved the right to terminate a chairman's appointment without notice if he became unfit to hold the appointment or incapable of acting, and also to terminate an appointment by one month's notice if there was any likelihood that confidence in a chairman's impartiality might be impaired because of stated events e.g. prominent connection with national politics. Other circumstances which might lead to termination included being an employer or a company director; being actively connected in a paid capacity with any organisation "which exists to promote the welfare of its members"; and being a lawyer whose firm had a practice including cases arising under the National Assistance and National Insurance Acts, or a substantial amount of actions between work-people and their employers. These restrictive conditions must have had the effect of excluding many who might make good chairmen: they would certainly be likely to exclude such few lawyers as might be found who had knowledge of working-class conditions.

Subject to the 1948 Act and the statutory rules, procedure at a tribunal was such as the chairman might determine. "In view of the personal nature of the matters discussed, and the fact that many of the persons applying for assistance are aged and frail, the proceedings are kept as simple and informal as possible." There was no formal provision for cross-examination, but it was expected that the chairman would ensure that all the relevant facts were obtained from the appellant and the Board's officer, and that if the appellant wished to question the Board's officer, he would be given every facility to do so. No reasons were given for a tribunal's decision. "Each case referred to the tribunal is dealt with on its own facts and the tribunal does not create case law by its decisions. No question arises, therefore, of publishing digests."[32] The decisions of the tribunals were "conclusive for all purposes."[33]

Oral evidence was given by the Board's Secretary, Sir Harold Fieldhouse. According to Sir Harold, consistency in tribunal decisions was not a paramount consideration. As circumstances in individual cases varied, the Board expected there to be variation in the decisions. So far as the Board's staff were concerned, discretion obviously had to be controlled and kept within reasonable bounds, and departmental instructions tended to produce uniformity. But each tribunal had a wide discretion and the Board had never had reason to complain of the way it was exercised. The clerk of the tribunal might call a tribunal's attention to regulations, but departmental instructions were not put to the tribunal. There was "absolutely no reason at all" why reasons should be given if there was no further right of appeal. It would, indeed, be very difficult for a tribunal to give its reasons, for, if it confirmed the officer's decision, it would do so for his reasons. "If not, it would be possible but not very easy for a tribunal to give its reasons." (Does this suggest that all reasonable tribunals would be disposed to uphold the official decision?) It had not been the subject of public notice that the clerks were members of the Department, an arrangement which was "very useful to the chairman". The Board did not consider representation of claimants to be necessary. Where a claimant did not attend, "we would expect the chairman to take good care that the Board's officer brought out any facts that might tell in favour of the claimant".[34]

The value of this evidence was diminished by the fact that the witness admitted that he did not know very much about the inside of these tribunals. "I have kept away, myself. But I did go to see one, because I knew that I would be coming here."[35] It is a matter for speculation whether members of the NAB themselves would have known more or less about the tribunals than this. But this was the nearest that the Franks Committee came to studying the actual operation of the tribunals!

As the deliberations of the Franks Committee proceeded, the NAB were asked to submit additional comments on certain issues of principle as they might affect NATs. The Board reiterated the nature of the main task assigned to the tribunals. In the typical case, a local officer's decision involved first an arithmetical computation of need in accordance with the rules set out in regulations for calculating requirements and resources, but this computation was subject to discretionary variation, either up or down. "The real issue in nearly all appeals is whether these discretionary powers should be exercised . . . Questions of law hardly ever arise. When they do they are usually resolved without difficulty by reference to the plain requirements of the Act and the Regulations. The tribunal's job is to decide what appears to it the most appropriate—not the only lawful—action that could be taken in a particular instance. Thus they are quite different from the National Insurance Appeal Tribunals, which interpret statutory provisions in their application to given sets of circumstances and in relation to statutory rights. The Assistance Tribunals do not make case law" . . . "The appellants are usually simple people; most of them are old and some nervous. Care is taken that the proceedings shall be informal and indeed friendly, without any of the atmosphere of a law court." While the Board agreed that some things should be formally regulated (e.g. composition of the tribunal; and notification to the appellant of the hearing), the Board believed that extreme simplicity in procedure was required and could not be maintained if the chairman's hands were tied. Hearings were necessarily held in private: "It has been the policy of Governments since 1948 to give every encouragement to persons in genuine need to apply for national assistance, and any whittling down of the present rules ensuring complete privacy could undo much of the good that has been achieved over many years by the application of that policy."[36]

As for the question of legally qualified chairmen, the departmental view was that the qualities required in a chairman included "a knowledge of working class conditions, an orderly mind, and a sense of fairness, possession of which he ought to be able to communicate to the kind of people appearing before him". If a lawyer had these qualities equally with a layman, the lawyer would be appointed, "but he will not come across much legal work in the course of his duties"—a deeply significant statement, which reflects an extremely narrow conception of a lawyer's work. The ban on legal representation had been imposed in part because in matters of a discretionary nature there was no ground for allowing a contest between professionally qualified advocates, but mainly to safeguard the simple and summary character of the proceedings.

Regarding a possible further right of appeal, the Board had this to say:

"Since questions of law hardly ever arise with the Assistance Tribunals the Department has no view on the question of an appeal from administrative tribunals on a point of law. It is considered, however, that there should not be a right of further appeal from the Assistance Tribunals on a point of fact. It is difficult to conceive on what principle one could justify superimposing a second tribunal upon the first or what one could hope to gain by doing so . . . In the absence of case law a superior tribunal could not have a co-ordinating mission: it could only retread the ground covered by the original tribunal (and earlier by the Board's officer) by way of considering the facts and forming a decision on them. The issues are not of a kind to be decided by a central authority remote from the cases, so that the second tribunal would have to be a body much much like the first. One such body could scarcely have pre-eminence in wisdom or experience over another. Moreover long drawn-out disputation about how much money should be allowed to provide a current subsistence seems contrary to common sense; and it could have an enervating effect on assistance administration, of which the essence is prompt service and speedy decision."[37]

This is again a most significant passage.

Apart from the NAB evidence, the Society of Labour Lawyers suggested that the work of NATs should be transferred to National Insurance local tribunals, for two reasons (1) in order that the local tribunal might be completely independent of the NAB and (2) in order that there should be a further appeal to the National Insurance Commissioner.[38] Less radically, the National Citizens' Advice Bureaux Committee reported that bureaux were in general satisfied with the NATs but doubed whether appellants always knew their rights of appeal, pointing out that some citizens found difficulty in presenting their cases in writing.[39]

The conclusions of the Franks Committee

It is well-known that the Franks Committee stressed that openness, fairness and impartiality should mark both inquiry and tribunal procedures. The Committee rejected the view that tribunals should be regarded as part of the machinery of administration, a viewpoint which had been reflected in much of the official evidence. "Tribunals should properly be regarded as machinery provided by Parliament for adjudication rather than as part of the machinery of administration. The essential point is that in all these cases Parliament has deliberately provided for a decision outside and independent of the Department concerned . . . (The) intention of Parliament to provide for the independence of tribunals is clear and unmistakable." The Committee continued:

> "In the field of tribunals openness appears to us to require the publicity of proceedings and knowledge of the essential reasoning underlying the decisions; fairness to require the adoption of a clear procedure which enables parties to know their rights, to present their case fully and to know the case which they have to meet; and impartiality to require the freedom of tribunals from the influence, real or apparent, of Departments concerned with the subject-matter of their decisions."[40]

The significance of these broad conclusions can scarcely be over-estimated. They led to the Tribunals and Inquiries Act 1958, the establishment of the Council on Tribunals and other measures for improving tribunals. The national assistance tribunals derived some benefit from these general improvements. But in some important respects the application of the Franks principles to the NATs and their successors was severely restricted. As will appear below, NATs (and their successors the SBATs) have been consistently regarded as special cases amongst tribunals: whether rightly or wrongly is a matter for present discussion.

One clarification of the Franks recommendations needs to be

made. It was one thing for the Committee to reject the view that tribunals are not "mere appendages" of government departments. It
was another thing to reject the view that tribunals should be
regarded as part of the machinery of administration "for which the
Government must maintain a close and continuing responsibility".[41] It is salutary to remember the opinion quoted by Robson that
judicial administration is merely a specialised form of general
administration which "has acquired an air of detachment".[42] When
Government and Parliament establish a social security system, they
must arrange for the determination of disputes which arise out of
individual claims. Excessive delays or undue emphasis on legalistic
procedure would defeat the aims of the system. Whether justice is
being administered by courts or tribunals, Government and Parliament are responsible for ensuring that the machinery of justice is
working well. Responsibility for the system need not endanger the
independence of court or tribunal in deciding individual cases.
Indeed, the main theme of the Franks report is that adjudication
will not be effective except in conditions which make for independent tribunals. For example, the principle of independence requires
that all policies which Government intends a tribunal to follow
should be defined and publicly declared in the form of regulations
or published directions. As Professor Robson had argued, "The
control exercised by the Minister over the work of the tribunal
should be exclusively confined to instructions contained in public
documents of this kind."[43] So too, the Franks Committee said, to
entrust decisions to a tribunal rather than a Minister requires that
"every effort should be made to express policy in the form of regulations capable of being administered by an independent tribunal".[44]
For this and other reasons, it is especially important to clarify the
proper extent of departmental responsibility for the operation of
social security tribunals, which have such a close relationship with
their 'parent' department.[45] If departmental responsibility includes
the duty of ensuring that decisions are taken by tribunals free of
departmental influence except that which is exercised openly by
means of the public rule-making functions of the department, it
must be asked whether this duty has been adequately discharged by
DHSS and its predecessors in respect of NATs and SBATs. Probably one of the primary weaknesses of adjudication in this field has
been a failure by the Department to grasp this difficult nettle with
sufficient firmness.

Detailed recommendations of the Franks Report

The Committee rejected proposals for amalgamating all social security tribunals into a single structure on the National Insurance

model. The Committee were not satisfied that the functions of the
various tribunals were sufficiently cognate to permit integration.
And, citing the Pensions Appeal Tribunals and the NATs, the Committee considered that amalgamation would be unacceptable on
political grounds. The Committee also doubted the practical value
of placing too wide a range of jurisdictions upon part-time members.[46]

The Committee considered that the chairmen of all tribunals
should ordinarily have legal qualifications: "objectivity in the treatment of cases and the proper sifting of facts are most often best
secured by having a legally qualified chairman". Moreover, "the
presence of a legally qualified chairman should enable the tribunal
to attach the proper weight to such matters as hearsay and written
evidence".[47] But suitable chairmen could be drawn from fields other
than law: only for second-tier tribunals should it be obligatory for
chairmen to have legal qualifications.[48] Nonetheless the Committee
recommended that the chairmen of all tribunals should be
appointed by the Lord Chancellor (in Scotland the Lord President
of the Court of Session).

As for the other members of the tribunals, the Committee recommended that the proposed Council on Tribunals should make all
appointments, but this recommendation was not accepted by the
Government.

As for the practice of appointing departmental officials to serve
as clerks of tribunals, the Committee considered, but rejected, the
proposal that a central corps of clerks for all tribunals be established under the Lord Chancellor's Department. The Committee
did not wish to prevent social service departments from giving staff
members a period of service as clerks, since this was "doubtless valuable in developing the outlook appropriate to the administration of
a social service".[49] The Committee recommended that the clerk
should be debarred from retiring with the tribunal when the members considered their decision, except if he was sent for to advise on
a specific issue. But this recommendation was not accepted by the
Government.

The Committee preferred to enunciate general principles of
procedure rather than attempt to draw up codes of procedure. The
committee were certain that in some instances informality had been
secured at the expense of orderly procedure. In most tribunals, the
object to be aimed at was the combination of a formal procedure
with an informal atmosphere. The Committee felt that the nature of
the issues involved before NATs justified a departure from the principle that tribunals should sit in public, in the interests both of the
actual appellant, whose privacy was at stake, and of future appel-

lants who might be deterred from appealing if any publicity was given to NAT proceedings.[50] One change recommended was that in place of a complete ban on legal representation, the chairman of a NAT should have discretion to permit legal representation: in the event the ban was removed entirely.[51]

As for procedure after the hearing, the Committee were convinced that if tribunal proceedings were to be fair to the citizen, reasons should be given to the fullest practicable extent. A decision was apt to be better if the reasons for it had to be set out in writing; the giving of reasons would enable the citizen to decide whether it was worth enforcing any further right of appeal.[52] The Committee recognised that in the simpler types of case, only a brief statement of reasons might be given, but thought that in general fuller reasons could be given. Thus the views of the NAB and Sir Harold Fieldhouse on this point were completely rejected.

Possibly the most important indication that the Franks Committee regarded NATs as a special case is to be found in the rejection of the need for a right of appeal from NATs to a higher tribunal. The Committee considered that the ideal structure was that from the first tribunal there should be a full right of appeal (on law, facts or merits) to a higher tribunal. Appeal was not needed, however, when the tribunal of first instance was "so exceptionally strong and well qualified" that an appellate tribunal would be in no better position to review its decisions. Where a second tier of tribunals existed, the higher tribunal should publish reports of leading cases for circulation to lower tribunals, and as a guide to appellants and their advisors.[53]

Although the Committee had rejected the view of the NAB that reasons should not be given for NAT decisions, the Committee was persuaded by the official evidence that no appeal was needed from the local NAT.

"Although in form these Tribunals hear and determine appeals against decisions of local officers of the National Assistance Board and therefore exercise adjudicating functions, in practice their task much resembles that of an assessment or case committee, taking a further look at the facts and in some cases arriving at a fresh decision on the extent of need. For this reason and also because by their very nature questions of assistance require to be finally determined as quickly as possible, we do not think that the provision of a further appeal on merits from the Tribunals is appropriate."[54]

Did this view amount to a conclusion that NATs were exercising judicial functions only in form, and not in substance? While this view may possibly have been a correct perception of the situation as it existed in the 1950s, it is not certain that this had been intended by the Minister in 1948. Indeed, in so far as "case-work", e.g. concerning the work-shy, was undertaken by persons outside the NAB, this was a matter for the local advisory committees. In setting up these advisory committees, the Minister had been at pains to emphasise the difference between them and the appeal tribunals.[55] If social case-work was the proper task of the tribunals, then the nomenclature and procedure of tribunals were ill-suited to the task. It needs to be considered whether with the passing of the 1966 Act and its emphasis on statutory entitlement to benefit, and with the growth of the welfare rights movement, the verdict of the Franks Committee if valid in 1957, remains valid today. Recent research indicates, however, that the "case committee" view is still held strongly by many tribunal members.

A related matter was the scope for review of tribunal decisions by the ordinary courts. The Act of 1948 had provided that tribunal decisions should be "conclusive for all purposes"[57] which at that date may have been thought to exclude judicial review altogether. The Franks Committee considered that all decisions of tribunals should be subject to review by the courts on points of law. For most tribunals, the Committee recommended that a statutory right to appeal on points of law should be provided to the High Court in England or the Court of Session in Scotland, but not in the case of the National Insurance Commissioner or the NATs. In both these cases, the Franks Committee held that it would be sufficient if review was by means of the English remedy of certiorari.[58]

The difficult technical aspects of this subject are summarised in Appendix B. What needs to be stressed here is that although the Franks Report treated national insurance and national assistance adjudication alike in that no appeal to the superior courts was provided on points of law, the two tribunal systems were and still are so dissimilar that different arguments must justify the common treatment. It is one thing for no appeal on law to be provided from the National Insurance Commissioners, who are lawyers of standing and have unrivalled expertise in national insurance law. They form in effect a national tribunal exercising a uniform jurisdiction throughout Great Britain. It is another thing for there to be no appeal from 120 tribunals, who typically have no legal members, are unaccustomed to basing their decisions on relevant statutory authorities and find difficulty in formulating adequate reasons for their decisions. Unfortunately this distinction was rarely drawn in Parliamentary discussion of the Franks Report, the case of NATs usually passing by default.[59]

Parliamentary discussion of the Franks Report

When the Franks Report came to be debated in Parliament, NATs were seldom mentioned. The Home Secretary stressed that there were many NAT chairmen who had no legal qualifications but nonetheless performed their duties extremely well. In the House of Commons, Reginald Prentice was alone in urging that an appeal on points of law should lie from NATs; he argued that at least in those appeals which were not simply based upon the scale-rates of assistance, the tribunal was "not merely a case committee but had to interpret what the Act intended"; it was unsatisfactory that, when so many chairmen of tribunals were not legally qualified, diverse interpretations of the Act could be made. In the same debate, James Griffiths endorsed the general view that tribunals must be looked at not as part of the administration, but as bodies to adjudicate. He went on: "It is important therefore that no Government shall give to these tribunals matters to decide which they cannot adjudicate except by subjective considerations . . . we should not give to any of these tribunals . . . the power to decide matters on which there is no criterion by which any body of men can actually come to a practical decision."[60] Whether or not the former Minister who had established the NATs had in mind the wide discretion exerciseable by these tribunals, the comment helps to explain why difficulties arise if unstructured and uncontrolled discretion is vested in lay tribunals.

Making his maiden speech in the House of Lords debate, Lord Denning said, basing his remarks on experience gained in hearing appeals from Pension Appeal Tribunals, "Unconsciously and unmeaningly, a tribunal may slip into error and may need to be corrected, but that is not the only purpose of an appeal. Another purpose is to get uniform decisions." Lord Chorley urged the provision of an appeal on a point of law from the National Insurance Commissioners to the court: "There ought always to be the chance of thinking again by another group of people in regard to any decision."[61] In the House of Commons debate, Peter Rawlinson stressed the value of an appeal to a second-tier tribunal being available: "The fact that there is an appeal tribunal over any court always helps with the proper administration of justice; . . . the fact that there is an appeal tribunal brings to the lower court a very much more careful and proper sense of sanction than if there is no appeal tribunal."[62] But none of these three distinguished lawyers applied their remarks to the special case of NATs.

The Tribunals and Inquiries Act 1958 and subsequent developments

Despite the apparent view of the Franks Committee that NATs

were judicial in form only, many provisions of the 1958 Act were applied to them. Thus they became subject to the supervision of the Council on Tribunals. Chairmen of NATs in future would be appointed by the Minister from a panel of persons appointed by the Lord Chancellor (in Scotland by the Lord President).[63] Members and chairmen could not be removed without the concurrence of the Lord Chancellor or the Lord President[64] although such concurrence was not needed if an appointment lapsed by process of time and was not renewed. Reasons had to be given by NATs but only if requested on or before the decision being given,[65] a limitation which, at least for inexperienced and unrepresented claimants, made the duty to give reasons of little practical value. Legal representation before NATs was permitted when new regulations were made.[66] But no further appeal was provided, whether on the merits to a higher tribunal or on a point of law to the civil courts. And the NATs continued to sit in private.

The immediate effect of these changes was not considerable. Between 1959 and 1965, the number of appeals heard by NATs showed a general tendency to rise, although not as sharply as after the 1966 Act. Little use was made of the new right to legal representation, at least in the first few years after 1958.[67] A small number of visits were made by members of the Council on Tribunals to NATs, and a number of miscellaneous points about the tribunals were considered by the Council from time to time. The accommodation provided for the tribunals was not at first considered satisfactory and was later improved.[68] In 1959 Tribunals visited were found to be giving a "fair and patient hearing" to appellants but a year later, some tribunals "seemed markedly more efficient than others" and in three tribunals, the clerk was permitted to take too active a part.[69] In 1962, members of the Council were favourably impressed by the "sympathetic hearing" given to appellants at the seven tribunals visited.[70] Infrequent visits of this kind may have some value, but the Council did not have the resources, nor possibly a sufficient foothold within Whitehall, to review the working of NATs at all systematically, even if this had been felt necessary. The involvement of the Lord Chancellor and the Lord President in the appointment of chairmen did not, as might have been supposed, lead to more legal chairmen being appointed. In fact a sharp trend away from legal chairmen occurred: in 1956, 37 of the 151 chairmen of NATs were legally qualified; in 1969, only 11 out of 205 chairmen of SBATs were lawyers.[71] In its report for 1963, the Council on Tribunals reported that NATs were functioning satisfactorily without legal chairmen but it is not certain that this view would today be held by the Council as regards SBATs.[72] When SBATs were established under the 1966 Act, the Council on Tribunals was consulted on the new rules of procedure.[73]

In 1966, national assistance gave way to supplementary benefits. While much of the legislation was simply re-enacted in the Act of 1966, significant alterations to the legal nature of the scheme were made. The framers of the 1966 Act were anxious to narrow the gap which had developed in administration between contributory benefits and non-contributory, means-tested benefit, particularly as many people were in receipt of both. The new Ministry was created to provide a framework within which both kinds of benefit could be jointly administered. The Supplementary Benefits Commission was set much more plainly within the Ministry than the National Assistance Board had been. The most important change for present purposes was the introduction of the concept of entitlement to benefit. Whereas the National Assistance Board had been under a duty to give assistance and the claimant had at best an implied right to assistance, the 1966 Act gave an express right to benefit and the concept of assistance disappeared. According to the Minister's explanatory memorandum, "In the future there will no longer be the sharp distinction which now exists in the administration of contributory and means-tested benefit."[74] And in Parliament, the Minister said: "under the new scheme, there will be a clear statutory right to benefit for anyone who fulfils the conditions set out in the Bill".[75]

The extent to which the concept of entitlement replaced that of administrative discretion is discussed in later chapters. To give some effect to the notion of entitlement, it was necessary to develop the legal framework of rules. Thus the Act allowed the SBC no discretion to reduce supplementary pensions below the scale rates.[76] Several rules appeared in legal form for the first time—e.g. the disqualification of persons completing secondary education; the cohabitation rule; the long-term addition; the rules on deliberate abandonment of resources; and authority was conferred on the SBC to review all decisions of the Commission and of appeal tribunals.[77]

But the 1966 Act did not alter the tribunal structure. The tribunals were renamed and, as in 1948, existing tribunals were deemed to have been constituted under the new Act. Parliamentary debate on the 1966 Act was sharply curtailed because of the imminent general election. Almost nothing was said about the tribunals. Some M.P.s unsuccessfully supported an amendment requiring a written explanation to be given of the calculation of every pension and allowance and every refusal or reduction of benefit, but no M.P. appeared to grasp the potential significance for the tribunal system of the concept of entitlement. Mr. Pentland, Joint Parliamentary Secretary, stated, "I do not think that the fact that adjudication (i.e. on claims) is done under the authority of the SBC rather than by the local insurance officer will make any difference one way or the other to the pensioner."[78] This statement ignored the "sharp distinction" which continued to exist between the two adjudication schemes and which had the direct effect of producing one form of entitlement for national insurance benefits, and another lesser form of entitlement for supplementary benefit purposes.[79]

Subsequent events have confirmed that the failure in the 1966 Act to take the opportunity of reforming the tribunal structure was not inadvertent.[80] In 1970, when Family Income Supplement was introduced, appeals were entrusted to SBATs. Now FIS, although a means-tested benefit, is exclusively a matter of entitlement and in no way dependent upon administrative discretion. In the debate on the bill, Michael Meacher suggested that FIS had much in common with Family Allowances and should therefore be entrusted to the national insurance scheme of adjudication. The Minister replied that national insurance procedure was more formal and less friendly than that of SBATs, and "would tend to legalise and make more difficult, remote and forbidding to the individual the procedure that we are proposing."[81] This was a strange description for the Minister to give of social security tribunals for which he was himself responsible. Are national insurance tribunals, which hear Family Allowance appeals, "difficult, remote and forbidding to the individual"?

Conclusions

I have sought to demonstrate the strong element of administrative continuity which underlies the development of supplementary benefit adjudication. Neither in 1948, nor in 1966, nor in the debates on the Franks Report, was Parliament enabled to explore the scope for reform in the adjudication machinery for means-tested, non-contributory benefits. Necessarily the Franks Report was a product of its time and restricted in the depth of its findings by the extremely wide examination of all tribunals and inquiries which it was asked to make. Probably the general principles laid down by the Franks Report have still something to offer SBATs, if only because they have never been fully applied. But in the light of developments in the social security system since 1957, the views of the Franks Committee on the structure and purpose of these tribunals should not be accepted today without thorough re-examination. Far more research has been done into SBATs than was ever done into their predecessors. Even the discreet reports of the Council on Tribunals have in recent years provided evidence of shortcomings in the present system. Have any other tribunals experienced the acute difficulty in giving adequate reasons for their decisions which the SBATs are still experiencing, sixteen years after the duty to give reasons was first introduced by the 1958 Act?

Across the broad span of government in the 1960s there developed new tribunals and new techniques for enabling executive discretion to be exercised in a manner conforming more closely to modern notions of administrative justice. The immigration appeals system, created in 1969, is a striking example of the application of tribunal procedures to an area formerly reserved to executive discretion. Evidence of administrative continuity tenaciously maintained over a period of 40 years does not in itself prove that the system should be changed. But the available evidence does suggest that the case for innovation has not yet been fully explored by those directly responsible for developing social policy.

NOTES
[Report = Report of the Franks Committee on Tribunals and Inquiries, Cmnd. 218, 1957. Evidence = Evidence to the Franks Committee, 1957.]

1. George Lach, in *Administrative Tribunals at Work*, ed. Pollard, 1950, p. 56.

2. Old Age and Widows' Pensions Act 1940; Lach, p. 44.

3. 1948 Act, ss. 2(2) and 4.

4. H.C. Deb., 24 Nov. 1947, cols. 1606 and 1616. Bevan was in fact referring to the passing of the unpopular 'household' means test; see chap. 2 above.

5. H.C. Deb., 24 Nov. 1947, col. 1640.

6. Standing Committee C, 11 Dec. 1947, col. 2398.

7. See the repeated discussion of the use of discretionary powers in the reports of the U.A.B. for 1935-1939. That for 1935, at p. 170, quoted the Manchester office: "Area Officers have come to feel that the arithmetical calculation is merely a background for the exercise of discretion ... Imagination and experience have enabled them to evolve a welfare service which is doing a good deal to restore the self-respect of our people."

8. Stdg. Ctee. C. 11 Dec. 1947, cols. 2373-2382. After surviving various changes of name and structure, the advisory committees were eventually abolished by the Social Security Act 1971.

9. H.C. Deb., 24 Nov. 1947, col. 1714 and Stdg. Ctee. C, 11 Dec. 1947, cols. 2385-2386.

10. H.C. Deb., 24 Nov. 1947, col. 1646 (Carmichael), 1659 (Macpherson), 1688 (Wingfield Digby); cf. H.C. Deb. 5 Mar. 1948, col. 720 (Molson).

11. Stdg. Ctee. C, 18 Dec. 1947, col. 2464 (Carmichael).

12. Stdg. Ctee. C, 18 Dec. 1947, col. 2465 (Griffiths)

13. N.A. (Determination of Need) Regulation 1948 (S.I. 1334), regns. 3 and 6.

14. Stdg. Ctee. C, 18 Dec. 1947, col. 2465.

15. H.C. Deb., 24 Nov. 1947, col. 1715.

16. Stdg. Ctee. C, 11 Dec. 1947, cols. 2402 and 2481. For the practice of the U.A.B., see chap. 2 above.

17. Stdg. Ctee. C, 17 Dec. 1947; col. 2463.

18. 1948 Act, s. 14(2): this requirement was quietly dropped from the 1966 Act.

19. H.C. Deb., 24 Nov. 1947, col. 1659 (Macpherson).

20. Stdg. Ctee. C, 17 Dec. 1947, col. 2420 (Webbe).

21. H.C. Deb., 5 Mar. 1948, cols 681-686.

22. H.C. Deb., 5 Mar. 1948, col. 728.

23. Lach, p. 52; 1948 Act, sched. 6, para. 7

24. Act of 1948, sched. 5, para. 3.

25. Lach, pp. 52-53.

26. N.A. (Appeal Tribunals) Rules Confirmation Instrument 1948 (S.I. 1454), rule 11(1).

27. The power still survives: see 1966 Act, sched. 3, para. 5.

28. The written evidence by the N.A.B. is in Memoranda submitted by Government Departments, Vol. I, pp. 27-34 and in Appendix II to Evidence, pp. 159-162. The oral evidence is in Evidence, pp. 42-49 and pp. 1124-6.

29. Evidence, Appendix II, p. 161.

30. Annual Report of U.A.B. for 1935, chap. 4.

31. Memoranda, pp. 33-34.

32. Memoranda, p. 31.

33. 1948 Act, s. 14(4). See also Appendix B.

34. Evidence, pp. 44, 48, 46.

35. Evidence, p. 47.

36. Evidence, App. II, pp. 159-160.

37. Evidence, App. II, p. 161.

38. Evidence, p. 516.

39. Evidence, p. 574.

40. Report, paras. 40, 42.

41. Report, para. 40.

42. W.A. Robson, *Justice and Administrative Law*, 2nd edn., p. 12.

43. Robson, p. 505.

44. Report, para. 406.

45. R.E. Wraith and P.G. Hutchesson, *Administrative Tribunals*, 1973, p. 165.

46. Report, para. 138. cf. Harry Calvert's arguments, chap. 14 below.

47. Report, paras. 55 and 90.

48. Report, para. 58. Tribunals and Inquiries Act 1958, s. 6.

49. Report, para. 60.

50. Report, paras. 64, 79 and 180.

51. S.I. 714 of 1958. See now S.B. (Appeal Tribunal) Rules 1971, S.I. 680, rule 11(3).

52. Report, para. 98.

53. Report, paras. 106 and 102.

54. Report, para. 182.

55. H.C. Deb., 24 Nov. 1947, col. 1714 (Griffiths).

56. See chap. 8 below.

57. 1948 Act, s. 14(4). 1966 Act, s. 18(3).

58. Report, paras. 107-109. Tribunals and Inquiries Act 1958, s. 9.

59. H.L. Deb., 27 Nov. 1957, col. 527 (Lord Reading), col. 582 (Lord Kilmuir). H.C., Standing Committee B, 15 July 1958, cols. 71-77 (Renton).

60. H.C. Deb., 31 Oct. 1957, cols. 406 (Butler), 458-9 (Prentice) and 504 (Griffiths).

61. H.L. Deb., 27 Nov. 1957, cols. 548 and 558.

62. H.C. Deb., 31 Oct. 1957, col. 1633.

63. Tribunals and Inquiries Act 1958, s. 3; now 1971 Act, s. 7.

64. 1958 Act, s. 5; 1971 Act, s. 8.

65. 1958 Act, s. 12.

66. Note 51 above.

67. Report of N.A.B. for 1958, Cmnd. 781.

68. Report of Council on Tribunals for 1959, para. 100; for 1960, paras. 54-56.

69. Report for 1959, para. 100; for 1960, para. 53.

70. Report for 1962, para. 51.

71. Kathleen Bell, "Administrative Tribunals since Franks", *Social and Economic Administration* 4 1970, p. 289.

72. Report for 1963, p. 29; cf. Report for 1972-73, para. 70-73 and Appendix B.

73. Report for 1970-71, para. 48.

74. Ministry of Social Security Bill, Explanatory Memorandum, Cmnd. 2997, 1966, para. 2.

75. H.C. Deb., 24 May 1966, col. 340.

76. 1966 Act. Sched. 2, para. 4(1).

77. See, respectively, in the 1966 Act: s. 9; Sched. 2, para. 3; Sched. 2, para. 12; Sched. 2, paras. 27 and 28; s. 17(1)(c).

78. H.C. Deb., 24 May 1966, col. 410.

79. Lynes, *Penguin Guide to Supplementary Benefit.* 1972, pp. 24-25.

80. See e.g. R.M. Titmuss, "Welfare 'Rights', Law and Discretion", *Political Quarterly* 42, 1971, pp. 113-132.

81. H.C. Deb., 18 Nov. 1970, cols. 1357-1358 (Dean).

IV DISCRETIONARY BENEFITS*
Richard Wilding

Two main kinds of discretionary benefit are paid under the supplementary benefits scheme: the regular additions to weekly benefit known as exceptional circumstances additions (ECAs) and the lump sums known as exceptional needs payments (ENPs).

The benefits and disregards which make up a person's entitlement are laid down in detail in the legislation.[1] The powers providing for the two main kinds of discretionary benefit that may be paid in addition are expressed in very different legislative language. Section 7 of the 1966 Act, which provides for the occasional lump sums or ENPs, says: "Where it appears to the Commission reasonable in all the circumstances they may determine that benefit shall be paid to a person by way of a single payment to meet an exceptional need."

Paragraph 4(1)(a) of the Second Schedule, which provides for regular weekly additions to benefit or ECAs, says: "Where there are exceptional circumstances, benefit may be awarded at an amount exceeding that (if any) calculated in accordance with the preceding paragraphs . . . as may be appropriate to take account of those circumstances."

In both cases the need or the circumstances have to be exceptional. But apart from this proviso, Parliament has placed no limit either on the kind of need that may be met or on the amount that may be paid. A large responsibility is therefore placed on the Supplementary Benefits Commission to devise their own methods of administering these discretionary benefits. They face three main problems:

*This chapter is abridged from a lecture given to first year graduate social work students at the University of Oxford as part of a series on aspects of discretionary powers in the social services. It was first published in *Social Work Today*, 5 October, 1972 and is reprinted here with the permission of the editor and the author.

(1) Where is the line to be drawn between the needs that should be regarded as *universal* and those that should be regarded as *exceptional*?

(2) How far should it be the objective of the supplementary benefit scheme to exercise discretion in a manner which is *equitable* as between one person and another?

(3) How far should the Commission *delegate* the discretionary power provided by Parliament to the nearly 20,000 staff, mainly in relatively junior grades, in the 400 local offices up and down the country?

First, universal versus exceptional. A person's needs are all of a piece. If he needs extra heating or a special diet, this is no less a part of his essential need than the basic weekly scale-rate or the rent. In this respect there is no distinction between what he is entitled to and what he gets as a result of discretion; and both are rightly measured together against his resources. This at once modifies the concept of discretion as something entirely free in this context; however much it is left to discretion to decide whether an exceptional need exists, once it is decided there is something at least of an obligation to meet it. The point emerges most clearly where normal needs are already met by existing resources and it is the discretionary decision that determines whether supplementary benefit is to be paid at all. Once established, the special need is part of the situation which adds up to a person's entitlement to benefit, even if it is not itself the subject of a statutory right.

So the question is not one of entitlement versus discretion as two wholly separate and opposite things. It is one of distinguishing those needs which can usefully be expressed in the form of a universal entitlement because they are part of everybody's requirements from those that are better provided for in a general discretionary power because they are exceptional and because one cannot give a statutory description of them which will satisfactorily cover all circumstances which need to be met. The problem is to determine where from time to time the one ends and the other begins.

Universal and exceptional

It is illustrated by the long-term addition (LTA), introduced in 1966, which is required to take the first strain of special needs: ECAs are only paid in long-term cases where the total of a person's exceptional needs exceeds 50p a week.[2] A problem now arises whenever additional money can be found for the improvement of the supplementary benefit scheme over and above the annual increase in the basic rates. The extra sum can go to increasing the LTA, thus increasing universal provision but decreasing discretionary provision, since those with special needs over 50p then receive more in LTA but less in ECAs. Or it can go to improving ECAs, with the effect of increasing discretionary provision while keeping the LTA's level of universal provision static—or decreasing in real value as prices rise. Unless the sum is equally divided between the two, one or the other must be favoured.

The necessity of this choice between improving the universal at the expense of the discretionary or *vice versa* could only be eliminated if:

(a) the universal rates were raised to the level of the highest discretionary addition; or

(b) the Commission ceased to provide for some of the exceptional needs which it covers at present.

On the first of these, discretionary additions can amount to several pounds a week, e.g. for some sick people needing domestic help; and it is difficult to imagine that any government will regard it as its highest social priority to raise the universal rates to that level, involving as it would a vast increase in the numbers of people on supplementary benefit. On the second, it is equally hard to imagine the Commission feeling that the right way of promoting universal benefits was to cut back the exceptional ones. In practice, therefore, the question is one of adjustment from time to time, depending on the situation, the resources available and the ability of the local offices to take on more discretionary work.

In considering discretionary provision, the Commission is bound by the word 'exceptional'. Its application can be illustrated by reference to extra heating — extra because normal heating needs are included in the basic scale-rate. 'Exceptional' here can mean two things. One is an exceptional situation external to the claimants themselves. Thus, for example, during exceptionally prolonged cold winter weather, local offices have standing instructions to give extra help, for example with meeting electricity bills. More commonly, however, 'exceptional' means an exceptional need of the individual — by comparison with the general run of claimants. The guidance given to the staff thus provides that ECAs may be allowed in those situations where people commonly need more heating than usual. These are chronic ill-health or accommodation which is exceptionally difficult to heat or a combination of the two. The three rates of benefit, 30p 60p and 90p a week, depend on the severity of the case.[3]

Two points are worth bringing out here. First, the Commission may not use its discretionary power to provide extra heating for the generality of supplementary benefits claimants in normal circumstances, that is, as a more or less covert way of supplementing the basic rates of benefit. If claimants generally are cold — or hungry or ill-clad — this is a situation which only the government can deal with, by increasing the basic rates payable under the Act. Secondly, the criteria for extra heating illustrate the reasons why it is desirable and perhaps even essential to keep the statutory authorisation of this kind of help in general and discretionary terms. A statutory description of the terms of eligibility would have to take the form of a list of prescribed diseases and accommodation criteria in which cubic footage, and index of humidity and rates of heat-loss would all have to appear. It is not difficult then to imagine the extensive bureaucratic apparatus which would have to be erected in order to determine, and to check in cases of appeal, whether each individual qualified, and for how much. And even then, it is a safe bet that cases of genuine need would arise which the statutory criteria failed to cover.

Concepts of discretion and equity

At first sight, the two concepts of discretion and equity are uncomfortable bedfellows; indeed, the equitable exercise of discretion could be argued to be a contradiction in terms. In this context however it is not only not a contradiction; it is an essential objective. It has two aspects: equity as between one supplementary benefit claimant and another; and equity as between claimants and their neighbours in full-time work.

The point can be illustrated by ENPs (occasional lump sum payments). These cover a wide variety of needs. Just over half the total are paid to help with clothing and bedding; but ENPs can also cover repairs to the houses of owner-occupiers, fares, removal expenses, furniture, curtains and floor coverings, fireguards, on rare occasions funeral expenses and a multitude of other things. To avoid hardship, they may on occasion cover expenses which are intended to be met out of the scale-rate. Minor items of clothing for example are covered by the scale-rate; and the cost of heating is covered by the scale rate and any ECA that may be allowed. But if a claimant is badly in need of underclothes, or has run up an electricity bill which he cannot pay and hardship to old people or young children will result if the supply is disconnected, the Commission may use its discretionary powers to help out in exceptional cases.

The discretionary power is thus wide; but the Commission has to be correspondingly careful about the use it makes of it. Take for example the payment of a fuel bill. People get into debt for a variety of reasons. They may have moved into new housing with a new form of heating which they have not yet got used to. Or illness may have produced a need for which an ECA could have been paid if the need had been picked up at the time. In such cases the local office will readily foot the bill. But where the claimant has plainly neglected to budget, the problem is more difficult. The local office must weigh his need against the demands of equity — fairness to the great majority of claimants who have paid their electricity bills out of their regular income. This is equity between one claimant and another. Where old people or young children are at risk, equity has to go under and the bill must be met (though the local office will take what steps it can to prevent it happening again). But in other cases the claims of equity must be asserted.

Similarly, if a claimant needs a winter coat, this is normally too expensive to be met out of the scale-rate, and it will often be right to make an ENP. The payment should be enough to buy a decent article of durable quality. But it is evident that the Commission will be in trouble — and rightly — if it provides a coat which is well beyond anything that the neighbours in full-time work could buy for themselves. This is equity as between claimants and the rest of the community. Regard must be had to the standards and expectations which are normal to the claimant and his neighbour.

These rival concepts of welfare and equity can perhaps best be reconciled if one looks on discretionary benefits as paid not on top of the normal rates of benefit but in support of them. The scale-rates provide something more than a bare subsistence level: they are some 75 per cent higher in real terms than they were in 1948.[4] Within them, there is a small margin: income which a claimant can choose how to spend. It may be nicer food, a television licence, household amenities, pocket money for the children or an occasional outing or a shampoo and set. The object of ECAs and ENPs is not only to provide those goods or services which represent an essential need, but also to restore that small element of choice in situations in which it would otherwise disappear. A family should not have to go without all these things in order to keep itself clothed or fed or warm. The use of ECAs and ENPs is thus in one sense to restore the situation — but not, by doing more than that, to raise claimants above the general standard of living which the general rates of benefit imply.

The delegation of discretion

Finally, the third and most difficult problem: how far to delegate the Commission's discretionary powers. The discretion is the Commissioners' and they are finally responsible for the way it is exercised. Equally, the Act talks of what appears "reasonable in the circumstances" and "when there are exceptional circumstances", clearly implying that discretionary decisions should take all the circumstances into account. No set of rules of thumb promulgated by the Commission could discharge this duty. The question is: how much should be left to the officer on the spot who alone can say what all the circumstances are, and how much laid down in the instructions and guidance which the Commission issues to its staff? If the instructions are too vague, there will be no consistency in practice; if they are too detailed, they will fail to fit the variety of need and the staff will not be able to digest them.

In practice the answer varies. At one extreme, little if any discretion is left to the local officer. This is so for special diets. The list of conditions for which a special diet is essential is promulgated by the Commission on medical advice. The question whether Mr Brown has the disease and ought to have the diet is decided by Mr Brown's doctor. Discretion hardly comes into it at all. At the other extreme come some ENPs. Mr Jones, who has a wife and four children, claims an ENP to buy a new pair of shoes. He had a payment for the same purpose three months ago; he is behind with the rent and probably drinks the rent money; he is or should be looking for work, and less likely to go out if his shoes let in the wet; he produces an old pair of shoes which could just — but only just — be repaired. The decision is, has to be, left to the local officer almost entirely. The Commission offers general guidance, but at the end of the day only the officer's own experience and commonsense can provide the answer in the individual case.

His decision, of course, is not necessarily the end of the story. The claimant may appeal against it, and quite a number do. And if a third party or his MP takes up the case on his behalf, and if inquiry shows that not all the relevant facts were taken into account, the decision can be altered. But subject to these safeguards, the Commission will stand behind a discretionary decision which the local officer has responsibly taken with all the facts before him.

Hard-pressed local officers

It is sometimes said that this system puts too great a weight of responsibility on local officers, who are relatively junior in rank, not trained as professional social workers, paid at the normal civil servant rates for their grades, hard-pressed by a flood of work which seems constantly and inexorably to increase, and may have been drafted into supplementary benefit work with little liking or natural aptitude for it. This is commonly said when mistakes, both real and imagined, are brought to light; and the argument is then advanced that the Commission ought to tie the hands of the staff more closely; the instructions should be made more precise and exhaustive, and they should be published so that everybody knows what they are.

This is a respectable view, sincerely held. The pressures on our local offices are heavy, and have been greatly increased by the relatively new pressures brought to bear ·by claimants' unions, the CPAG, some students and some social workers who in different ways have begun to act as representatives of claimants, both collectively and individually. This development was bound to come and is entirely to be welcomed except in the few instances where it takes a disruptive form. It does not add to the responsibility of the job, but it increases the demand on time and on the ability of the local office to explain and defend what it is doing. But is there now a convincing case for a radical change in the system?

The answer to this question lies not in pretending that the scheme works perfectly, which it does not, but in considering whether any better alternative can be devised. The criticism should be seen in perspective. Quite certainly mistakes are made. But not as many as some think. A good many cases come my way. More often than not, the person who refers the case has heard one side of the story only — the claimant's — and has not checked it; and more often than not the story has become distorted in the telling. It is important to say this, both in defence of our staff and because unchecked horror-stories, when given publicity or passed from mouth to mouth, create a prejudice which must sooner or later deter some needy person from claiming benefit.

When one looks at the mistakes that are made, moreover, few of them are attributable to the lack of a professional social worker's training. Most arise at a relatively simple level. People make mistakes in arithmetic; they fail to ask the relevant question they have been trained to ask; and sometimes, not very often and usually under stress, they attach too much importance to an impression of bad faith on the part of the claimant. All these, and others, are mistakes which an experienced clerical or executive officer, properly trained, can avoid. The great majority do in fact avoid them nearly all the time. It is possible greatly to underestimate what the experience and good sense of the average officer in the local social security office can do in this field. And when he finds a problem which really does need the expertise of the social worker or other professional, he is instructed to enlist it. If this analysis is right, or even three-quarters right, then most of the necessary improvement in the administration of supplementary benefits can be brought about by improvements in training, in managerial supervision and in communications between the Commission and its staff.

A restrictive alternative?

The alternative of elaborating and publishing rules and instructions seems a lot less attractive from the point of view of the claimant's interest. It is a fallacy to believe that discretion can be virtually abolished in this field. If, to borrow Professor Titmuss's example, it were a rule that everybody should possess a serviceable toothbrush, there would still be room for argument about whether the old toothbrush was worn out.[5] The effect of multiplying rules is not to abolish discretion but to transfer it to a narrower and less fruitful area. As rules define, moreover, they necessarily also restrict. If the Commission attempted precisely to define the circumstances in which help could be given, it would have to rule some circumstances and some categories of claimants out. But it is certain that among them there would be some cases of genuine and pressing need. Rules will not tell you which they are, but the local officer, looking at all the circumstances of each case, will get at least some of them right.

The question of publication is more complex. It is one thing to publish a broad account of the principles that the Commission has developed for the exercise of its discretionary powers and the general nature of the guidance it has issued. This is surely desirable; the Commission has advanced along these lines in the Supplementary Benefit Handbook, and is taking it further in its special reports. But it is another thing to publish the precise instructions given to staff. What then inevitably follows is a series of confrontations, in which the claimant or his advisers argue that the instructions provide for extra benefit in his case and the local office argues that they don't. The response of any bureaucracy to the stress which this sets up is to elaborate its defences by multiplying the rules and tying down the cases. The restrictive effect of multiplying rules is thus compounded by publishing them. And as rules multiply, so do the procedures for applying them, and so does the number of civil servants needed to do the job — and to do it, as I have suggested, less well.

I have tried to indicate some of the constraints that are inherent in the system, the need to adjust from time to time the balance between universal and exceptional provision, recognising that it is not possible to escape the dilemma by making the whole benefit structure universal; the need to balance the claims of welfare against the claims of equity; and the need to accept some unevenness in administration as the price paid for the flexibility which can only be kept by preserving and standing behind the discretionary judgment of the local officer. There is no room for complacency about the system, but it is not beyond our reach to make it work well. Without doubt, one of the essential conditions of that achievement is that the scheme should be understood, in both its limitations and its possibilities, by those who work in closely related fields, so that social security staff can work effectively with them in ensuring full use of its potential for bringing help to those who need it.

NOTES

1. The Supplementary Benefits Act 1966 and the regulations made under it.

2. Since this article was first published the LTA has been incorporated in long-term scale rates of which 50p (75p for those over 80) is offset against special expenses, other than heating additions. The change does not affect the argument.

3. These rates have since been increased and are subject to further amendments with time. Current rates and a fuller description of the circumstances in which they apply are discussed by Henry Hodge, chapter 5 below.

4. As of July 1974, they were over 100% higher.

5. Richard Titmuss, "Welfare 'Rights', Law and Discretion", *Political Quarterly* 42, 1971. p. 113.

V DISCRETION IN REALITY
Henry Hodge

The supplementary benefit system provides for all or part of the financial needs of nearly 4½ million people in our society. The scale of operation of the Supplementary Benefits Commission (SBC) is massive. In 1973 there were over 4½ million claims for supplementary benefit and on average over 2,600,000 regular weekly payments to heads of households or single claimants. The effect of the Supplementary Benefits Act 1966 is to give an entitlement to benefit. There are, however, four preconditions which must be met before benefit will be paid: the claimant has to be in Great Britain, he must be over the age of 16, his resources have to be insufficient to meet his requirements and he must fit his case within a series of provisions contained in the 1966 Act. Broadly, benefit will not be paid if the claimant is in remunerative full-time work or undergoing full-time education in school; and if the claimant is on strike he cannot get benefit for himself.

When a claim is made, the SBC has an obligation to work out the claimant's statutory requirements (including rent) and resources, and then deduct those resources from his requirements to arrive at the figure which prima facie should be paid as benefit. Entitlement is therefore assessed by a means-test and the Commission's wide discretionary powers can then be used both to the advantage and the disadvantage of claimants. The power to increase or reduce benefit makes discretion the dominant element in the system.

The role of discretion in the system

The number of claimants who have discretion exercised in their favour is very considerable. Over 750,000 people have their weekly benefit increased by exceptional circumstances additions (ECAs) which range in amount from a few pence to £3 or more. In 1973 over 800,000 single payments to meet an exceptional need (ENPs) were made by the Commission. On the negative side, in 1973 there were

65

just under 13,000 claimants whose full rent was not being paid and between October 1968 and May 1973 about a quarter of a million claimants had their benefit withheld four weeks after they made a claim.

When a claim for benefit is made the Commission will first satisfy themselves that the four preconditions set out above have been met. Then, using Schedule 2 of the 1966 Act, they have to decide if any other person's requirements and resources should be aggregated with the claimants. Discretion can operate when calculating requirements: thus, under para. 13 of Schedule 2, the rent addition for claimants need only be what "is reasonable in the circumstances". The Commission may also be obliged to limit the claimant's requirements to the amount he would receive if he were in work under the wage stop rule.[1] In theory, even if he ought to be wage stopped, the Commission need not apply the rule if there are exceptional circumstances.

In practice that discretionary decision is never made at a local office but is reserved for the Commission's head office. Discretion may also be exercised when calculating resources. The Commission might decide that the claimant has deliberately abandoned resources in order to obtain benefit, or that some resource that is not specially mentioned in Schedule 2 should not be included in full as an asset so as to reduce his requirements. But discretion as it is most commonly understood does not come into play until these first calculations have been done.

The three most important powers under which discretion is exercised by the Commission and the appeal tribunals are contained in sections 7 and 13 and para. 4 (1) of Schedule 2 of the 1966 Act. Under section 7, where it appears to the Commission reasonable in all the circumstances, they may determine that benefit should be paid to a person by way of a single payment to meet an exceptional need. Under section 13, they may pay benefit in an urgent case without having any regard to the Act, the regulations or the rules contained in Schedule 2. Under para. 4 (1) (a) of Schedule 2, where there are exceptional circumstances, benefit may be paid at an amount which exceeds the calculation of entitlement. Those who receive a supplementary allowance (people under pension age) rather than a supplementary pension can also, by para. 4 (1) (b), have their benefit reduced or withheld completely.

The problem of how to exercise discretionary powers has exercised a number of statutory bodies which Parliament has entrusted with the administration of successive means-tested income support systems. They have each tried to provide answers to questions such as: what are exceptional circumstances?, what are exceptional needs?, what is reasonable?, and what is urgent?. The Unemployment Assistance Board, the National Assistance Board and now the Supplementary Benefits Commission have all resorted to giving guidance on these questions to their staff in policy codes, the details of which are kept secret. These codes have grown in complexity since the 1930's. There are now thought to be something like 16 secret codes but little is known of how the policy contained in them is formulated. It is reasonable to assume that major policy matters are decided by the Supplementary Benefits Commission itself. However Government in the shape of the DHSS also involves itself in the exercise of discretion and it was as a result of a Government decision that the notorious four week rule was introduced in 1968. For five years the Supplementary Benefits Commission, acting under Schedule 2, para. 4(1)(b), used to withhold benefit after four weeks from unemployed, single, fit, unskilled men under 45 when there were thought to be good job opportunities in the area where they were claiming. Those factors were thought to provide a satisfactory legal basis for saying that the individual claimant's circumstances were 'exceptional' and so justified a withholding of benefit. Equally it appears to have been a policy decision by the Government to abandon this procedure and to replace it with an alternative, whereby such claimants are specially interviewed at the end of four weeks and may then have their benefit withheld.

In mid 1975, the four week rule was not being operated, again as the result of a Government decision, but we do not know whether this was promoted through representations from the SBC, the Department of Employment, or Ministers themselves. What is obvious to anybody who has looked at them is that the secret codes are a tribute to the ingenuity of successive statutory bodies and civil servants who have attempted to define every possible situation that classes of individuals may meet. At the same time, because of the complexity of trying to deal with the individual needs of millions of claimants the codes are difficult to understand, difficult for any but the most industrious to know in detail and, more importantly, rarely provide answers on how to deal with an individual's personal problem. The most they can hope to do is to provide a framework within which to consider that problem.

Discretion is therefore operated within a framework of policy rules and it is perceived in different ways by individuals with different positions within the system. Discretion is, in the writer's view, most real to the administrators. But the administrators are not a homogeneous group. The members of the Supplementary Benefits Commission appear to have the widest discretion; they decide the policy rules and the Chairman can, and occasionally does, exercise his discretion in individual cases. The civil servants who draft the codes also exercise a wide discretion. Thereafter the power to make discretionary decisions outside the policy rules decreases according to the administrator's position in the hierarchy. Staff who make the decisions at headquarters have more power than those who make decisions at regional office level, who in turn have more power than those at local office level while tribunals, technically, have all the powers of the Commissioners, discretion becomes almost mythical for claimants who want their own personal needs to be considered. Their needs must fit within the policy. Help is most likely if the need is objectively assessable and least likely if the need is entirely personal. This arises because of the conflicts which are inherent in attempts to exercise discretionary powers for large numbers of people. The adminstrators work so as to promote equity between one claimant and another and to promote equity between claimants and non-claimants at about the same levels of income.[2] The administrators also clearly attempt to use their powers to satisfy society at large that hardship will be alleviated. But a further criterion appears to operate, namely how deserving is the individual claimant in society's terms, both as a person and according to the hardship he or she faces?

Against this background this chapter examines the policy used in awarding heating allowances and clothing grants, then looks briefly at the adjudication system, and finally considers this policy in the context of the equity arguments outlined above.

Heating and clothing grants — the policy

What happens when a claimant wants help with his heating costs? It is CPAG's experience that the majority of claimants are not aware of the existence of ECAs and studies in Coventry and Birmingham confirm this. If they get so far as to claim them they often meet with "begrudging obstructionism".[3] In addition they run up against the Commisssion's policy rules. A claim for an ECA for heating will first be considered in the local office and a visitor may then be sent to the claimant's home. If the ECA is granted it will be fitted into one of the 40p, 80p or £1.20 bands. The banding is sophisticated and is as follows:

"The following extra heating additions are payable for a claimant or dependant where:-

(a) mobility is restricted because of general fraility or old age.   40p

(b) extra heating is required because of chronic ill health (e.g., chronic bronchitis, rheumatism, severe anaemia or chronic debility)   40p

(c) the claimant or dependant is housebound (including one whose mobility is so restricted that he is unable to leave the house unaided)   40p

(d) there is a serious illness requiring extra heating   80p

(e) the claimant or dependant is bedfast (or his mobility is so restricted that he requires assistance in walking in the room) and needs extra heating day and night   £1.20

(f) serious illness requires a constant room temperature day and night   £1.20

or if the claimant is a householder and:-

(g) the accommodation is difficult to heat adequately (e.g., on account of damp or because the rooms are unusually large)   40p

(h) the nature and condition of the accommodation is such that it is exceptionally difficult to heat adequately   80p

Any one of the health criteria (a—f) may be aggregated with either one of the accommodation criteria (g—h) subject to an overall maximum addition of £1.20. In very exceptional cases an addition of more than £1.20 may be made."[4]

The absolute discretion conferred by para. 4(1)(a) is clearly limited so as to enable "a lay officer to decide what is a reasonable level of additional expense in given circumstances" (Handbook, para. 7). The individual's assessment of his own needs is irrelevant in these circumstances. It is occasionally possible for claimants or their advisors to present the local DHSS office with fuel bills which show an average expenditure of over or between the 40p, 80p and £1.20 tariffs. Such details are invariably ignored at local office levels. Their criteria ignore actual expenditure.

Some guidance as to why this happens is given in the way in which claims for extra expenses for central heating are now dealt with. The published policy referred to above indicates that if a fixed charge exceeds £1.60 the extra will be paid and indeed that appears to have been the practice until recently. But now the secret policy is different. A recent copy of the 'A' code (Circular A/199) has this to say about central heating:"Common figures of average expenditure on central heating will be established in liaison, as appropriate, with fuel authorities and local authorities and a heating addition will be payable of the amount by which this figure exceeds £1.60. If different figures for different sizes of accommodation can be established these will be used in both full and partial central heating cases. There will be no need to have regard to actual expenditure or to make enquiries about what is actually spent". Administrative simplicity thus takes precedence over the claimant's wants and the money he spends on heating is irrelevant.

Weekly benefit is also supposed to cover normal replacement of clothing. Grants for exceptional needs can however be made under section 7 of the 1966 Act. The Commission say that need for such grants for clothing should only normally arise when:-

"(a) the claimant has lived at or below supplementary benefit standards for some time before making a claim and may therefore be in difficulty over the replacement of major items;

(b) there are dependent children (where ordinary clothing is concerned; school uniforms are the responsibility of local education authorities);

(c) the claimant or one of his dependants is suffering from a chronic or serious disease where an adequate stock of warm clothing is essential e.g., respiratory tuberculosis or other serious bronchial conditions;

(d) hardship will result if a payment is not made to meet an urgent need."[5]

If the conditions are satisfied then the visiting officer must refer to a standard list of clothing (B/O.40) and decide on and price the items according to another standard list provided by the SBC based on national prices. The B/O.40 list is not, it is said, a "kit list" and it is supposed to provide, in Lord Collison's memorable phrase, "neither a maximum nor a minimum" standard. It is also for the claimant to express the need. The visiting officer can take the initiative only "if he can see for himself that the claimant or his dependants has been on benefit for some years without receiving an ENP".[6]

The adjudication process

Claimants with high heating or clothing needs can deal with them in a number of ways. Many claimants are apparently thought to work on the side, although, notwithstanding the Fisher Report, I share Molly Meacher's view that "it is difficult to see how any objective person can conclude that abuse by wrongful claim is a serious problem".[7] Cohabitation is another method of keeping warm but is unlikely to deal with a clothing need, so the best way is to ask for more benefit. But unless this claim fits the policy guidelines set out above, then it will be refused in the first instance. Robert Coleman has pointed out that when a claimant is aggrieved by a determination of the Commission and issues a complaint he sets in motion a complex administrative proceedure.[8] First the complaint is considered by the local office. Whether it is clearly an appeal against a decision or simply a question which has arisen as a result of a decision, the procedure is exactly the same. The local office will first of all review the case and the claimant may be visited to clarify what has happened. Sometimes the visiting officer will try and persuade the claimant to withdraw an appeal if one has been lodged.

One of three decisions will then be taken. First, the local office may decide to change the original decision. Second, the local office may decide that the original decision was correct but that it should now be altered because of a change in circumstances. Third, the local office may decide that there is no reason to change the decision. In this case, the papers are then sent to regional office. All this is done under the regulations which give the Commission power to review its own decisions. The regional office may make a further investigation of the case and will very occasionally refer it to headquarters. Only after this process has been completed and only if no changes are made in the original decision does the case get sent to the appeal tribunal. Something like 17% of appeals result in the decision being revised in the claimant's favour as a result of this administrative review process.[8]

Once the complaint reaches the appeal tribunal there appears, on 1973 figures at least, to be a 20% chance of having the original decision reversed.[9] But an executive officer, possibly a local manager, a regional official, and on occasions, where discretion might really have to be individualised, the Commission's London office are all consulted before the case reaches the only independent element in the system. The tribunals however, as argued later, seem to consider themselves bound by Commission policy as much as do the Commission's officers.

Objectifying discretion

The Commission then has attempted to provide as far as possible objective criteria by which to guide their officers who exercise discretion. Heating needs are most easily decided by such criteria. A claimant's ill health is observable, a doctor can report on it; the condition of his property can be seen and judged. An ECA for heating may then be awarded or warm clothing bought with a lump sum grant (ENP). We are all presumably thought to feel that hardship and ill health should be alleviated. Equity is thus maintained among claimants and between claimants and non-claimants. Even the poor law allowed the infirm special treatment. They are thought to be deserving of sympathy. The level of help is left to the individual officer or the appeal tribunal, but the officer's discretion is limited to the three bands, 40p, 80p or £1.20p. If he wants to go above the top figure he must refer the case to his local office. But there is freedom to choose between the bands and experience suggests that officers are careful to use the lower bandings in most cases. The tribunals on the other hand have complete discretion. CPAG have shown in a number of cases by producing bills that heating expenditure exceeds the banding plus the amount allowed in the scale rates. Yet it is a major event when a tribunal plucks up courage to exceed the fixed levels. Claimants need both poor health, age and a good advocate to win, and if they do win the tribunal will give a careful explanation in its reasons why it had exceeded the guidelines. Tribunals appear ready to accept the fixed levels in preference to the real costs incurred by the claimant. Do they simply not believe the bills or have they accepted that equity between claimants is preferable to meeting individual needs? If they really exercised an individualised discretion and did not simply follow the rules laid down by the Commission, we would see far more heating additions set at levels which reflect actual expenditure than we now do.

But what of the position of claimants without the 'advantage' of an objectively observable disadvantage, who want some clothes? People who leave work having been living below the supplementary benefit scale rates are supposed to merit special treatment. They will in any event be wage-stopped and have their benefit pushed below the basic poverty line. Wage-stopped claimants are supposed in any event to get special treatment with grants although the reality is usually different from the theory. The chronically sick or those with a serious disease are equally accorded special treatment in the policy on clothing grants. Again their needs are objectively assessable. Claimants with dependant children and those suffering hardship are the people who are least likely to have an objectively assessable need. If they do claim they at least consider they have a need which should be met. How then do they get a grant?

The Commission's view is that needs should be recognised as primarily those which an individual feels and expresses. They accept that they cannot lay down rules of thumb so they leave the problem to individual officers. They appear to be motivated by a number of factors. First, how many grants have been given previously? Second, how well does the household manage its financial affairs and has there been mismanagement? Third, what effort has the claimant made to find work, where this is relevant? Fourth, how long has the claimant been on benefit? Those who represent claimants also know that grants for clothing come more readily to old people and less readily to those with a poor work record. The single mother with dependant children is sandwiched somewhere between. Sympathy from a visiting officer is most crucial. If that sympathy does not exist, either because it was never there or has gone as a result of a past conflict between claimant and visitor, then "begrudging obstructionism" is again the most common reaction to claims for clothing grants.

Questions of hardship tend to become subjective. Clearly some people, whether claimants or otherwise, find it easier than others to live within their income. Benefit levels are low and grants are not designed to lift people above the scale rates. The punitive approach to poverty which characterised the Poor Law seems, at least to many of CPAG's clients, to continue to dominate the system, particularly when discretionary grants are being considered.

Tribunals and equity

At their best, supplementary benefit tribunals hear evidence and consider the facts of cases before them, apply the law, reach a decision and give reasons for that decision. However, tribunal members are given no training, virtually no guidance from the Council on Tribunals or anybody else and consequently they learn about the system on the job. This learning comes about in a number of ways. Members read the tribunal papers prepared by the DHSS in which the Commission's submissions quote the legislation and the policy. These submissions are almost always better argued and set out at greater length than the claimant's appeal statement. The tribunal members are provided with copies of the Acts and regulations governing the system and with the published handbooks setting out the Commission's policy. They participate in hearings and hear from the Commission's presenting officer both the Commission's view of the facts and more details on the policy which has been applied. They thus work within a framework of the law, and the policy used in applying that law, as these are understood by one party to the appeal. Claimants face a double problem. They have to contend with an experienced and knowledgeable advocate and a policy system that has not, in their view at least, reflected properly their individual need.

Yet tribunals cannot avoid considering individual cases in the context of the system as a whole. They hear similar cases in which claimants are asking for discretion to be exercised to meet their needs. But the condition of, or the lack of, clothes is extremely individualised. The actual cost of heating or the proper amount to be spent to keep warm are almost as personal. We do not know with any great precision what motivates tribunals or their individual members to reach their conclusions. But Ruth Lister's research does provide a guide.[10] Forty-three of seventy-four chairmen and members of SBATs whom she questioned felt either bound or guided by Commission policy. The majority of respondents knew there were no limits on the items for which they could make grants but some said they set their own limits and others thought they were limited by regulations. A factor apparently taken into account was whether the appellant had had any grants before; and there was a reluctance to help people who were felt to be bad managers. Ruth Lister concludes, "comments suggested a general tendency to follow the rules established by the Commission; . . . in some cases this was done to preserve uniformity and in an attempt to attain a balance between appellants and non-appellants but in many cases it was clearly believed that these rates established by the Commission had the same status as the basic scale rates established by Parliament."

It seems likely then that tribunals when using their discretionary powers are inclined to follow Commission policy. Equally, whether consciously or otherwise, they seem to attempt to preserve equity among claimants, and between claimants and non-claimants, whatever the individual need. Again experience suggests that if the tribunal's sympathy can be aroused then there is a greater chance of success. Sympathy comes most easily to those with obvious problems such as ill health.

This occurs in a system where tribunals are virtually immune from challenge. Despite a number of attempts, it has been rare for a claimant to challenge a tribunal decision successfully in the High Court.[11] In particular it is virtually impossible to challenge discretionary decisions in the courts. What is "exceptional need" is largely a question of fact. So long as there is the merest hint that the tribunal has considered the facts of the case the court will not investigate the correctness of the decision. Lord Denning has even said, "the courts should leave the tribunals to interpret the Act in a broad reasonable way, according to the spirit and not to the letter, especially as Parliament has given (the tribunals) a way of alleviating any hardship".[12] There are thousands who feel that their hardship has not been alleviated.

Discretion appears to be exercised by the Commission and the tribunals in a rigid way. Individual needs may be satisfied if they fit the policy guidelines or if they are thought to deserve sympathy. The claimants are immersed in a system which few people understand fully, where rules are kept secret or are published in the broadest terms, where they must take the initiative if they want further help and where their prospects of further help are greatest according to unacknowledged criteria about which they can do little. Meanwhile the numbers on supplementary benefit continue to increase. We are left with the pious hope expressed by Richard Titmuss, the great apologist for the scheme: "I believe that it is possible to develop a system of flexible individualised justice, based on considerations of dignity and self-respect. But not with millions of clients and inadequate resources in man-power".[13] Only benefits at a higher level paid as a matter of right will cure the problem.

NOTES

1. 1966 Act, sched. 2, para. 5. The wage stop was discontinued on 28 July 1975.

2. For an administrator's account of the system, see Wilding, chapter 4 above.

3. AFFOR, *Strangled by the Safety Net*, 1 Findon Road, Birmingham 19. p.18.

4. *Supplementary Benefits: Help with Heating Costs*, DHSS Leaflet OC2, 1974.

5. *Exceptional Needs Payments*, SB Administration Paper 4, 1973, para. 25.cf. Handbook, paras. 70-71.

6. As above, para. 26.

7. Molly Meacher, *Scrounging on the Welfare*, 1974, p.5

8. Robert Coleman, *Supplementary Benefits and the Administrative Review of Administrative Discretion*, CPAG Poverty Pamphlet 7, 1971.

9. In 1973, SBATs confirmed the Commission's decision in 18,449 cases (79.7%) increased benefit in 4,662 cases (20.2%) and reduced it in 13 cases (0.1%). Figures from *Social Security Statistics 1973*, Table 34.20.

10. Ruth Lister, *Justice for the Claimant*, CPAG Poverty Research Series 4, 1974, pp. 37-38.

11. *R. v. Greater Birmingham SBAT ex parte Simper*[1973] 2 All E.R. 461; also *ex parte Oliver* 6/3/1972, *ex parte Sullivan* 8/5/1972 and *ex parte Barnett* 11/4/1973, Divisional Court, unreported; and also *R. v. West London SBAT, ex parte Taylor* [1975] 2 All E.R. 790 and *R. v. West London SBAT, ex parte Clarke*, 31 July 1975, *The Times*.

12. *R. v. Preston SBAT, ex parte Moore*, [1975] 2 All E.R. 807, 813.

13. R.M. Titmuss "Welfare 'Rights', Law and Discretion" *Political Quarterly*, 42, 1971, p.132.

VI DISCRETIONARY JUSTICE AND THE SUPPLEMENTARY BENEFITS SYSTEM

Norman Lewis

The Supplementary Benefits Act 1966, (hereafter the 1966 Act), though spawned by a liberal-minded administration which waxed lyrical about the "right" to economic security, afforded a considerable degree of discretion to the Supplementary Benefits Commission, and hence to the appeal tribunals established by the Act. That was perhaps inevitable at the time but nearly a decade later the system of discretionary justice administered under the legislation is badly in need of review. Part of the problem is that, a few instances of political.partisanship aside,[1] the intervening period has seen no re-assessment of the scheme by Parliament. It was predictable that wide-ranging discretion should harden over a period into policies, standards and rules, some of which work manifest injustice, some of which are controversial and some of which would doubtless be widely acceptable and capable of being translated by Government into official policy, whether by legislation or otherwise. The problem of individualised justice versus policy is a familiar and intractable one but it is clear now that much of the individualised justice that both the Act and official literature speak of[2] is a chimera. That should not surprise us. What should is that no real attempt has been made to re-assess the role of discretion in the system after so much experience has been gained. It may have been that in 1966 the Minister, Margaret Herbison, entertained hopes that the appeal tribunals which she established would have held the right balance between law, policy and inidividual need. If so she must now be a very disappointed woman. It is these concerns that form the subject matter of this chapter.

The range of discretion under the 1966 Act is considerable,[3] a fact well appreciated by the higher echelons at least of the Supplementary Benefits Commission, though less well so by the tribunals established to hear appeals from it. It should be emphasised that when an appeal is taken to a tribunal against a

77

supplementary benefit decision, the tribunal may confirm the decision "or substitute therefor any determination which the Commission could have made".[4] In other words, the range of discretionary choices available to the appeal tribunal is as wide as that available to the Commission and, subject to the statutory power of review, the authority of the tribunal is greater since it is expressed to be "conclusive for all purposes". In legal parlance the tribunal is empowered to hear the appeal *de novo*. This is an important point which will be enlarged shortly but the evidence now emerging indicates that this fact is inadequately appreciated by members of the tribunal themselves, who do not consistently dispense individualised justice, who appear unduly deferential to SBC policy and who recognise neither the legal parameters of their jurisdiction nor other juridical constraints. It would be superfluous to particularise these assertions since they have been catalogued elsewhere.[5] Nonetheless the nature of those legal parameters will be explored here and during this exercise more specific criticisms of the tribunals will emerge.

The nature of the discretion given by the 1966 Act differs considerably within the body of the statute itself, though not with any obvious respect to the context or subject-matter being entertained. So, for instance, an exceptional needs payment (ENP) may be made "where it appears to the Commission (and therefore to the appeal tribunal) reasonable in all the circumstances...".[6]

In other words the discretion is framed in highly subjective terms; this gives a reviewing court more limited powers of intervention than if the discretion were objectively expressed. Similar broad powers are to be found in other provisions of the 1966 Act.[7] By contrast an exceptional circumstances addition (ECA) is to be payable simply "where there are exceptional circumstances" the only constraint being that the amount of benefit payable shall be "determined by the Commission".[8] Yet another provision seems to leave the Commission's discretion straddling somewhere between an objective appreciation of needs and their own perception of the limits of the normal statutory formula.[9] It is doubtful whether Parliament in 1966 was very conscious of these differences for the debates in both houses avoided legal niceties or indeed any analysis of discretion. The only information vouchsafed was that ENPs would be dispensed "as generously and wisely as .... in the past",[10] being a reference presumably to the objective compassion of the National Assistance Board. It is legitimate to assume that Parliament in 1966 intended the various discretionary formulae to be interpreted according to common legal standards; but if this were not the case, then perhaps further impulse is given to the need for an overall review of the legislation. However, even supposing that an intention to vest a wholly subjective set of discretions in the Commission and the tribunal system could be elicited, it is clear as a matter of law that the discretion must be operated within legal limits. In other words the supervisory jurisdiction of the superior courts remains as a theoretical check upon abuse of discretion within the supplementary benefits system as elsewhere.

The Queen's Bench Division of the High Court is the traditional repository of reviewing powers over inferior tribunals within the English legal system.[11] Briefly this means that although a statute may confer "final" or "conclusive" jurisdiction on the merits of a decision to a body possessing appropriate expertise, that body is not free to err in law. If it does then its decisions may be impugned in the superior courts, a costly and cumbrous process though one not infrequently used (in company with appeals on points of law afforded by individual statutes) in relation to subject matter outside the welfare field, e.g. planning, licensing etc. It is precisely because the reviewing machinery is expensive and cumbrous that by the end of 1974 only one challenge in the matter of supplementary benefits had ever been successfully achieved in the courts.[12]

Recipients of welfare benefits have neither time, inclination nor resources to launch complex legal challenges to those who deny their requests, a fact that has contributed to both the SBC and the tribunals remaining ignorant to a considerable degree of the limits and extent of their powers. Nonetheless limits do exist and should operate to restrain even the most subjective discretions within the general policy of the empowering legislation.[13] Even despite their traditional reluctance to do so, the courts in recent years have struck down the exercise of discretionary powers by Ministers of the Crown where they have not been exercised in conformity with the implicit intentions of parliament.[14] There have been many contexts, mostly involving property ownership, in which ostensibly unfettered discretions have been limited by the courts. In aggregate the decisions of the courts show that administrative authorities and those exercising jurisdiction do behave improperly from time to time but that abuse of power is litigated in some areas and not in others. As the leading academic authority on such matters has put it:

"On analysis, then, few discretionary powers are found to be absolutely unreviewable when they have a direct impact on private rights; and judicial review is conducted by applying flexible principles of legality in a flexible way".[16]

The submission being made here is that were SBAT members aware of the concept of jurisdiction and the parameters of legality, they would not act in the way they do. They would recognise that considerations alien to the philosophy of the legislation must be discounted, that individualised judgment is a legal requirement, that self-imposed policy restraints are unlawful and that they must address their minds to the strict requirements of the legislation. This theme will be developed in context shortly but first it might be instructive to re-examine the breadth of the discretion afforded to a tribunal.

The nature of an appeal on the merits

An appeal to a tribunal on the merits of a decision reached by a subordinate authority requires the appellate body to hear and determine the issue afresh. To that extent it is unlike a court reviewing the legality of administrative action, which is concerned only to supervise error. An appellate body then is not concerned with supervision of the inferior authority but is directed to examine the full merits of a case *de novo*. In the case of SBATs this means a requirement to adjudicate upon a claimant's case uninfluenced by what the SBC had previously done. As we shall see, due weight may be given to policy considerations, whether of the SBC or the tribunals themselves, but the merits of the individual case form the subject-matter of their jurisdiction. The law reports are full of instances where bodies considerably more learned in the law than SBATs have been directed to re-address their minds to their appellate functions instead of simply asking themselves whether the body exercising original jurisdiction had behaved unlawfully, capriciously or against the general weight of evidence.[17] The courts of superior jurisdiction have impugned the decisions of magistrates, local licensing authorities, recorders and numerous others simply on the grounds that they did not recognise the full amplitude of their discretion in particular cases but simply sought to supervise the activities of the inferior authority.[18] As Lord Parker C.J. once remarked, in a case concerning the scope of an appeal to a court against the refusal of a licence for a fruit machine,

> "There is no question here of the exercise of judicial discretion; the matter is wholly at large on the merits of the case."[19]

One need go no further than Ruth Lister's research to draw conclusions from this brief legal detour. With nearly 25% of her sample of tribunal members regarding their primary responsibility as being to the SBC or Ministry itself,[20] over half not cognisant of the range of discretion open to them[21] and 21% totally convinced that they were bound by Commission policy,[22] it is clear that the *Simper* case would not be such a rare example of judicial criticism of tribunal behaviour were the supervisory jurisdiction of the High Court to be more readily accessible than is the case. Other research indicates that the vast majority of tribunal members do not see themselves as exercising adjudicative functions,[23] while all the recent research findings adverted to indicate an unbecoming deference by the tribunals to the decision-making of the SBC. If the justification for discretion is indeed individualised justice then perhaps SBATs have failed to justify their existence. There appears to be a credibility gap between the actuality of tribunal adjudication and the SBC's statement that "each claimant has to be dealt with individually".[24]

If indeed, as the Commission remarks, "There is an inescapable element of judgment as to what constitutes essential need in an individual case",[25] one would expect there to be considerable scope for disagreement between two decision-making bodies addressing their minds freshly to individual claims.

Abuse of discretion

Even though the determination of an appellate tribunal is expressed to be "final" or "conclusive", a tribunal may nonetheless be supervised by the courts for abusing its discretion. In other words, it must not err in law by e.g. taking improper considerations into account, ignoring relevant considerations or fettering its discretion by giving undue weight to policy. directives (whether these are imposed by itself or others). There is considerable evidence that SBATs offend these injunctions frequently by unseemly deference to SBC policy, by considerations of social virtue and life-style predominating over concepts of "need" and so on. It is clear that their deliberations are characterised neither by judicial aloofness nor by judicial self-restraint. A brief examination of the principles of judicial review should make it clear that the insistence by tribunal members that the law be expelled from their reflections[26] is an admission of their unsuitability for their allotted tasks.

Let us first take the issue of "acting under dictation". Authorities empowered to exercise statutory discretion, whether executive officers, tribunals or other inferior jurisdictions, are usually entitled to take into account considerations of public policy, whether laid down by Government department or independent agencies; but personal judgment on individual cases must be exercised at all times. As has been said by one of the most distinguished judges in the Commonwealth, in a case concerning the refusal of the Australian Director-General of Civil Aviation to grant operating and import licences to an aviation company, one must not "automatically obey" general policy, even that which is "considered to be in the best interests of the country".[27] Indeed the extremely resistant problem of the relationship between acceptable policy guidelines and the exercise of judicial discretion was tortuously argued through the judgments in this case. Anyone with experience of SBATs is left with the very strong feeling that such sophistication is beyond the unaided sensitivities of the tribunals. Even in the area where broad matters of national policy affecting the central direction of the economy are concerned and where the discretion is vested in a Minister of the Crown the courts have insisted that he does not "shut his ears to an application".[28] The following is a useful summary of the position:

"... a factor that may properly be taken into account in exercising a discretion may become an unlawful fetter upon discretion if it is elevated to the status of a general rule that results in the pursuit of consistency at the expense of the merits of individual cases".[29]

Most of the cases where the courts have been faced with these issues have concerned licences and permits but the relevant principles are of general application.[30] Without detailing the many areas where both the SBC and the SBATs fail to give adequate individual attention to individual cases which appear to fall within the ambit of a general policy, mention may be made of the much-criticised "four-week" rule.[31] This Commission policy was presumably based upon the power to withhold benefit where "there are exceptional circumstances".[32] It is highly dubious whether a policy stated in the Commission's terms should ever be applied so as to pre-judge exceptional circumstances but the reliance placed on the four-week rule both by the Commission and the tribunals has frequently offended the canons of legality described here.[33] So also the power under the 1966 Act to make exceptional circumstances additions (ECAs) is open-ended[34] but the scale rates of the SBC are often treated as holy writ by the tribunals; in the case of many tribunal members it is "clearly believed that these rates had the same status as the basic scale rates established by Parliament".[35] Vital discussion of when ECAs should be payable assumes metaphysical proportions in this climate.

Improper considerations

When a decision has been taken by an interim body on the merits of a case without being influenced by extraneous considerations, the courts will not interfere with the decision even though they might have arrived at different conclusions themselves. This is a principle which has been consistently stated over the centuries but its reverse side is that where a body has been influenced by matters outside the proper sphere of its authority, then the courts will intervene. Again this is a principle of general application: it has been applied to the refusal of charabanc licences by a local authority on the grounds of dislike of the applicant's business ethics rather than the transport needs of the community,[36] to the refusal of a local authority's sanction for an access road on the grounds of pedestrian convenience rather than the engineering considerations envisaged by the legislation[37] and so on.

The SBC (and in consequence the SBATs) is directed by the legislation to exercise the functions conferred upon it "in such manner as shall best promote the welfare of persons affected by the exercise thereof".[38] This is, of course, language of the highest aspirational generality and considerable difficulty would accompany an attempt to enforce it as a positive duty, but it does serve to indicate something of the boundaries of discretion envisaged by the Act. Although "welfare" is nowhere defined in the legislation its general usage imports prosperity, well-being etc. rather than, say, belonging to a particular social group such as the old, the young, the unmarried etc. Yet the tendency of the tribunals is to divide applicants into the deserving and undeserving on the basis of what can only be described as extraneous considerations.[39] In many instances it would be difficult to elicit the alien factors in a tribunal decision in the absence both of adequate reasons for decision, and of a need to observe something like a substantial evidence rule (of which more below); but examples abound where an accurate record of an SBAT decision would establish the most manifest abuse of discretion reviewable by a superior court. In a recent cohabitation case which I attended, the official line of questioning was insistently concerned with contingent events should the decision go against the claimant, allied to a clear statement that it would be in her best interests to expel the man from her home. Moral propriety was clearly involved as, no doubt, was a highly subjective perception of what would be in the best interests of the claimant.[40] What was not involved, sadly, was a determination objectively made as to whether, according to legal criteria, cohabitation had been established. Such confusion is by no means limited to cohabitation cases but it lends support to the common observation that SBATs often regard themselves as case committees rather than adjudicative bodies. Perhaps they should be accorded that role by the law. Currently they are not.

Discretion and legal order

The general burden of the argument made so far is that it is only the absence of an accessible reviewing court that has allowed SBATs to evade the legal requirements of the 1966 Act; and that without some infusion of legal technique and without added safeguards, the tribunals are unlikely to operate according to law. The argument for stronger procedural safeguards has been made elsewhere[41] but in the field of discretion they seem particularly desirable. In fact there is increasing evidence of the tribunals being unable to be guided on the law even where assistance is offered. In the cohabitation case adverted to, the chairman was asked whether he would be guided by decisions of the National Insurance Commissioner. He reluctantly agreed but said that since he did not have access to them they would necessarily carry little weight. The same response emerged in relation to disputes about the onus of proof, something which most chairmen seem incapable of understanding. This has caused observers to call for tighter directions on this matter through the S B regulations.[42] While this may be welcomed, there is no reason to believe that it would have more than a marginal impact on decision-making if the requirement to state reasons for decisions is any guide. The deficiencies of tribunals in meeting the statutory requirements in this respect have been observed by numerous commentators, and the Council on Tribunals has now issued specific guidance on this matter.[43] Nonetheless personal experience suggests that the direction is either still misunderstood or deliberately avoided, not least in a case where the whole of the guidance from the Council on Tribunals was read out to the tribunal. The continuing evasion of the obligation to state reasons simply disguises the fact that Commission policy is often rubber-stamped or that the tribunal is indeed basing its judgments on irrelevant considerations.

Allied to the duty to give reasons is the question of the weight to be given to the evidence heard; this matter is recognised by most National Insurance local tribunals and given force through their practice of summarising the evidence when stating their decisions. It is no doubt possible to satisfy the general requirement to state adequate reasons and still deliver a judgment which is totally against the weight of evidence. The importance of this distinction has recently been recognised by the English courts[44] and long-recognised in North America.[45] The nub of the new doctrine, which is known as the substantial evidence rule, is that a decision should be based upon "evidence of a kind which would justify a reasonable man in reaching the conclusion . . . ".[46] The doctrine is currently of somewhat tenuous validity in English law but its acceptance would, if regularly applied to SBATs, make a considerable impact upon their practice. The meticulous collation of evidence, the breaking down of a presenting officer's testimony, the making of a reasoned case against a Commission policy often counts as naught when set against nothing more than the presenting officer's written submission.[47] If no further appeal on the merits is to be allowed from SBATs then it is becoming clear that a statutory requirement to observe a substantial evidence rule supervised by a readily accessible superior authority should be introduced.

A somewhat specialised and abstract analysis of the constitutional defects of SBATs has been undertaken here for the simple reason that a professional assessment of the shortcomings of the adjudication system might have some hope of showing tribunal members and the SBC itself that the act of adjudication is more complicated than they have previously assumed. Their somewhat easy assumptions have been shared by many other decision-making bodies over the years. Being aware of this fact, Parliament rarely grants conclusive adjudicatory powers to bodies without any legal expertise. So long as an exception is made for the supplementary benefits system, the *raison d'etre* of SBATs is in danger of being destroyed.

Discretion-rules-legislation

"Perhaps the most frequent deficiency of legislative bodies has to do with failure to follow through in the development of policy after the delegation has been made."[48]

Parliament has made no comprehensive review of the supplementary benefits scheme since its inception. It is clear from what has gone before that the adjudicatory system needs to be re-examined, but more than that is almost certainly required. It was perhaps inevitable that very broad legislative standards should have been adopted at the outset of the scheme when no experience of its working was available and when the legislature would itself have been unable to predict desirable standards. This is the classic situation requiring a broad delegation when at the outset statutory standards to govern the exercise of discretion are neither possible nor desirable; but, as Davis has said, "a legislative body still has to face the question of when and to what extent a statement of standards is desirable".[49] It is a common experience that time shows many statutory delegations to be deficient in their failure to clarify known objectives. To quote Davis again:

"A clear statement of legislative objectives in every delegation of power is unarguably desirable whenever the legislative body is itself clear about its objectives. Furthermore, legislative bodies should unarguably strive for such clarity."[50]

The position adopted here is that much would be gained if Parliament were to give legislative force to those practices of the SBC which are found acceptable,[51] were to outlaw those practices which did not recommend themselves and were to cause the Commission to publish its other rules and practices. It has been seen in relation to the four-week rule that certain assumptions of doubtful validity have been made which ought now to be pronounced upon by the legislature. Equally some criteria have hardened into rules which would undoubtedly find general acceptance. If this exercise were undertaken, it would offer the opportunity to provide a much-needed public discussion of the changing face of welfare, while removing unnecessary discretion and publicly confirming that which was deemed necessary. At the same time the opportunity could be taken to confine and give direction to certain discretionary formulae: this would give claimants and their advisers pegs upon which to hang their claims, while making it easier to keep the decision-makers within the policy objectives of the scheme. This ought to make it considerably clearer that SBC rules which had not been legislatively sanctioned or proscribed lay in the area of broad discretion and must give way to individual requirements. It would also allow the monitoring of Commission decisions against declared policy.

Conclusion

The general weight of published evidence has called seriously into question the quality of decision-making by SBATs. Were the theoretical legal restraints upon the excesses of the tribunals to have become real, then this fact would have been known very much earlier and remedial action taken. There can now be no excuse for allowing the position to remain in its present state, for allowing the tribunals to operate contrary to the will of the legislature, or for expecting tribunals to appreciate the limits of their jurisdiction without benefit of legal advice and technique. There is no threat to informal and expert decision-making implicit in this argument, any more than there is in causing medical appeal tribunals to be presided over by legally qualified chairmen. Whether or not SBATs are special cases, they are not so special that they should be allowed to operate outside the legal framework which Parliament has required them to observe. They must certainly not be allowed to frustrate the legitimate expectations of claimants by acting as *ersatz* legislatures themselves. In a sense, the nature of the structural reforms required is less important than the recognition that they are needed. Parliament will no doubt find a plethora of good advice if it cares to listen. It should also take the opportunity nearly ten years on to re-assess the supplementary benefits system as a whole.

NOTES

1. E.g. Social Security Act 1971, s. 1, which reduced the SB entitlement of certain categories of unemployed person and those affected by trade disputes.

2. E.g. *Exceptional Needs Payments*, SB Administration Paper 4, 1973.

3. cf. chapters 4 and 5 above.

4. 1966 Act, s. 18(3).

5. See the present writer's article in [1973] *Public Law* 257 and the researches there adverted to; and Ruth Lister, *Justice for the Claimant*, CPAG Poverty Research Series No. 4, 1974.

6. 1966 Act, s. 7.

7. E.g. ss. 9(1), award of benefit to persons attending school; and 14(1), award of benefit in kind.

8. 1966 Act, sched. 2, paras 4(1) and 5(1).

9. 1966 Act, s. 13(1), overriding discretion in cases of urgency.

10. H.C. Deb., vol. 729, col. 1147 (Harold Daves M.P.).

11. See Appendix B.

12. *R. v. Greater Birmingham SBAT. ex parte Simper* [1974] Q.B. 543. In 1975 the Court of Appeal decided *R. v. Preston SBAT. ex parte Moore* [1975] 2 All E.R. 807. A refusal to grant certiorari was upheld where two students had sought review of their vacation claims to benefit. Lord Denning MR took the view that the courts should interfere with an SBAT's decision only when it was manifestly unreasonable, natural justice was offended or an excess of jurisdiction was clearly established. The court should not necessarily interfere with a tribunal's decision, he stated, "even though it may be said to be erroneous in law". The courts should "hesitate long" before interfering with decisions of tribunals, though they should be ready "to consider points of law of general application". This approach would seem to leave lay tribunals much too free to rubber-stamp administrative decisions. For further criticism, see Harry Street, LAG Bulletin, May 1975, p. 118.

13. See e.g. *Pocklington* v. *Melksham U.D.C.* [1964] 2 Q.B. 673, esp. at 682 (Salmon L.J.)

14. See e.g. *Padfield* v. *Minister of Agriculture* [1968] A.C. 997, esp. at 1054 (Lord Pearce).

15. S.A. de Smith, *Judicial Review of Administrative Action*, 3rd edn., 1969, pp. 259-262.

16. de Smith, p. 261.

17. See e.g. de Smith, pp. 249-51.

18. See e.g. *Stepney B.C. v. Joffe* [1949] 1 K.B. 599, *Godfrey* v. *Bournemouth Corpn.* [1969] 1 W.L.R. 47 and *Sagnata Investments Ltd.* v. *Norwich Corpn.* [1971] 2 Q.B. 614.

19. The *Bournemouth Corpn.* case at p. 51.

20. Lister, *Justice for the Claimant*, Table 10.

21. Lister, Table 21.

22. Lister, Table 22.

23. Ross Flockhart, chap. 8 below.

24. SB Handbook, 1974, para. 88.

25. *Exceptional Needs Payments,* para. 7.

26. Ruth Lister, *Justice for the Claimant,* p. 29.

27. Kitto J. in *R. v. Anderson, ex parte Ipec-Air Pty. Ltd.* (1965) 113 Commonwealth Law Reports 177 at 193.

28. *British Oxygen Co. v. Minister of Technology* [1971] A.C. 610, 624-5 (Lord Reid). For error of law in exercising a discretion, see the *Simper* case (note 12 above) and the remarkably similar *R. v. Vestry of St. Pancras* (1890) 24 Q.B.D. 371, 380 (Fry L.J.).

29. de Smith, *Judicial Review,* p. 275.

30. See e.g. *R. v. Flintshire C.C., ex parte Barrett* [1957] 1 Q.B. 350 anu *Lavender v. Minister of Housing* [1970] 1 W.L.R. 1231.

31. See Molly Meacher, *Scrounging on the Welfare,* 1974.

32. 1966 Act, Sched. 2, para. 4(1)(6).

33. See e.g. Lister, *Justice for the Claimant,* pp. 39-40.

34. Sched. 2, para. 4(1)(a).

35. Lister, p.38. For continuing complaints by claimants' representatives that law and policy are being hopelessly confused, see *New Society,* 15 Aug. 1974.

36. *R. v. Brighton Corpn., ex parte Thomas Tilling Ltd.* (1916) 85 L.K.B. 1552.

37. *Marshall v. Blackpool Corpn.* [1935] A.C. 16. See also *R. v. Birmingham Licensing Planning Committee, ex parte Kennedy* [1972] 2 Q.B. 140.

38. 1966 Act, s. 3(1).

39. See the present writer's article [1973] *Public Law,* pp. 277-8 and Lister, *Justice for the Claimant,* esp. at pp. 26-27.

40. Similar complaints have emerged from the Scottish Social Policy and Action Group of the British Association of Social Workers concerning general SBC policy which confuses "need" with social inadequacy (*The Guardian,* 31 Oct. 1974).

41. [1973] *Public Law* pp. 263-275.

42. Ruth Lister, p. 12.

43. A letter sent to all SBAT chairmen is reproduced in Annual Report of Council on Tribunals, 1972-3, Appendix B.

44. See e.g. *Ashbridge Investments Ltd. v. Minister of Housing* [1965] 1 W.L.R. 1320, esp. 1326 (Lord Denning M.R.); *Coleen Properties Ltd. v. Minister of Housing* [1971] 1 W.L.R. 433, 437 (Lord Denning M.R.), 441 (Buckley L.J.); *R. v. Deputy Industrial Injuries Commissioner, ex parte Moore* [1965] 1 Q.B. 456.

45. Schwartz and Wade, *Legal Control of Government,* 1972, pp. 228-35.

46. Buckley L.J. in the *Coleen Properties* case.

47. See too *New Society,* 15 Aug. 1974.

48. K.C. Davis, *Discretionary Justice.* 1971, p. 50

49. Davis, p. 45.

50. Davis, pp. 45-46.

51. As was done *ad hoc* after the *Simper* case: see National Insurance and Supplementary Benefit Act 1973, sched. 4.

VII   "WE GO BY THE LAW HERE"
Steve Burkeman

Whereas the other chapters examine aspects of the theory or historical development of Supplementary Benefit Appeal Tribunals (SBATs), I have tried in this chapter to complement those perspectives by one which is based on my experiences 'on the coalface' working at the CHECK Rights Centre in Liverpool, which handles 350-400 SB appeals a year as well as many more cases which never reach the tribunal stage. A mixture of trained volunteers, some of them law students, and full-time staff achieves an overall success rate of approximately 44% in those Supplementary Benefit appeals which reach tribunal stage. Of all appeals lodged, something approaching 30% are superseded by a decision favourable to the claimant. Thus, the Centre may claim an overall success rate of appeals lodged in the order of 60% (we define 'success' as meaning some additional income accruing to the claimant as a result of the appeal, though that is a contentious definition since, for example, one cannot claim any real success when one is appealing for £50 for an exceptional needs payment towards a gas bill and the tribunal makes a token gesture of £10, which is insufficient to get the gas switched on again). The 44% figure compares with an overall figure of 30% for claimants represented by groups such as CPAG, claimants' unions, trade union officials, and CHECK.[1]

These figures are important, not only because Merseyside tribunals have, statistically, among the lowest percentage of successful appeals in the country. The figures do, I hope, add credibility to our perception of what is happening in SBATs, and to the observations which follow. At the very least, it should be apparent that, as demonstrably proficient technicians, we do not need to allege falsely in order to excuse our own failure. Yet if what we found in Merseyside is in any way symptomatic of the way in which tribunals operate generally, then there must be cause for concern.

Examples of tribunal decisions

I begin by giving some illustrations of the grosser forms of abuse of the Supplementary Benefit Appeal Tribunal system that we have experienced.

Mr. Jones was a shipbuilder for Cammel Lairds at Birkenhead. The recurrence of an old war wound meant that he had become chronically sick and had blackouts. We represented Mr. Jones at a tribunal. He was appealing against the SBC's refusal to pay for fares which would have enabled him to travel to hospital to see his son who had been injured in a motorcycle accident. Mr. Jones' blackouts meant that he could travel nowhere without his wife and he had also applied for fares for her to accompany him to hospital. Towards the end of the tribunal the truth of Mr. Jones' submission was tested to the limit: just as the chairman was thanking him for coming and me for accompanying him, Mr. Jones slumped sideways and fell out of his chair onto the floor, with another blackout. The tribunal chairman came round to the claimant's side of the table, an ambulance was summoned and Mr. Jones was taken off to hospital, this time in his own right. In the circumstances, one might have thought that a victory for the claimant was a matter of course. Had one thought that, one would have been wrong. Mr. Jones lost his case.

On another occasion Mr. Bradshaw was appealing against the Commission's refusal to make a single payment towards the cost of clothing needed for his children. The decision against which he was appealing had been issued some weeks previous to the actual date of the hearing, and by the time the hearing was held, Mr. Bradshaw was working at Fords at Halewood. Since he had borrowed money and incurred debts while unemployed he pursued his claim under the impression that his present circumstances were irrelevant, and that what mattered were his circumstances at the time he applied for help. While fetching his coat from the waiting room after the hearing, and after his CHECK representative had left, Mr. Bradshaw was approached by the clerk of the tribunal, who asked him, "Oh by the way, Mr. Bradshaw, what do you earn at Fords now?" Caught off guard, Mr. Bradshaw told him. A complaint to the Council on Tribunals led, 9 months later, to a detailed rebuttal of the charges laid against the clerk by Mr. Bradshaw.

While the *Simper* case was still law, before the enactment of the 1973 Social Security Act, our representative, a barrister, pleaded *Simper* in arguing against an automatic offset of a heating allowance against the long term allowance as it was then known.[2] The tribunal was unwilling to concern itself with a mere High Court case. The clerk, waving the 1966 Act in the air, said, "We go by the *law* here", meaning statute and not case law. Our man treated him to a brief lecture on the role of statute and common law, and came back to the office to draft a letter to Lord Collison. Meanwhile, the claimant lost the appeal.

A member of the Liverpool Trades Council, and a member of the panel of SB tribunal members, complained to us that he had rarely been called upon to sit on tribunals. The Trades Council, concerned at this, wrote to the clerks to ask which individuals *had* been called to serve and how frequently. The figures showed that the complainant—noted for his liberal views and union activities—had been called 9 times in a year, whereas a rather conservative retired schoolmaster had been called 25 times.[3]

The final example was an appeal that had a successful outcome. It owes not a little to David Bull, of Bristol CPAG, who had been pursuing for some time the question of Heavy Goods Vehicle qualifications. When new qualifications were introduced, drivers who were not in work at that time were required to take a test and to go through several hours of tuition prior to that test. Drivers caught out of work during the relevant period were in a difficult position. With no income, they had somehow to assemble the funds necessary to have the tuition, pay for the test, and buy the licence. It had been the practice of the SBC to refuse an application for an exceptional needs payment to meet this cost. David Bull successfully appealed against a decision to refuse this payment.[4] Our case was almost identical. Our claimant was the perfect appellant: he had done everything possible for himself, applying for every conceivable job. Through his M.P., his local office manager, through newspaper advice bureaux, he had tried to persuade the Commission to pay the required sum. Over the four years that he had been trying, he had received something approaching £4,000 in state benefits. At the appeal, which he won, the most significant argument which we were able to present was simply that a similar case had been decided in Bristol some months previously. It was this fact alone, amid a lengthy and detailed quasi-legal and social argument, that weighed most heavily with the Chairman who, having been persuaded of the merits of the case, did not wish to be seen as pushing back any frontiers.

Issues needing investigation

These illustrations raise some of the issues that may need more investigation. I believe we already know enough about many aspects of supplementary benefits tribunals. We know that it is better to be represented than not to be represented. We know that claimants find tribunals intimidating and inhibiting. We know that chairmen are selected from a restricted background and that very few are work people, women, or black. We know that if legal aid were available for tribunals then more people would be represented at them. But there are other questions which have not yet been answered. It is almost as if there is an assumption that in a judicial system as fair as Britain's, a quasi-judicial system such as Supplementary Benefit Appeals must be similarly fair. A closer look at some of the issues illustrated in the examples above suggests that that assumption is mis-placed.

One such issue concerns the role of the clerk to the tribunal. We are told time and time again that the clerk is independent. At CHECK we are accustomed to witnessing a little ritual when accompanying claimants' at which the clerk soothingly assures the claimant that 'It's just a cosy little chat really—nothing to worry about', and during the hearing itself the clerk generally remains silent. We do not dispute that the clerk fulfils his role according to the letter of the law during the actual tribunal hearing and during the minutes before it. What we are concerned with is his hidden role—before the tribunal ever meets, while it is deliberating on its decision, and after it has disbanded.

Is it right, for instance, that the clerk should be entrusted with the selection of those members of the tribunal panels who should sit on each occasion? What guidance is given to clerks in respect of this responsibility, and should not this guidance be published and generally available? It is hardly surprising that at times those members of the work-people's panel who are of the left have been ignored in favour of members who might be more likely to want to uphold the Commission's decision: since, after all, the clerk has come from the DHSS and will return to the DHSS when his stint as clerk is over. It seems strange, too, that the list of 'other members' of the tribunal is not published nor generally available. How is it possible for people to judge whether or not tribunals are competent to carry out their functions unless something is known of the personal backgrounds of members?

While the tribunal is deliberating on its decision, and in the absence of the claimant or his representative, we have little evidence to show how far the clerk's loyalties to the department interfere with his independence. Nor do I think that we will ever assemble such evidence through expensive research projects with pre-arranged access. We all behave perfectly when we are being watched. The only way that we will ever learn about this 'mystery time' is to work patiently with our local trades councils, and to persuade work-people's representatives on tribunals to become acutely conscious of the possibilities of abuse of the situation by the clerk, so that it can be dealt with there and then, and reported later. This, I am happy to say, has already begun in Liverpool.

Similarly—and here one risks being accused of paranoia—we have been led in the past to wonder whether the decision reached by the tribunal at its meeting is always the decision which reaches the claimant and his or her representative. Our suspicions on this lack sufficient evidence to back them, though they are not founded on mere speculation. They are, indeed, compounded when one realises that tribunal members themselves, in Liverpool at least, do not receive copies of the decision sheet, nor does the chairman himself write out the decision: it is written by the clerk, and merely signed by the chairman. We do not know whether it is thus signed before or after the decision has been written out. There is, therefore, no check at all by the independent tribunal that its wishes have been communicated by a clerk who, necessarily, is less than independent. This too is an area which is beginning to be examined in Liverpool.

The role of the work-people's representatives also gives grounds for concern. All too often, they appear to be asleep, or not to understand what is going on, or are trying so hard to be impartial that they end up singing the praises of the presenting officer. In Liverpool, this situation is changing thanks to continued close co-operation between CHECK and the Liverpool Trades Council. The calibre of the Council's tribunal panel has substantially improved: more militant members of the Trades Council now sit on the panel and they operate according to agreed policy decisions on specific areas of the Supplementary Benefit system—particularly the wage-stop, to which the Trades Council is officially opposed, and which, therefore, their people will oppose on principle each time the issue is presented to tribunals. However, more remains to be done. People nominated to tribunals should receive some kind of training and guidance, designed so as to protect them from over-zealous clerks, recently seconded from the DHSS and rather anxious to be able to return there in good favour shortly. This should be an ongoing process: members should receive full details of High Court cases, and interesting decisions of tribunals elsewhere. Guidance should be provided to members about the relationship of the Supplementary Benefits Commission to other sources of funds, so that glib advice to "ask for help from the local authority" is not offered without some knowledge of what is and what is not available. Perhaps tribunal members should be given local employment statistics and current average wage and overtime levels, broken down by industry, so that cases relating to Unemployment Review—particularly wage-stop cases—can be better dealt with. All this would be best done by an independent body—perhaps through a much strengthened Council on Tribunals.

The attendance of claimants at tribunal hearings

The importance of claimants attending the hearing of their appeals is generally accepted: though there is one alarming statistic which suggests that claimants who do not attend but are represented by a middle-class advocate have a higher success rate than those who attend, with or without a representative (to me this suggests that tribunals would far rather not be faced with the real consequences of poverty, and would prefer to reach an accommodation based on an understanding between people who 'speak the same language'—and that is not the language of the poor).[5]

Setting this aside for the moment, on the assumption that it is generally desirable, as a matter of principle if nothing more, for claimants to attend, what encouragement to them to do so is offered? In Liverpool, there is very little. Claimants receive at the most one full week's notice of their tribunal date and time, and since, by definition, few can afford telephones, communication with scarce advocacy resources in that time is made almost impossible. Grudgingly, the clerks have for some time now acknowledged CHECK's right to be informed of the date at the same time as the claimant, where it is named as representative in the claimant's original appeal: but what about those people who do not think about representation until faced with the actual appeal date? Why should it not be the practice for the 'right of appeal' notice to list local advocacy sources, with numbers and addresses? Why is it not possible to give at least a fortnight's notice of the date of appeal? Indeed, since the DHSS employ virtually full time presenting officers, why should not a reinforced independent tribunal system employ full time 'claimants' friends' available for consultation by claimants in connection with their appeals?

If a claimant does decide to go to the tribunal, and succeeds in finding a representative, the facilities accorded to them at the tribunal leave something to be desired. My request to the porter at the Liverpool tribunal premises to allow me to use the telephone to check a fact in our files before a case begun, was turned down, when the presenting officer told the porter that the phone was for her use only. There is no room offered or available for private interview before a case—unlike, for instance, Medical Appeal Tribunals or Industrial Tribunals. There are no facilities to buy coffee or cigarettes in order to settle an appellant's nerves, no toys or books to keep children amused, no magazines for adults—not even any social security leaflets. The Liverpool tribunal premises are located on the seventh floor of a large forbidding office block, with no sign from the outside of the block to indicate that the Supplementary Benefits Appeal Tribunal is therein.

The need for a system of precedent

Finally, I believe that the lack of a system of precedent in the Supplementary Benefit tribunal system is one which operates against the interests of the claimant. The rigidity which is supposed to be the main disadvantage of a system of precedent in this situation is offset in, for instance, National Insurance tribunals, by a good deal of flexibility within clear guidelines. For Supplementary Benefit appellants, there is no rigidity, but there are no guidelines either. There is instead pseudo justice based on arbitrariness, charity and prejudice. We do not need to wait for the official introduction of a precedential system to prove its merits. With careful monitoring, close cooperation and good organisation, the groups operating in this area could build for themselves a national system of precedent, which I believe would help to fill in those empty words about "benefits as of right". CPAG's Poverty Magazine and the Legal Action Group's Bulletin recognise this by including welfare law cases among their reports, but this is scratching at the surface: what is needed is a standard recording procedure, a central storage facility, and regular, e.g. weekly, mailings to local groups. I do not believe the cost of the operation would be prohibitive: and the possibilities are enormous. We fail the poor if we are not prepared to be better bureaucrats on their behalf than the bureaucrats we criticise. It is important to realise that most of the criticisms I have made would not occur if the tribunal system were rather more judicial: and we can help to make it so. The question is whether the welfare rights movement which we represent has enough organisational strength and willpower to establish such a system.

NOTES

1. Letters, *Social Work Today*, 9 August 1973. See also Coral Milton, Chapter 10 below, Table 5.

2. In *Simper's* case [1974] Q.B. 543 the Divisional Court quashed a tribunal decision which had automatically offset the appellant's ECA for heating against a long-term addition, holding that the Act required a discretion to be exercised. The legislation which followed laid down precise rules for offsetting various ECAs against the long-term addition. Since April 1975, the long term addition has been incorporated into new long-term scale rates.

3. *New Society*, 5 April 1973, p. 24.

4. David Bull. "SB Appeals: Advocacy Against Policy Decisions", *LAG Bulletin*, January 1975, pp. 18-20.

5. See Hilary Rose, Chapter 11 below.

VIII SOME ASPECTS OF TRIBUNAL MEMBERSHIP
Ross Flockhart

In the summer of 1971, a study of the membership of Supplementary Benefits Appeal Tribunals was carried out in Scotland, with financial assistance from the Department of Health and Social Security. The aim of this chapter is to comment upon those aspects of the study which are relevant to the current discussion of the operation and structure of the tribunals.

Scotland at that time was divided into twenty tribunal districts. With the co-operation of the Department, a questionnaire was posted to all the known members of the SBATs in Scotland. 205 questionnaires were sent out and 159 (77.5%) were returned. Of these, 148 (72.2%) were completed. The figures quoted in this chapter are based upon the 148 completed returns.

The background of tribunal members

Tribunal members fall into three categories:

(1) chairmen, appointed in Scotland by the Secretary of State for Social Services from a panel of persons approved by the Lord President of the Court of Session (who is head of the Scottish judiciary);

(2) persons appointed by the Secretary of State from among persons appearing to him to represent work-people. In practice they are selected from lists of names submitted by local Trades Councils. They are referred to here as Trades Council members (TCMs); and

(3) other persons appointed by the Secretary of State, here referred to as Other members (OMs).

Of the 148 respondents, the membership functions were:

Chairmen	26
Trades Council members	74
Other members	48

Of the 26 chairmen who responded to the questionnaire, all were lay-chairmen, i.e. none were lawyers. 19 of the 26 chairmen were over sixty years of age; ten were retired persons, three of whom were over seventy years of age. Three were appointed as chairmen without having any previous experience of SBATs. 22 of the remaining 23 had previously served as Other members; only one chairman was drawn from the ranks of the Trades Council members.

In terms of the Registrar General's Classification 78% of the chairmen and Other members, taken together, were from Social Classes I and II. The social class breakdown of all respondents is summarised in the table below:

Social Class	Chairmen	OM	TCM	All Members
I	4	4	0	8
II	15	35	14	64
III (Non-manual)	2	4	9	15
III (Manual)	1	0	38	39
IV	0	1	10	11
V	0	0	1	1
Unknown	4	4	2	10
Total	26	48	74	148

Table 1:   Social class composition of Scottish SBAT members (1971).

There is a case for arguing that a welfare tribunal should be composed of three "ordinary people" drawn from the local community, sitting together as lay persons to assess the extent of social need (cf. the membership of Children's Panels in Scotland). If so, it might be thought that these three lay persons should represent in themselves a reasonably varied and wide social experience. The membership of the tribunals in this study reflects a narrow grouping of social class and age amongst the chairmen and Other members but is significantly less narrow in terms of social class among the Trades Council members. In addition, of the 148 members only sixteen were women, i.e. 11%. When asked to rate the importance of having at least one woman member on a tribunal 60% said it was unimportant.

As stated above, 22 of the 26 chairmen were formerly Other members. As far as could be determined, a person's name appeared on a list of suitable candidates for appointment by the Lord President of the Court of Session only after his name had been passed through the critical filter of that part of the DHSS which deals with SBATs.

If tribunals are over-dependent on the SBC the roots of that dependence may lie in the selection process. However "objective" they try to be, departmental officials cannot avoid in some measure choosing or approving persons likely to be "good" and "reliable" in the eyes of the DHSS. Moreover, if a member knows, as some undoubtedly do, that he has been vetted or suggested by the DHSS and if he finds some personal satisfaction in tribunal service, then he is less likely, consciously or unconsciously, to take an independent line when contributing to a tribunal decision.

When asked if they would like to see changes in the kind of people appointed as their fellow-tribunal members the vast majority said "No". They seemed to be well satisfied with one another. There was, however, a significant minority of Trades Council members (13 out of 74) who wished to see a change in the kind of person appointed as chairman.

The motivations of tribunal members

Membership of a SBAT is a form of public service and is often not the only form of public work undertaken by the members. A number of respondents had been candidates at local elections (45), some had served as elected members (30) and some were currently active as elected members (18).

At tribunals, the chairmen receive a fee (£10 per sitting in 1971) but the Other members and Trades Council members can only claim appropriate travel allowances, subsistence and loss of earnings. Evidently members do not give this service for financial reward. Indeed nearly 20% of the Other members and Trades Council members incurred personal financial costs over and above the allowances mentioned above.

This public service is an expression of some kind of altruism and also provides a measure of personal satisfaction to the members. When asked if they would attend sittings more frequently 78% said "Yes". When asked if at the end of their present term of appointment they would accept a further term of service 90% said "Yes"! There is clearly no lack of enthusiasm among tribunal members. The reasons they offered for this willingness to serve were first, that tribunal service was enjoyable, interesting and personally educative, and second, that it was a necessary public service, a duty to be performed. They were also ready voluntarily to give time and energy in order to undergo some form of training. The popular thesis that altruism or public service should be without financial reward is somewhat modified, however, by the view expressed by over half of all the members that all members should receive a fee for their services.

The functions of SBATs

The conduct of each hearing is in the hands of the chairman. The chairman of an SBAT does not need to be a lawyer and in Scotland it is clear that a policy of appointing laymen has been followed by the appointing authorities. The reasons for appointing lay chairmen are directly connected with the way in which the task of the tribunal is understood. If an important function of the tribunal is to sift facts in a manner understood by lawyers, to understand the nature of evidence, and to determine, within a legal framework of regulations, the rights of the appellants then it may be appropriate to have a lawyer-chairman. If, on the other hand, it is of greater importance to elicit and assess, even in a general way, the degree of need in relation to financial assistance then it may be that the special skills of a lawyer are less appropriate for the chairman than an understanding of social need and the conditions surrounding it.

The role and qualifications of the chairman are thus dependent upon the task of the tribunal. The task of an SBAT contains within it elements that are in themselves inconsistent. The dilemma is summed up in the Franks Report (para. 182):

"Although in form these Tribunals hear and determine appeals against decisions of local officers of the National Assistance Board and, therefore, exercise adjudicating functions, in practice their task much resembles that of an assessment or case committee, taking a further look at the facts and in some cases arriving at a fresh decision on the extent of need."

To this should be added the words of the Chairman of the Supplementary Benefits Commission in 1970, Lord Collison, in the Introduction to the Supplementary Benefits Handbook:

"An exclusively legal approach to a non-contributory benefits scheme can only lead to a narrower not a broader concept of the 'rights' of claimants, since those rights are or should be social as well as legal."

When asked if it would be an advantage or disadvantage if SBATs were to have lawyer-chairmen, 56% of all respondents said it would make no difference and 25% said it would be a disadvantage. When asked to indicate, in the terms of the Franks Report, whether they considered the proper function of an SBAT to be adjudication or assessment of need, 87% considered that it was the function of an SBAT "to act like an assessment or case committee, taking a further look at the facts and in some cases arriving at a fresh decision on the extent of need." There can be no doubt about which way the great majority of the members understood the role of the tribunal. It could be argued, however, that because there were no lawyers amongst the respondents, they were predictably disinclined to recognise the more legal-style adjudicatory role as being the proper function of the tribunals.

The composition of SBATs

While it is clear that the Trades Council members as a group are of a different social and occupational class from the chairmen and Other members, it does not follow that they are necessarily typical of the claimants who appeal to the tribunals. In the case of National Insurance local tribunals, it is plainly sensible to have at least one member who can be regarded as a representative of work-people or employees, but many Supplementary Benefit claimants have never been "work-people". Perhaps SBATs should include a representative of "claimant-people" or "appellant-people". There is in any event reason to reconsider the composition of SBATs. Since so many chairmen were formerly Other members, the present situation is, in effect—two Other members and one Trades Council member. If the function of the tribunal is to act like an assessment or case-committee, perhaps consideration should be given to including a qualified social worker? It might also be helpful to consider a lawyer in a non-chairman role, and whether the chairmanship could rotate between different classes of member.

Training of members

There was a clear indication that members would like to have more information when first appointed and that members thought that special pre-service training would be of value. The evidence points to a desire for more careful preparation for tribunal service, for some in-service training and to a willingness on the part of members to participate in pre- and in-service training. Just over half of the members felt that the official literature received at the time of appointment was less helpful than it might have been. 53% would have liked further information, particularly:

(1) on the Acts and regulations, with an explanation of them in plain English, and also reference to the scope and limits of tribunal powers;

(2) SBC pamphlets and scales of payment.

An overwhelming majority of members would have valued special pre-service training (86%). They particularly referred to the desire to participate in group discussion as a method of training and to receive more explanatory material. Lectures were not highly favoured. The trades council members were the most in favour of pre-service training. A correlation with the school-leaving age of all members shows that the earlier the school-leaving age, the greater the desire for training. On in-service training, a clear majority (55%) considered that conferences for members, including chairmen, would be useful.

Very few members knew any other SBAT members, apart from those with whom they sat, and 74% had never discussed tribunal matters with other tribunal members, other than those with whom they sat. One member commented, "I wouldn't know who the whole local team are." Members are clearly isolated from each other. The interest in group discussions and conferences indicates a desire for a sharing of experience, problems and information, and also perhaps a reaching out for a corporate identity.

The organisation of tribunals

Some tribunals, such as industrial tribunals and pension appeal tribunals, have a full-time national president; other tribunals are organised regionally with regional presidents. The presidents exercise some supervisory and co-ordinating functions. SBAT members were asked if they would favour any similar arrangements. The majority (63%) thought not, but the reasons given were not very substantial. Many simply said that the present arrangements were satisfactory and that a president would interfere with the independence, impartiality and informality of the SBATs. These reasons are akin to those adduced by persons or organisations who are fearful that the quality of their work would be exposed as inadequate if observed by other knowledgeable people. Such fears are often groundless but do act as an inhibiting factor. On the other hand, 31% favoured some form of president, perferably regional presidents. They considered that it would be an advantage to have a regional president who could co-ordinate and advise, particularly about regional problems and conditions. Chairmen were the most in favour of a presidency system. It may be that such a system would also help the development of a sense of identity.

An SBAT sits in solitary confinement. The members have no way of comparing their methods or decisions with other SBATs. Still, it was surprising to find that 41% were in favour of circulating to all SBATs the recorded details of individual cases. The weight of paper involved would be monumental, but the response does indicate a desire to compare practice. A further question showed that if details of other cases, including the recorded decisions, were available for reference these decisions should in no way be regarded as binding precedents. A majority (60%) considered that recorded decisions available for reference should be regarded as a general guide for other tribunals, but that each case should be decided on its own merits.

This expression of opinion accords with the majority view that the function of an SBAT is more akin to assessment than adjudication and that a tribunal makes a fresh assessment of the appellant's claim. It also makes it clear, however, that deciding a case "on its own merits" has its drawbacks when there are no standards to refer to. The desire for general guidelines and the conviction that the particularity of each case must be preserved indicate that training of various kinds, including simulated hearings, would prove helpful.

The powers and independence of SBATs

At the moment the tribunals members are effectively left in the dark about the way in which they should exercise their powers. It may be this factor more than any other, including the selection procedures, which leads to an alleged degree of dependence on the SBC. If the only known standards or decisions are those of the SBC, then it is understandable that tribunal members who seldom meet the members of other SBATs and who have no information about the decisions of other SBATs tend to lean toward the known norms of the local officers and the presenting officers of the SBC.

One presenting officer will usually serve more than one tribunal district. A similar practice is followed with clerks, e.g. in 1971 two clerks serviced all the tribunals in the East of Scotland. These officers are, or become, specialists and are in possession of comparative information about decisions and the style of different tribunals which is denied to the tribunal members. It would not be surprising if the best of chairmen and members did not tend to depend upon the information and guidance of these officers. One Other member remarked, "I feel we should be loyal to the local SBC officer, he knows the situation. We trust him." The great majority (92%) of the members were in favour of the arrangement whereby the clerks are supplied from the staff of the DHSS; the main reason given for this apparent satisfaction was that the clerks are "professional and well-informed".

As the Franks Report (para. 40) pointed out: "Tribunals are not ordinary courts but neither are they appendages of government departments." The members studied seemed to be not wholly free of the criticism of being appendages of the SBC in their approach to the work of the tribunals. The cure for dependence is not necessarily to have a lawyer-chairman; it may more reasonably lie in better selection, preparation and training of members, regional meetings, the provision of comparative information and possibly a change in the composition of the tribunals. Educational and training developments should not be carried out by the DHSS but by an external agency such as the Council on Tribunals, or the Council in conjunction with universities.

Attendance at appeals

A well-known irritant to tribunal members is the unnotified non-attendance of some appellants. 70% of members acknowledged that non-attendance affected the decision of the tribunal and that the decision was less likely to be in the appellant's favour. If the adjudicative function is regarded as the primary function of an SBAT then it might be said that the appellant's failure to attend should not affect the decision so heavily. On the other hand if the primary function is to assess and to make a fresh decision on the extent of need then it is not surprising that if the appellant fails to attend, or to be represented, the members should feel that they cannot carry out their task of assessment. The main comment offered was that if the appellant is present it helps the tribunal to scrutinise and assess. The need for further enquiry into the reasons for the unnotified non-attendance of appellants was indicated by the survey. Some tribunal members remarked that "Non-attendance indicates a weak appeal". This may, however, not be so. Many non-attenders may have the strongest of cases but be frightened of appearing, or just feel that the system is against them and that they cannot win. Some may not realise that they have what the tribunal would have considered to be a strong case.

The representation of appellants

There is controversy about the value and function of an appellant's representative. Once again the issue raises the implicit function of the SBAT. In an adjudicative-style tribunal a representative is likely to be of great assistance to an appellant. A representative can provide moral support and can also, in instances where the representative is a "specialist", function as a skilled advocate. If SBATs are to be identified increasingly as adjudicative bodies then it would be proper to ensure that an appellant had the opportunity to use a welfare-rights lawyer, or similar person, as his representative in order to act as his advocate. In an assessment-of-need style tribunal a representative might provide moral support and in the case of inarticulate or low I.Q. appellants help them to answer questions, to explain their feelings and to describe their need. The assessment-method or style is more of an enquiry or an investigation than a legal debate. In this case a "specialist" representative might help an appellant to present his case in an attractive, more need-apparent way.

It is of interest that the majority (70%) of the members considered that where an appellant is represented the decision of the tribunal is unaffected by the presence of the representative. This response is probably a form of self-protection. By contrast, a minority of 25% were willing to say that when an appellant was represented the decision was more likely to be in favour of the appellant. They regarded representation as a positive aid to the appellant.

The table below ranks the categories of representative which the members considered to be the most effective in presenting the appellant's case, starting with those considered to be the most effective:

Representative	Rank
Claimants' Union	1
Trade Union	2
Social Worker	3
Friend	4
Relative	5
Local Councillor	6
Lawyer	7

Table 2: Effectiveness of representation as perceived by SBAT members.

The concepts of welfare and justice are both combined in the function of an SBAT. The concept of welfare contains the idea of individualisation and the need for discretionary decisions in order to meet particular needs. The concept of justice contains the ideas of consistency and of regulated rights. It is clear that these concepts do not sit easily together in an SBAT.

IX THE CONDUCT OF TRIBUNAL HEARINGS*

Michael Adler, Elizabeth Burns and Rosemary Johnson

The research described in this chapter arose out of our concern with the conduct of appeals in SBATs; from the fact that relatively little empirical research has been carried out on tribunal hearings[1] (the considerable amount of writing on SBATs is mainly based on reports of individual tribunal hearings by those who have acted as appellant's representative,[2] and on Ruth Lister's recent survey of tribunal chairmen and members[3]); and from an impression that, as others have suggested, many of the recurring reported criticisms of SBATs in action related to *structural* issues (such as the appointment of non-legally qualified chairmen, the dependence of the lay tribunal on the expertise of the clerk and the presenting officer, the irrelevance of precedent and the dubious status of Commission policy), all of which are at variance with the practice of NILTs. We therefore decided to undertake a systematic study of hearings of SBATs in the Edinburgh area; and to do so on a comparative basis, observing a comparable number of NILTs in the same area over the same period. Our reasons for so doing are that SBATs are often unfavourably compared with NILTs[4] and that the two tribunals differ markedly in structure (in that, for example, all NILTs have legally qualified chairmen and the system of adjudication is one based on precedent). We were thus concerned to assess the validity of some of those criticisms of SBATs which have been expressed in previous chapters and elsewhere, and to do so by comparing SBAT hearings with the hearings of NILTs which have been largely immune from criticism.

* The authors would like to thank the Trustees of the Moray Fund at the University of Edinburgh for a small grant which helped to defray research costs. They would also like to thank everyone who participated in the study.

Methods of investigation

(1)   *The sample*

Our findings are based on attendance at all but one SB and all NI tribunals in Edinburgh and East Fife, over a period of six weeks during October and November 1974. We attended 13 SBAT and 9 NILT sessions, and gathered data on 66 SB and 46 NI cases (all those heard at the sessions' attended, with the exception of one NI case from which we were excluded at the appellant's request).[5]

We make no claims to have attempted to obtain, still less to have succeeded in obtaining, a representative sample either of tribunals or of cases within them. It would therefore be quite wrong to make inferences about all tribunals from this study—some are undoubtedly better, others are possibly worse, while most probably differ in significant respects. However, because our observations frequently corroborate those of others and because of the comparative aspect of the study, we believe that some inferences about SBATs in general can be drawn from it.

Because of our interest in tribunal hearings, we had to devise ways of collecting information on the ways in which tribunals dealt with appeals. Unlike some tribunal researchers, we were not allowed to observe the tribunals' deliberations.[6] Thus the research focussed on the pre-deliberation stage. Information was collected by completing a written transcript of the hearing and a specially constructed questionnaire.

(2)   *Record of tribunal proceedings*

A group of 10 observers (from Edinburgh Citizens' Rights Office and from the University Departments of Social Administration and Sociology) attended tribunals and recorded as fully as possibly everything that took place at the hearings. After testing various methods of recording, we found it was possible for observers working in pairs to record the gist (and in a proportion of instances a verbatim transcript) of the entire proceedings. One observer focussed his attention on the members of the tribunal, noting as far as possible all that was said by the chairman and members and recording the contributions of others only by indicating their occurrence and source with the initials of the role of the person concerned (e.g. AP—to represent a spoken contribution from the appellant, PO—to indicate one from the presenting officer etc.) The other observer noted all spoken contributions from the insurance officer or presenting officer, from the appellant and his representative, or from the clerk and any witnesses, and, in a fashion complementary to that of his fellow-observer, noted the contribution of tribunal members only by initials which enabled an intervention by a particular member to be identified. From these two records it was usually possible to "reconstruct the dialogue" with a high degree of plausibility and, we hope, with some degree of accuracy. The observers also identified, at the time or immediately afterwards, the kinds and the substance of the evidence presented, using the categories: direct, hearsay, opinion, biographical, written, other (which included references to "trade usage" etc.) We do not, however, refer to the evidence data in this chapter. Immediately after each session, the two observers together completed one of the questionnaires described below for each case they had heard.

(3) *Questionnaire*

In formulating specific questions, it seemed appropriate to base these (as others have) on the criteria of "openness, fairness and impartiality" established by the Franks Committee.[7] We used many of the empirical observations and evaluative categories reported in other studies of tribunal procedure (in particular by Ruth Lister in *Justice for the Claimant*), to specify types of event which can be taken as indicators of the very general and diffuse Franks categories. This led us to develop a questionnaire which was directed to two kinds of information:-

(a)   general categories of response (recorded for subsequent analysis)—e.g. comments of tribunal members on the powers and duties of the tribunal; references to the law, or to Departmental policy and procedure (the latter not only by tribunal members but also by presenting officers or insurance officers or by the appellant and his representative); comments of tribunal members on representation and on the absence of the appellant; and references (again by any party) to the "burden of proof" on a particular issue.

(b)   specific categories of incident—e.g. did the chairman state that the tribunal was independent?; did he offer a definition of the nature of the appeal?; did tribunal members consult any documents other than the case-papers during the hearing?; if witnesses were present was the other party invited or allowed to question them?; was the appellant allowed to make his case without interruption?; was an adjournment requested and allowed?

A list of questions asked appears at the end of this chapter.

It is not always very easy to make complete sense of tribunal hearings without prior access to the tribunal papers and from the outset we hoped that we would be able to see not only the tribunal papers but also a copy of the tribunal's decision. However, we were only given permission to see copies of the tribunal papers and the tribunal's decision where we had the express permission of the appellant.[8] Moreover, the DHSS was reluctant to allow us to seek the appellants' co-operation with this study before the hearing, on the grounds that this might, in some way, affect the proceedings, so that our first opportunity of approaching the appellant was at (or immediately after) the hearing itself. Most of the appellants who attended a hearing willingly gave us access to their tribunal papers and gave permission for us to receive duplicate copies of the tribunal's decision but we had very little success at getting a response from those appellants who did not attend. Under arrangements agreed with the DHSS, a letter from us asking for their co-operation was enclosed together with the tribunal's decision. Unfortunately, the response to this was very small indeed. As a result we have complete documents on 23/66 (34%) of SB cases and 19/46 (41%) of NI cases and know the results of 28/66 (42%) of SB cases and 30/46 (65%) of NI cases. (See Table 1 below). The deficiency of the data in this respect is undoubtedly a serious shortcoming, although it is not a fatal one since our focus was on the hearing itself rather than the outcome of the appeal process.

	SBAT	NILT
Number of sessions	12	9
Number of cases	66*	46**
Number of cases where result is known	28 (42%)	30 (65%)
Number of cases with full documentation	23 (34%)	19 (41%)

*   includes one FIS appeal
** not counting one case from which observers were excluded at appellant's request.

Table 1:   Summary of sample data

In the following sections we first compare SBATs and NILTs in terms of the Franks Committee's three criteria (openness, fairness and impartiality), then look at the effects of attendance and representation on the hearing, and finally attempt to analyse the appeals and characterise the tribunal proceedings.

The Franks Committee criteria

According to the Franks Committee, *openness* "includes the promulgation of reasoned decisions, but its most important constituent is that the proceedings should be in public."[9] All 28 SB and 30 NI cases for which we have copies of the tribunal decision state reasons for the decision, although those of the SBATs were clearly inferior to those of the NILTs in several respects. In the first place, they were handwritten and often difficult to read (the NILT decisions were all typed). Secondly, they were extremely brief (most comprising a single sentence and none consisting of more than two such sentences) whereas the NILT decisions were often considerably longer and more detailed. Thirdly, where SBATs confirmed the Commission's decision, they frequently stated as a reason for so doing that benefit had been correctly calculated by the Commission or that the Commission's decision had been a correct one whereas NILTs in similar circumstances usually stated their own reasons in full. A frequently occurring form of entry under "Reasons for decision" in SBAT cases in which the appeal was rejected was : "The tribunal were agreed that the case had been correctly calculated in accordance with the Supplementary Benefits Act 1966". This should be compared with an example of the "grounds for decision" recorded in a NILT case where benefit was refused: "The tribunal took into account the claimant's past record, that he was usually certified fit to resume work on the Monday following his examination, that his injury does not appear previously to have affected him unduly and that he resumed work immediately after the visit of 16.9.74". This contrast may well reflect the difference between a tribunal reviewing an administrative decision and a tribunal hearing a case *de novo*—a point to which we return in the final section.

In spite of its general preference for public hearings, the Franks Committee exempted National Assistance tribunals on the grounds that "the issues to be determined involve the disclosure of intimate personal or financial circumstances".[10] The Committee, and successive Governments who have accepted its conclusions, were presumably concerned to protect the privacy of the claimant and to prevent possible embarrassments to him. It is therefore of some interest that when we sought SB appellants' permission to attend hearings this was not withheld on a single occasion and was frequently positively welcomed. Whether or not it was so in 1957, many appellants at SBATs appear to welcome the presence of others at a public hearing, perhaps seeing it as a form of protection. If SB appellants were given the right to have their appeals heard in private if they wished, in the same way as NI appellants currently are (during the tribunal sessions we attended, one person exercised this right), there would seem to be no reason why SBATs should not be open to the public.

Several items on the questionnaire were concerned with *fairness*, which the Franks Committee held "to require the adoption of a clear procedure to enable parties to know their rights, to present their case fully and to know the case they have to meet".[11] Although our data do not always substantiate the critical observations of others, we found that in a considerable number of SBAT hearings the conditions which would ensure a fair hearing were not satisfied.

In certain respects both SBAT and NILT appellants lacked help in "presenting their case fully". Very few tribunal chairmen introduced those present (Question 1), although on this single criterion SBATs were marginally more helpful than NILTs. Most appellants were presumably expected to know who everyone at the hearing was and what their roles were. At neither tribunal was the procedure ever adequately explained to appellants. The order of proceedings adopted in the two tribunals was in fact very different, and neither appeared unequivocally "fairer" in this respect. With one exception, in those SBAT cases where the appellant was present the hearing commenced with the presenting officer reading aloud the entire case papers, reading the appellant's statement first, then the Commission's observations and, finally, going through the calculation of benefit. In contrast, in every NILT hearing where the appellant was present, the chairman opened the proceedings by inviting the appellant to put his case. As we suggest later these procedural differences may be related to differences in the character of the hearing. In particular where, as often happened in the SBATs, the tribunal members took up points raised in the presenting officer's submission, the appellant often found it difficult to put his case. On the other hand, the SBAT procedure does ensure that the appellant is aware, if he can understand it, of the Department's case against him.

We note that in our sample neither SBAT nor NILT chairmen imposed the restrictive requirement (reported in *Justice for the Claimant*) that all questions should pass through him (Question 10).[12]

Neither at SBAT nor NILT hearings were appellants regularly helped to "know the case they have to meet". Although the grounds for the decision against which an appeal was being made were stated in the claimant's case papers, they often needed to be elucidated or expanded. The SBATs which we observed did little to explain the issues at stake, though in this respect they were little worse than NILTs. Chairmen offered definitions of the nature of the appeal (Question 4) in only 20% of SBAT cases (compared with 26% of NILTs), and when they did so it was sometimes only when the appellant's confusion had already become apparent and very rarely at the outset. Chairmen even less frequently made statements about the "burden of proof" (Question 23) on a particular issue (4/66 in SBATs, 3/46 in NILTs); and this was done just as infrequently by POs (4/66) and IOs (2/46). We should perhaps point out that we are making no distinction here between correct and incorrect definitions and references to the burden of proof, on the ground that any definition or reference is advantageous to the appellant in that it helps him to know where he stands. It must be remembered, however, that these deficiencies are likely to have relatively more serious consequences in the case of SBATs, since the case papers for NILTs are usually fuller and more explicit on these issues than are those prepared for SBATs. The former regularly contain references not only to the burden of proof but also to the standard of proof required as well as a reasoned statement of the grounds for the IO's decision. This statement is in general more detailed than that of the PO.

In other respects also, SBATs were more frequently and/or more seriously deficient than NILTs in providing the conditions for a fair hearing. Our general impression was that SBATs were less orderly than NILTs. Interruptions were more frequent (Question 26)—20/66 SBAT cases involved interruptions compared with 8/47 NILTs—and fewer appellants were able to put their case without interruption (Question 25). In only 2/66 SB cases the clerk intervened on his own initiative (Question 22) but these two cases were serious violations of the principle of fairness. On one occasion he urged tribunal members to make a decision when they were considering an adjournment and on another occasion he suggested that three cases, in which the appellants were all absent, should be heard together. (In fact, five sets of three SB cases and one set of two SB cases were heard together in this way in a manner which clearly offends against the principle of fairness).[13] There were no comparable cases of questionable intervention during the hearing by NI clerks, whose general involvement in the hearing was considerably less than that of their SB counterparts (and there were likewise no examples of cases being heard together with others).[14] In only 3/66 SBATs was fresh evidence put to the tribunal by the presenting officer (Question 29) but this did not happen at all in the NILTs. Although there were no restrictions on the calling or cross-examining of witnesses, very few were called by either side in either tribunal (Questions 27 and 28). In the case of SBATs, 3/5 witnesses were relatives of the appellant while, in the case of NILTs, 3/5 were "experts" and, in contrast to the SBATs, all witnesses were closely examined by the tribunal. In both tribunals it was usual for the hearing to be terminated by the chairman (Question 33), but in NILTs the chairman more often asked the appellant first if he had any more to say, and gave him an opportunity to sum up. 5/36 appellants at SBATs were given this opportunity compared with 7/31 at NILTs.

In view of the relatively greater amount of information given in NILT papers, it is disconcerting to find that even among the NILT cases observed there occurred not only three apparently "mistaken" appeals, but also a number of instances of apparent confusion and misunderstanding which should have been resolved by the Insurance Officer. By "mistaken" appeals, we mean appeals which were outside the jurisdiction of the tribunal and which therefore stood absolutely no chance of succeeding.[15] In the SBATs we detected at least seven "mistaken" appeals (in four cases against statutory deductions from Supplementary Benefit on the grounds that the appellant had left work voluntarily or had been discharged through misconduct). This number does not include appeals "against the scale rates" which we consider separately below. There was no indication that any of these appellants had previously been advised to appeal elsewhere or to take more appropriate courses of action. It is true that they were sometimes so informed at the tribunal (most often by the Trades Council member) but by then most appeals would have been "out of time". As an example of confusion and misunderstanding which had led to an unnecessary NI appeal we can cite the case of a local government officer who appealed against the Department's decision that he should refund an over-payment of family allowance. He did not understand the IO's submission that he had failed to exercise due care and diligence in avoiding over-payment and suggested in his written submission that the Department's "inspector" would confirm that "any money received by me was used with care and diligence". There were many similar examples of confusion and misunderstanding among SB appellants.

The Franks Report held *impartiality* "to require the freedom of tribunals from the influence, real or apparent, of Departments concerned with the subject matter of their decisions"[16] and many items on the questionnaire were concerned with impartiality, both in this narrow sense and in the broader sense of competence and freedom from bias towards or against appellants. SBAT chairmen mentioned the independence of the tribunal at 8 of the 36 hearings at which the appellant was present (Question 3). Although the independence of the tribunal was mentioned in the literature which appellants received along with their tribunal papers, the infrequent statement of independence at SBAT hearings is unimpressive unless contrasted with the fact that NILT chairmen did not refer to the independence of the tribunal on a single occasion. SBAT members were in general far more likely to make references of some kind to their powers and duties (Question 17). They did so in 17 cases, as compared with three such references by NILT tribunal members, all of them "mistaken" appeals. However, the SBAT references were largely negative; in 10 cases they referred to the limitations of their powers ("we can only operate within the rules", "we can't depart from the scale rates except for fringe benefits" [*sic*]). In addition, in three cases (with two chairmen) the SBATs' powers were seen as limited strictly to the appeal "exactly as it is written before them"; and in two cases the related point was made that an SBAT was not the place to initiate claims for ENPs (of particular importance when the appeal is a simple statement that the appellant "wishes to appeal to an independent tribunal" or that he cannot manage on his supplementary allowance). In our sample, only two positive references were made to discretion (one qualified by "within the rules"). As a result, and this is confirmed by an examination of the records of the proceedings, it is extremely unlikely that any of the eight appeals "against the scale rates" resulted in any additional help for the claimant although, in a number of instances, appellants were advised to request exceptional needs payments from the Commission.

SBAT members were·in general conscious of limits to their powers rather than aware of their power to exercise discretion under the Act in a creative manner (even once or twice to the point of explicitly denying their discretionary powers, e.g. to pay more than the level laid down in the Handbook as a dietary allowance, and implicitly denying them on numerous occasions). Thus, it is very unlikely that any of the four people (all of whom had incomes slightly in excess of the scale rates) who appealed after being refused exemption from NHS charges received any help. Yet some SBAT members were critical of the SBC and its officers. There were 13 instances of such comments (none, incidentally, from Trades Council members), which ranged from case-specific issues such as the inadequacy of particular ENPs, to comments on Departmental procedure (e.g. that all giro cheques should be sent by recorded delivery), and Government policy (e.g. that scale rates are not related to average earnings). Only five critical comments were noted in the NILTs, and of these two referred to a specific change in regulations. The relative frequency of critical comment in SBATs might be taken as evidence of a proper independence from the SBC and its officers; but there are a number of indications to the contrary. First, there was a small number of remarks which seemed to align the SBAT with the SBC (one chairman remarked on the general nature of grants; another, after questioning the PO, said, "when you ask the Commission's Officer something he always knows the answer"; a third refused to allow the appellant to express criticism of the SBC on the grounds that the SBAT is "not the proper place for such criticism"). Secondly, we noted at least seven instances where there seemed to be good grounds for criticism of the SBC (for example, where an appellant said that if her entitlement had been explained to her she would not have appealed, and where an appellant's letter was omitted from the case papers), but where no criticism was expressed. The same could be said of the "scale rate" appeals mentioned above, most of which would have been unnecessary if the Commission had informed the claimant about ENPs and, in some cases, ECAs. Thirdly, the generality of most of the criticisms, so general that the PO could hardly have disagreed with them, casts a good deal of doubt on their seriousness and significance. Examples of such criticism are that the scale rates should be wage related and that all giro payments should be sent by recorded delivery. Conversely, the much smaller number of adverse comments from NILTs were seriously critical of Departmental policy and procedure.

· We now turn to the issue of the competence of tribunal members to act independently. Not surprisingly, more discussion of Departmental policy and procedure (Questions 16 and 24) took place in SBATs than in NILTs (the PO referred to policy and procedure in 26/66 SBAT cases, the IO did so in 5/46 NILT cases). However, on no occasion did an SBAT so much as imply that it was not bound by Commission policy or suggest that the 1966 Act could be interpreted in another way. Conversely, when the IO referred to Departmental policy it tended to be in response to an NILT's suggestion that the policy was not apt or that it perhaps penalised the appellant. In some SBATs there was clear evidence of the dependence of members on the PO—in almost half the cases the PO was asked for or gave his views on relevant statutes, regulations and policy, in addition to those expressed in his routinised opening statement, and his views almost invariably went unchallenged. In two instances NILT chairmen asked the IO about precedents not mentioned in the case papers. In both cases the IO was able to recite the precedent but there did not appear to be the same dependence on what he said. In several cases the PO's advice was asked on non-SBC matters (e.g. on Local Authority policy on rent arrears). The impression that the members relied on the PO's version of the relevant regulations is supported by our observation that in no case did any SBAT member consult the Act or the Handbook or any official publication during a hearing (Question 12). To be fair, it should also be said that NILTs never did so on their own initiative, although they did so once or twice at the request of an appellant or his representative. Moreover, our observations suggest that in 27 SBAT cases there are indications that tribunal members did not know about or did not understand relevant aspects of the law or of Departmental policy as against only three such instances in NILTs (Question 14). However debatable specific instances may be (and we readily admit that inclusion is based on value judgements) there remains very little in our record to suggest that SBAT members are operating with authority and familiarity in their discussion of law and policy, and much to the contrary.

Finally, moralising attitudes to appellants may also affect the impartiality of the tribunal. We noted only two instances of "accusatory" behaviour by SBAT members, and four of "moral exhortation" (e.g. an employer's representative to a recent graduate who left Edinburgh to take part in a job interview elsewhere, "why have you not taken a job to tide you over? . . . I've known chaps taking labouring jobs for a fortnight"). Even this small number, however, contrasts with the complete absence of such episodes in our sample of NILT cases, even in those which hinged on the credibility of an appellant's repeated claims for Sickness Benefit.

The effects of attendance and representation on the hearing

Table 2 below shows how many appellants were present at their appeal and how many were represented.

	SBAT	NILT
Appellant present with representative	18	18
Appellant present alone	16	13
Appellant absent but representative present	2	1
Appellant absent	30	14
Total	66	46

Table 2: Number of appellants present and represented

10 of the 20 SBAT representatives and 16 of the 19 NILT representatives could be described as "experts"—the former were mainly rights workers, the latter trade union officials. The most obvious effect of the presence of the appellant and/or his representative was on the duration of the hearing and the subsequent deliberations.

	SBAT	NILT
Appellant present with representative	20 mins	19 mins
Appellant present alone	17 mins	19.5 mins
Appellant absent but representative present	12.5 mins	20 mins
Appellant absent	4.5 mins	9.5 mins

Table 3: Effect of presence of appellant and representative on average length of hearing (including deliberation)

We should point out that the times in Table 3 probably overestimate the length of the proceedings since we had to assume that the time between cases was all spent discussing the previous case. This is somewhat unlikely. The most disturbing feature of the above table is the speed with which the cases of absentee appellants are dealt with by SBATs. We have already referred to the practice of taking cases together; in addition to the five sets of three SB cases and one set of two SB cases which were heard in this way, a number of other cases were despatched in incredible haste (i.e. in less than one minute), with few, if any, questions asked. In these circumstances, it is instructive to look at the comments of tribunal members (if any) on the presence (or absence) and representation of appellants, and at the use of their power to adjourn hearings. At both tribunals, the few comments that were made about attendance (Question 21) were mainly neutral although three SBAT chairmen made critical comments; one said that it was "a pity the appellant hasn't appeared", another that "it is difficult when appellants are not here" and a third (to us) that it was "a pity *for you* (i.e. the observers) that appellants aren't here since their cases cover a wide range of issues and it would, no doubt, have been useful *for you*. Likewise, two NILTs made similar comments, one member remarking that he would have liked to have questioned the appellant and a chairman commenting that it was a pity the appellant wasn't present to give his views on one aspect of his case. But despite the large number of absentee appellants (32/66 at SBATs, 15/46 at NILTs) absence in itself was *never* taken to be sufficient reason for adjournment. Five SBATs and three NILTs were, in fact adjourned. In one SB case this was the result of a letter from an absent appellant explaining that he was ill, supported by a request from the PO to adjourn the hearing, but for the rest, it was because one of the parties (tribunal members, Department's officer or appellant's representative) requested further information. Two requests for adjournment (from the PO at an SBAT and from a Union representative at an NILT) were refused. Written or spoken explanations from appellants accounting for their absence, which could sometimes be construed as requests for an adjournment, never produced this result. Three communications from absentee SB appellants, expressing a desire to be represented, likewise had no effect (once because the clerk failed to inform the tribunal although he showed the letter to us).

The only significant comments concerning representation (Question 20) occurred in NILTs. On two occasions an NILT chairman asked an appellant if he wished to be represented and offered to adjourn the hearing. Sadly these offers were misunderstood by the appellants, who thought they would be represented by the Department and declined. One NILT chairman commented on the advantage of representation for the tribunal, since there was much less explanation for them to do.

Before looking, finally, at the effects of the presence or absence of appellants on the conduct of the hearing, we first analyse the appeals and the character of the hearings. Because of our focus on the hearing itself and our incomplete set of tribunal decisions, we make no comments on the effects of appearance and representation on the outcome of the appeal.

The nature of appeals and the character of the proceedings

The Supplementary Benefits system and, by extension, Supplementary Benefit Appeal Tribunals, are frequently characterised by their concern with individual financial need and by their overriding discretionary powers.[17] However, as we try to argue in this section, the decisions of the SBC and of SBATs are not predominantly concerned with the exercise of discretion. The right to benefit established under the 1966 Act, together with the various statutory requirements and procedures therein contained, and the increasingly uniform policies adopted by the Commission, ensure that most decisions are initially arrived at by the Commission in a routine way through the application of a body of administrative rules to a particular set of circumstances.[18] As Harry Calvert argues in Chapter 14, this is not so different from the application of a body of precedents to a particular set of circumstances, as occurs in the national insurance system. Of course, there are differences for the tribunals in that the administrative rules are not binding on SBATs in the way in which precedents are binding on NILTs and the powers of SBATs are correspondingly greater. However, we contend not only that SBATs frequently fail to exercise their overriding discretion to meet financial need when it would be appropriate to do so, but also that a substantial proportion of SBAT appeals hinge on disputes which do not call into play these discretionary powers. We distinguish three categories of such "non-discretionary disputes"—those about facts (e.g. whether or not a claimant was working and, if so, what his earnings were), those about the interpretation of those facts and the appropriate application of policy (e.g. whether or not a set of circumstances admitted by the claimant constitutes cohabitation, whether or not a claimant's actual dietary expenses should be taken into account in awarding an ECA, or whether or not rent is "unreasonably high") and those about the law (e.g. whether or not the claimant is a householder, whether the requirement to register for work is mandatory or discretionary, or whether benefit has been calculated correctly). In Table 4 below, we analyse what was in dispute in the 66 SB appeals, using the categories described above but also distinguishing those disputes about law which were concerned with the calculation of entitlement.

Nature of dispute*	Number of disputes	Percentage of cases in which disputes occur
Existence of an exceptional need	25	38
Facts	14	21
Interpretation of facts and appropriate application of policy	31	47
Law	7	11
Calculation of entitlement	21	33

* Many of the cases involved more than one dispute. Where a case involved more than one dispute each dispute was recorded. The number of disputes therefore exceeds the number of cases.

Table 4:   Analysis of disputed issues in SB appeals

We judge that the possible existence of an exceptional need could have been an issue in 25/66 (38%) of SB appeals. However, in a substantial number of cases (involving six cases which were treated as appeals against the scale rates and another four cases involving exemption from NHS charges) this issue was not recognised as such by the tribunal. In six of these 10 cases, the appellant was absent and in none was he accompanied by an "expert" representative. If these cases are excluded, the possible existence of an exceptional need was an issue in only 15/66 (23%) of SB appeals. At the same time three out of every four cases heard by SBATs involved disputes about facts, the interpretation of those facts and the appropriate application of policy (including the appropriate payment for an exceptional need once established) and the law, i.e. precisely those disputes which characterise NI appeals. We consider that the existence of a minority of disputes concerned with the recognition of financial need is insufficient justification for maintaining tribunals within the supplementary benefits scheme which differ so markedly in structure and procedure from NILTs. We also consider that NILTs, with their legally qualified chairmen, would appreciate their discretionary powers more fully and be less reluctant to exercise them in an independent way, if they were given responsibility for hearing SB appeals.

We turn finally to a discussion of the style and character of the hearing. The following analysis is largely provisional and will need to be substantiated through a more rigorous analysis of our data. However, a preliminary survey of the detailed transcripts of the tribunal hearings points to differences between and within each type of tribunal. Analysis of the nature and extent of communication between those present suggests that the SBATs we observed resembled attempts to review decisions taken by the SBC whereas the NILTs more closely resembled attempts to hear cases *de novo*.[19] The following factors support this conclusion:

for SBATs—

(1)   the dominant position of the presenting officer's opening statement,

(2)   the discussions between the tribunal and the PO which frequently followed when an appellant was present,

(3)   the lack of assistance by the tribunal to appellants in putting their case,

(4)   the lack of a proper hearing when the appellant was absent,

(5)   the "reasons" given by SBATs for confirming decisions which were frequently expressed in terms of the correctness of the Commission's original decision;

for NILTs—

(1)   the emphasis on the appellant's statement,

(2)   the efforts of some tribunals to ensure that he made a coherent case,

(3)   the generally subordinate role of the IO in the proceedings,

(4)   the way in which the tribunal papers frequently referred

not only to the burden of proof but also to the standard of proof required,

(5) the tribunal decision, which was not only written by the chairman but also gave the tribunal's own reasons for the decision it had reached.

The appellant's presence and representation also had some effect on the hearing. At SBATs, the appearance of an appellant did at least ensure that some kind of hearing took place while representation, in particular expert representation, seemed to affect the rigour with which Commission decisions were reviewed. However, even when an expert representative was present, SBATs were very reluctant to hear appeals *de novo*. At NILTs, the attendance of the appellant likewise influenced the effectiveness with which the appeal could be heard without changing its essential style or character.

Conclusion

Nearly 30 years ago, the Franks Committee described the task of the National Assistance Appeal Tribunals as one resembling "an assessment or case committee taking a further look at the facts and, in some cases arriving at a fresh decision on the extent of need". Our study indicates that, for a number of reasons, they do not perform this task particularly well. Moreover, we maintain that very complex issues of entitlement arise in connection with the 1966 Act and that adequate protection of claimants' rights requires a different system of adjudication. Although, as our study showed, NILTs are not immune from criticism, we conclude that a greatly superior system of adjudication would result if supplementary benefit appeals were heard by NILTs and if these tribunals were bound by a set of precedents which would give interpretations of statute law and specify the circumstances in which discretion could be exercised. Although difficult problems would arise concerning the status of Commission policy we believe that such a structure is an appropriate one for the kind of adjudication we consider necessary in the supplementary benefits scheme.

NOTES

1. The major exception is Melvin Herman, *Administrative Justice and Supplementary Benefits*. 1972.

2. Most of these are published in CPAG's quarterly journal *Poverty* and in the *LAG Bulletin*.

3. Ruth Lister, *Justice for the Claimant*. CPAG Poverty Research Series 4, 1974.

4. See, for example, Norman Lewis, "Supplementary Benefit Appeal Tribunals", [1973] *Public Law*, 259.

5. In the case of both SBATs and NILTs, the majority of cases were drawn from the Edinburgh tribunals. We observed SBATs in four areas and NILTs in three.

6. Such access has recently been granted to Professor Kathleen Bell who is carrying out a study of SBATs for the DHSS.

7. Report of the Committee on Administrative Tribunals and Enquiries, Cmnd 218, 1957 (Franks Report); para. 25.

8. This is again in contrast to the facilities provided for Professor Bell.

9. Franks Report, para. 76.

10. Ibid., para. 180.

11. Ibid., para. 42.

12. It is significant that, in spite of having legally qualified chairmen, NILTs were no more formal in this respect.

13. Many cases in which the SB appellants were absent were heard so rapidly that no real hearing can be said to have taken place. See Table 2.

14. NI clerks frequently came in and out of the tribunal room during the hearing and the subsequent deliberations. SB clerks, on the other hand, were always present throughout since they took whatever record of proceedings was taken and wrote out the tribunal's decision.

15. The existence of such appeals is, of course, a reflection on the Department, not on the tribunals.

16. Franks Report, para. 42.

17. See for example, Richard Titmuss, "Welfare 'Rights' Law and Discretion" *Political Quarterly*, 42, 1971, pp. 113-132.

18. See chapters 4 and 5 above.

19. See chapter 6 above.

20. Franks Report, para. 182.

QUESTIONNAIRE

For reasons of space, the full questionnaire is not included here. In addition to recording information on the time, place and duration of the hearing, the individuals who were present at the hearing and during the deliberations, the personal characteristics of the appellants (e.g. age, sex, employment status) the following questions were asked. Answers to questions were later checked against the transcript.

1. Did chairman introduce those present?

2. Did clerk or chairman ask appellant's permission for observers to be present?

3. Did the chairman state that the tribunal is independent?

4. Did the chairman offer a definition of the nature of the appeal?

5. If yes, was the definition challenged? If so, by whom?

6. What was case about (in brief)?

7. What was Department's case?

8. What were IO/PO's arguments (if different from above)?

9. What were appellant's arguments?

10. Did the chairman require all questions to pass through him?

11. Did the chairman use the same form of address (usually Mr...) to (or about) appellant and IO/PO? If no, specify.

12 Did tribunal members consult any documents other than tribunal case papers? Specify documents if possible.

13. Were any references made to precedent? If so, by whom? If yes, what was the tribunal's response?

14. Did tribunal members display apparent ignorance of the law? departmental policy/procedure? work conditions in general? or the local situation?

15. Did tribunal members demonstrate any other incompetence (e.g. by confusing cases)?

16. Note any critical comments of tribunal members on DHSS procedure etc.

17. Note any references by tribunal members to the powers and duties of the tribunal.

18. Note any references by tribunal members to the law.

19. Note any procedural or "control" comments by tribunal members.

20. Note any comments of tribunal members on representation.

21. Note any comments of tribunal members on the absence of the appellant.

22. Did the clerk intervene on his own initiative? If yes, specify.

23. Were any references made to the "burden of proof"? If so, by whom? If yes, specify.

24. Were references made to "policy", "normal practice", etc? If so, by whom? If yes, specify.

25. Was the appellant (or his representative) allowed to make his case without interruption? If not, specify.

26. Who interrupted whom? how often? Note any regulation of interruption by the chairman.

27. Did anyone ask to call witnesses? If so, who did? If yes, note chairman's response.

28. If witnesses were present, was the other party invited to cross-examine? What was the chairman's response?

29. Was new evidence introduced? If so, by whom? If yes,

specify. Note chairman's response.

30. Did appellant refer to his rights, or to the law? If yes, specify. Note tribunal's response.

31. Was an adjournment requested? If so, by whom? If yes, on what grounds? What was chairman's response?

32. Did the tribunal consider adjournment in the absence of the appellant (or his representative)? What did they decide?

33. How did the hearing end?

34. What was the nature of the dispute? (Was it about the existence of an exceptional need, about facts, about the interpretation of facts or the appropriate application of policy, about the law, or about the calculation of entitlement?)

35. What was the decision (if known)?

36. Note any special features of the case, e.g. any special features of setting, seating, order of admission etc., any indication that tribunal members had met the appellant or his representative before, whether the representative was questioned about his personal knowledge of the appellant.

X APPELLANTS' PERCEPTIONS OF THE TRIBUNAL PROCESS
Coral Milton

This chapter is based on research carried out by the Legal Advice Research Unit of the Nuffield Foundation into three different "welfare" tribunals: Supplementary Benefit Appeal Tribunals, National Insurance Local Tribunals and Rent Tribunals (operating prior to the implementation of the 1974 Rent Act), hereafter referred to as SBATs, NILTs and RTs.[1] Although this chapter concentrates on those findings which relate particularly to Supplementary Benefit appeals, material from the full study will be used to give some comparative basis to these findings. I hope to indicate briefly how different policies, structures, and procedures relate to variations in the attitudes of appellants towards the different tribunals.

The intention is to describe the kinds of perception brought to the tribunal process by one major group of participants in hearings, the appellants. They are the primary consumers of the judicial process offered by a tribunal structure. Their attitudes are often very different from those held by chairmen, members and representatives, who tend to be better informed about the structure of tribunals, the form of proceedings and the areas of policy under dispute. Nevertheless, as users of the appeals process, appellants have valid interpretations and criticisms to offer which require wider articulation.

Information was gathered through observation of 276 cases, heard at two different sets of inner city, suburban and outer area tribunals. (Table 1). Detailed interviews were carried out with a different sample of 229 appellants who had appeared previously at those same tribunals. (Table 2). Samples of chairmen and members on tribunal panels and representatives were also interviewed. Fieldwork was completed by July 1974.

	SBAT	NILT	RT	Total
Observed cases	113(41.0%)	101(36.5%)	62(22.5%)	276(100%)

Table 1: Observed cases according to type of tribunal

129

	SBAT	NILT	RT	Total
Appellants	96(41.0%)	94(41.9%)	39(17.0%)	229(100%)
Chairmen & Members	49(42.6%)	51(44.3%)	15(13.0%)	115(100%)
Representatives	43(41.7%)	43(41.7%)	17(16.5%)	103(100%)

Table 2: Breakdown of interviews by type of tribunal

Social characteristics of appellants

The appellants who were interviewed tended to come from a restricted sector in society and in many respects constituted a disadvantaged group in the general population. The largest number, (41%) of appellants, fell into Social Classes IV and V, (that is unskilled and semi-skilled workers). A high proportion (20%) of all appellants were unemployed and a further 12% were retired or pensioners. Among Supplementary Benefit appellants, 29% were unemployed and 21% were retired.

Incomes tended to be low, with the Supplementary Benefits appellants worst off. (Table 3). 58% of them were found to be living on an income of less than £20 per week. This group also had the largest number of dependants, approximately 30% came from households of five or more persons. This group was most dependent on state benefits over long periods and, not surprisingly, a very high proportion (88%) stated that they had experienced or were experiencing financial hardship.

	SBAT % Appellants	NILT % Appellants	RT % Appellants
Under £20 p. wk.	57.9	28.2	34.2
£20—Under £40 p.wk	40.0	45.7	47.4
£40 or more	2.1	24.0	13.2
Unwilling to disclose	0.0	2.2	5.3
TOTAL	100.0 (n=92)	100.0 (n=94)	100.0 (n=38)

Table 3: Income of appellants according to type of tribunal

(Note: Cases where there was no information have been omitted from this table).

A large number of appellants were under thirty-five years of age and we infer that many were under pressure of responsibility for young families. Quite a number of single-parent families were interviewed but data on family circumstances were not specifically collected.

Appellants in general do not constitute a highly educated group. 48% of them went to a Secondary Modern or Comprehensive school and 34% left by the age of 15. 62% had no further education and 59% had no qualifications. We occasionally came across appellants who were illiterate. While capability cannot be equated in any narrow way with formal educational qualifications, we were not surprised to find that a large proportion of appellants were baffled by the tribunal process, particularly when it came to dealing with forms and correspondence or trying to interpret rules and sections of the relevant Acts. Supplementary Benefit appellants also tended to suffer more from educational as well as financial handicaps compared with the National Insurance and Rent tribunal respondents. In fact, their only advantage over one of the other groups lay in having superior accommodation to Rent tribunal applicants. 60% of them lived in local authority houses or flats, whereas 85% of Rent tribunal applicants (mostly tenants) lived, of course, in private furnished lettings, mostly in very cramped circumstances.[2]

This picture of appellants, particularly of the markedly disadvantaged Supplementary Benefit respondents, contrasts strongly with the social characteristics displayed by the chairmen and members of tribunal panels who make the decisions on each appeal.[3] The differences are perhaps predictable and indicative of the social distance existing between the two groups. Chairmen and members were a much older group than appellants, over half of them over 60 years of age. 31% of chairmen and members interviewed had a professional qualification or degree. Data on income was not available for this group, but it is reasonable to suppose that by virtue of their qualifications, their ages and social status (three-quarters of them came from Social Classes I and II), they were in a much superior financial position to the average appellant.[4]

Representatives were much closer to appellants in terms of age range and present levels of income. However, they constituted a highly qualified group (58% had a professional qualification or degree) and were also differentiated from appellants by social class (81% come from Social Classes I and II). Their prospects were significantly better than those of the average appellant as many were at the beginning of legal, social work and community work careers. A minority had some experience of poverty through claiming supplementary benefits, usually over a temporary period as students. A very few were themselves long-term claimants, whose involvement with a Claimants' Union had led them to pursue representation on behalf of fellow claimants.

The appellants' viewpoint

Generalisations are difficult to make since, as may be expected, appellants hold a wide variety of views about the tribunal process, reflecting not only differences in personal circumstances and wider attitudes but also differences between the geographical areas studied and between types of tribunals attended. Interviews with appellants took place after their cases had been heard, whether or not they attended, and their overall attitudes were usually directly related to the outcome of the appeal.

Positive responses to the tribunal system were given most frequently when the case had been "won" (i.e. the appeal allowed and the decision reversed or modified in the appellant's favour in the case of NILTs and SBATs). In part, this explains the much higher level of satisfaction reported by applicants to the Rent Tribunals, since it was in our experience difficult to clearly identify a "lost" case though a Rent Tribunal may have averted distress only temporarily, being unable to deal with the long term need for security. Actually "winning" a case was therefore important to overall response, even if appellants made other more specific criticisms of tribunals. However, a posititive response would be reinforced if the case had not only been "won" but the appellant also felt that he had been given a "fair" hearing. Occasionally an appellant would say that he had been given a "fair" hearing despite losing his case if he became convinced that the subject of the appeal lay outside the tribunal's jurisdiction, or if he came to believe that the source of dispute lay in genuine confusion about scale rates or eligibility. Conversely, some "successful" appellants remained dissatisfied, either with the details of the decision, such as the amount of their award, or with other aspects of their hearing.

It is difficult to say precisely what the concept of "fairness" means to different appellants. For some the informality of the proceedings was a pleasant surprise. However, only a minority of appellants mentioned this as a positive factor, and paradoxically Supplementary Benefit respondents were least likely to mention this. Chairmen and members were much more likely to stress the benefits of tribunal informality without realising to what extent any appearance before a judicial type of body can cause feelings of nervousness and disorientation.

Being given enough time to present the case in the appellant's own way, even where this meant bringing in facts not normally considered to be relevant to the issue, was also important to a positive response, especially for old people, the inarticulate or the confused. Allied to this was the question of support during the hearing, from a friend or relative or official representative. Represented appellants were more likely to say that they had been given a "fair" hearing on the grounds of balancing the odds with departmental officials or landlords' representatives and giving confidence to a nervous respondent.

Feelings of fairness were also very much influenced by the extent of "need" as perceived by the appellant. Where need was not total, but referred to a partial benefit or to the extension of benefit, even a negative decision could be accepted. On the other hand, where the appellant saw his need as desperate, then even partial refusal was unlikely to be regarded as fair, whatever the merits of the case. (Panel members at Rent Tribunals appeared to be generally more aware that their decisions will affect the lives of applicants to a very marked degree; since the social consequences of depriving a tenant of a roof over his head are well recognised. It seemed to be more difficult for the relatively affluent members of SBATs and NILTs to appreciate that in the case of appellants with strictly limited budgets, quite trivial sums of money have a very real significance.)

Negative responses to the tribunal system on the part of appellants often represent the opposite side of the coin, i.e. "losing" the case and feeling that it was "unfairly" handled. According to national statistics only about 19% of cases result in a revised or reversed decision in favour of SBAT and NILT appellants.[5] The level of dissatisfaction reported is therefore likely to be much greater than that of satisfaction, but criticism is not restricted to resentment concerning the practical and financial implications of a failed appeal.

Stereotyping

Appellants often see themselves as being categorised by tribunal members either in individual or in group terms. Notions such as "malingering", or "undeserving" are felt to attach to individuals; while "unmarried mothers", "students", "strikers", "squatters" and "immigrants" are examples of group stereotypes, all bearing a pejorative connotation which appellants feel may be held against them. Appellants report the feeling that members and official tend to pry into what are felt to be irrelevant factors.[6]

Rent Tribunal applicants do not on the whole seem to feel that negative stereotypes are attached to themselves as individuals. Where it does occur however, the categorisation of applicants may affect the extent of protection offered. Thus where the old or the sick are concerned or those with children, more sympathy is extended than would be, for example, to a young single man. However, there seemed to be a more general awareness amongst Rent Tribunal panel members that the shortage of adequate housing provision is a socio-political issue and hence becomes a societal responsibility rather than remaining an individual problem. Some moral approbation may be felt towards the kind of tenants who have been described as people "who have no stake in society", but we found that the distinction between the "deserving" and "undeserving" is by no means made so clear as it is to recipients of National Insurance and Supplementary Benefits.

Lack of independence

Very few SBAT and NILT appellants feel that tribunals are really independent of ministerial control or departmental influence, even though they may hold positive views of tribunals in other respects. Their criticisms in this area were generally directed against Presenting Officers and Insurance Officers who were accused of having undue influence over the tribunal in various ways. Most appellants did not mention the role of the clerk or the way members are chosen as they were largely unaware of the implications of these factors. Rent Tribunals were seen to be much more independent in practice than the other types of tribunal studied. The absence of a departmental representative and obvious lack of connection between the decision-makers and the opposition (i.e. landlord or agent) helps to avoid a situation where the appellant suspects some in-built bias towards the department.

Irrelevance of tribunal membership

There was a general feeling expressed, particularly at SBATs, that current tribunal membership is inappropriate because members lack the relevant experience and knowledge upon which to base decisions. Age, for example, may be important not simply in terms of the "generation gap", but at a very practical level in as far as members may be out of touch with the commitments and financial responsibilities of the appellant at his or her particular point in the life-cycle. Many appellants are actually ignorant of where tribunal members are drawn from and have a tendency to class them as judges or lawyers, and "local worthies", i.e. people very much out of touch with their own day-to-day experiences. This kind of social gap is also experienced by Rent Tribunal applicants, but the home inspection gave them greater expectations of the real situation speaking for itself.

The relevance of information provided

It seems that appellants over-estimate the interest of tribunals in facts which they as appellants see as relevant, for example, complaints about treatment at the local office, a general account of budgetary difficulties,[7] descriptions of illnesses among other members of the family, or in the case of Rent Tribunal applicants, complaints about fellow tenants and standards of cleanliness. This difference of perception results in feelings of frustration, since such differences of emphasis are rarely made explicit. It is perhaps not always realised by tribunal members that many appellants live daily in a situation of multiple stress and it is very difficult for them to restrict their comments to the limited area of appeal.[8]

Other aspects of the tribunal situation which affect response

(1) Accessibility

This factor was felt to be very important not simply in terms of geographical distance, but also in terms of other considerations such as the availability and cost of transport to the tribunal, the amount of time away from work, and the availability of child-minding arrangements. Rent Tribunal applicants were actually worst off in this respect since they are not offered expenses and would sometimes have to lose a whole day's pay to be at an inspection in the morning and a hearing in the afternoon.[9] Preference for evening hearings was advanced by those people who did not wish to take time off work.

(2) Speed of hearing

In general, it was thought that tribunals compared favourably in this respect with courts, but the concept of need was very important in this connection. Where need was felt to be acute, there was much criticism of the delay (approximately six weeks) and it was suggested that a system of immediate appeal to the manager of the local office (within 24 hours) should be instituted. It was further suggested, mainly by representatives, that benefits should not be cut off until the appeal had been decided. In the case of Rent Tribunal applicants seeking security, some delay was often welcomed, since any implementation of a Notice To Quit would be suspended until the outcome of the hearing was known.

(3) Availability of information

This issue was regarded as crucial and received perhaps the strongest criticism. Appellants were often unaware of the importance of a personal appearance in terms of outcome, of the availability of representation and its relevance in terms of likely outcome (Table 4), of the right to an adjournment, or of the changes in legislation. [10]

Appellants	No. of cases	% decisions in appellant's favour
Attended & represented	2,315	37
Attended, not represented	3,969	25
Not attended, represented	614	32
Not attended, not represented	7,647	6

Table 4: National statistics on attendance and representation at SBATs, related to outcome of appeal, October 1972—March 1973.

Source: DHSS computer print-out.

Only about half of the appellants interviewed by us took any advice before going to the hearing, the SBAT respondents tending to approach voluntary agencies, rights groups, advice centres and also Social Services Departments. As 68% of all appellants found prior advice helpful, it would be useful if those who do not currently seek advice could be enabled to do so. Appellants living in outlying districts have most difficulty in this respect, as there are usually only a limited range of agencies available for consultation.

(4) Tribunal procedure

Failure to introduce appellants to the members and to explain the different interest groups present, did at times add to the general sense of confusion about what was happening. Where tribunals were reaching the end of the session, appellants sometimes felt inhibited from presenting their case fully because of remarks made by members or meaningful glances at watches. We noted that the much busier inner city tribunals were more likely to convey this sense of the pressure of time available and to cut short expansive presentations.

There remains the problem that most unattended cases are awarded scant attention compared to attended ones, and we have already pointed to the likely result in terms of outcome of appeal. (Table 4). At the same time, respondents who did not attend usually posited valid reasons why they could not in terms of family and job commitments, sickness, transport difficulties and nervousness without support. [11] The dismissive attitude of tribunals towards unattended cases would seem to require a new approach, perhaps in terms of sending visitors to ascertain the degree of difficulty in making an appearance, which should then be taken into account during decision-making.

Approaches based on status identification

(1)   Social competence

Those who were able to handle the "business" of the tribunal exhibited more markedly positive responses. This was clearly associated with class position, level of education, social contacts, awareness of helping agencies and perhaps a sense of personal confidence. The less socially competent felt the whole "system" (not merely tribunals) to be difficult to manage. Such respondents needed assistance in approaching a situation with which they felt they could not cope. Unfortunately, a large proportion of appellants, especially Supplementary Benefit recipients, do suffer educational, social and financial deprivation, which together with a nervous attitude to appearing before tribunals seriously affects their competence to deal with the situation they encounter at the hearing.

Respondents who had prior experience of tribunals tended to be more knowledgeable and confident in their approach, if only because they knew what to expect and in some cases were better informed as to their rights.

(2)   Working class deference

Some appellants see tribunal members as "superior", being better educated than themselves and coming from a higher social class. This group regard it as legitimate that these members should make decisions and are therefore more likely to concur with the outcome. Yet others identify with middle-class values, and particularly the work ethic which the tribunal is seen by them to represent. Their attitudes and approach do not reflect feelings of inadequacy in the situation, except in the case of persons who feel that they have now come "down in the world" and are unwillingly forced to look to "charity".[12]

(3)   Hostility to the social system

There are a growing number of people whose negative attitudes reflect the idea that our wider society is unjust, who see tribunals as one means of supporting an inequitable system. Such people have a strong awareness of class differentiation and of social inequality which they experience as the reality of deprivation in everyday life. Some of the long-term Supplementary Benefits claimants are possibly the most militant in this respect, together with some active trade unionists appearing before National Insurance tribunals.

Appellants' views on representation and Legal Aid

Of the appellants interviewed by us, 53% of Supplementary Benefit appellants, 46% of National Insurance appellants and 28% of Rent Tribunal applicants were represented at their hearing.[13] Of these, over half felt that it had had a positive effect on the hearing, though a considerable number said that they thought it had little effect in either direction. However, people are aware that the effect of representation is not entirely predictable. One man commented:

"It's a great help to have a representative to present the case, but if he weren't there, they might be more sympathetic. If I'd gone by myself with such a case, they might have said, it's your fault, why didn't you get someone to help you."

Quite a few others said in effect: "It gave us moral support rather than affecting the decision". The very old or inarticulate appellants who were fortunate enough to have the responsibility for handling their case taken over by a representative usually had nothing but praise for the person concerned.

Almost half of the unrepresented (excepting Rent Tribunal applicants) felt that they would have had a better chance with their case if they had had a representative, but many did not know how to find one or were confused by the tribunal papers:

"I think they should give you one automatically, not make it hard to find. An ordinary person doesn't know lawyers."

"On the letter you weren't allowed a solicitor, you could just take a friend."

Appellants to different tribunals had different preferences as to which kind of representative they preferred. Subsequent to the hearing, 41% of Rent Tribunal applicants said that they would not want a representative, presumably because they felt that their interests had been protected without one. The next largest group, 38% said that given the choice, they would have liked to have a lawyer. NILT appellants also would have preferred solicitors or barristers or legally-qualified union representatives. Supplementary Benefit appellants were more divided in their opinions of who could provide the best representation and indicated their preference for people from non-statutory agencies, like the Citizens' Rights Office, the Free Representation Unit, Task Force, or a neighbourhood law centre. Such choices were always prefaced by the statement that it should be a legal type of service but "free", as most Supplementary Benefit claimants cannot afford financial contributions. This particular group could be considerably assisted by the recommended extension of Legal Aid to representation before tribunals,[14] though the exclusion of lay advocates from a scheme of funded representation would be particularly unhelpful to Supplementary Benefits appellants, since voluntary representatives seem to provide the most effective advocacy. (Table 5)

Representative	% total represented	% award increased
Friend, relative	65.4	33.1
Trade Union official	1.6	43.5
Solicitor	2.8	28.6
Social worker	9.4	54.7
CPAG	2.0	66.7
Claimants' Union	13.8	46.1
Other	4.9	46.6
Total	100.0 (n=1477)	

Table 5: Effectiveness of different types of representation at SBATs

Source: Table supplied by DHSS for quarter ending 13.3.73

However, our analysis of interviews indicates that very few appellants knew anything about the provision for Legal Advice which already existed at the time of our study.[15] 78% of respondents had never heard of it at all. Even those who claimed to have some knowledge were very confused as to what Legal Advice meant and who was eligible to receive it. When we explained how the scheme worked, the general response was favourable, though most appellants were quick to point out that advice from a lawyer could be wasted without his personal appearance to interpret the facts at the hearing. The real problem was identified as poor information services. Many appellants said that they would utilise any service which would assist them to win their case, but that they very often did not know where or who to turn to for the necessary information and assistance.

Conclusions

The attitudes which appellants adopt towards the tribunal experience are quite complex and cannot simply be equated with the outcome of the case, though this is an important factor in itself. Subjective criteria play an important part in influencing the appellant's views regarding the degree to which the system is felt to be just. These subjective criteria include the perceived seriousness of the need and the extent to which it is met, the extent to which tribunal members are willing to hear the material that appellants feel is relevant and the level of social competence which appellants feel they attain in providing this.

As far as representation is concerned, appellants do not always share the tribunal members' confidence that their rights are being protected without such assistance. Although their views about the role of representation may be contradictory, the mere presence of an advocate or a supportive figure is experienced as a means of closing the social and formalistic gap between appellants and the tribunal and affords them a considerable improvement in self-confidence. It has been suggested by appellants themselves that the onus should be on the system to offer access to and information about representation, rather than being on the appellants to find it. At SBATs in particular, the relative nature of "need" and the high degree of discretionary power available to the tribunal would seem to make representation essential at the individual level. However, there is currently a good deal of feeling that the system and the law itself are unjust in certain respects and that representation alone without other major policy and structural reforms cannot alter this situation.

At the moment, appellants are disadvantaged by insufficient provision of information and advisory services, and by the absence of co-ordination between tribunals and the related resource agencies which are concerned with appellants' wide-ranging needs.

NOTES

1   I would like to thank Ann Frost, who also worked on the Tribunals Research Project; she provided the data for the tables and made a number of general comments on this paper. A detailed report on the entire study is currently being prepared for publication.

2   A small number of landlords was included in the Rent Tribunal sample.

3   Cf. Ruth Lister, *Justice for the Claimant*, CPAG Poverty Research Series 4, 1974 pp. 6-7. and Ross Flockhart, chapter 8 above.

4   We were advised not to ask chairmen and members about their income for fear of causing offence. No-one thought appellants would be offended and, indeed, they did not seem to be.

5   DHSS Annual Report for 1973, Cmnd. 5706, H.M.S.O., 1974.

6   A particularly unpleasant example concerned the SBAT hearing where a West Indian woman, appealing over Family Income Supplement, was asked if the same father was responsible for both her children.

7   Melvin Herman has pointed out that some frustrated Supplementary Benefit appellants appeal against the low level of the basic scale rates, although SBATs have no power to alter these. See his *Administrative Justice and Supplementary Benefits*. Occasional Papers on Social Administration 47, 1972, p. 37.

8   Cf. Pauline Morris in Morris et al, *Social Needs and Legal Action*, 1973, p. 52.

9   According to our interview sample, only 73% of appellants at SBAT and
    NILT hearings were *offered* expenses although all were entitled to claim them.

10 Form LT 204 B, which is sent to all appellants with Supplementary Benefit
    appeal papers, says (para. 3) "You have a right to attend the hearing of your
    appeal" and (para 8) "THE Tribunal would like you to attend if you can do
    so". Nowhere, even in the small print, is it mentioned how much difference a
    personal appearance is likely to make to the outcome of the appeal. Form
    LT204 B has now (July 1975) been revised and in the opinion of DHSS the
    importance of personal appearance is sufficiently stressed. DHSS does not
    wish appellants to believe that attendance is synonymous with success. How-
    ever, our original opinion is still held for the reason stated.

11 Extreme cases of respondents who were stone deaf, had serious heart diseases,
    or were suffering a nervous breakdown were contacted during the course of
    the study. Such people were clearly unable to attend hearings and often had
    no one to send in their place. See Julian Fulbrook, *The Appellant and his
    Case*. CPAG. Poverty Research Series 5, 1975 for confirmation of the econ-
    omic, social and psychological reasons why some appellants find difficulty in
    attending hearings.

12 See Roger Gomm. "The Claimant as Mendicant". *Social Work Today*, 19
    Sept. 1974, for a description of attitudes adopted by claimants of social secu-
    rity in uneasy defence of their position.

13 The figures for representation of appellants interviewed are much higher than
    the rate of representation observed at hearings (19% SBATs, 18% NILTS and
    15% RTs). This weighting was intentional as we wished to compare repre-
    sented and unrepresented groups.

14 Lord Chancellor's Committee on Legal Aid and Advice, Report 1973-74, pp.
    47-55.

15 Under the Legal Advice and Assistance Act 1972, the £25 scheme permits a sol-
    icitor to advise an appellant and draw up papers for a tribunal hearing, but
    does not provide for representing the appellant at the tribunal.

XI WHO CAN DE-LABEL THE CLAIMANT? *
Hilary Rose

Recent years have seen important research and practical work carried out by lawyers, social workers and administrators in the field of welfare rights, a great number of whom have been associated with the Child Poverty Action Group (CPAG) and have had social security as their priority service[1]. The work has focused on the administrative process, in order to improve the fairness and functioning to the claimants' advantage. The rights approach has fostered a shift in the professionals' attitude towards the claimant, who is seen as more of a citizen with welfare rights, than a client with welfare needs. During the course of a larger project studying community action, we became very interested in what welfare rights strategies meant to social security claimants[2].

Working as researcher participants with claimant unions we became conscious that there were differences, which were more significant than mere style, between the approach of CPAG and the claimant unions (CU) to the prosecution of a rights strategy. In order to explore those possible differences systematically, we devised the strategy of making a comparative study of tribunals which we attended in a variety of roles, from solely observing to actively participating. It is this material, despite the not inconsiderable methodological problems it raises, which is presented and discussed here[3].

* This chapter was first published in *Social Work Today*, 20 September 1973, and is reprinted here with the permission of the editor and the author. The author wishes to express her thanks to members of the claimant unions; to Patrick Ainley and Caroline Griffiths who helped gather the material together; to Norman Dennis, Mary Mackintosh, Richard Mills, John Spencer and Peter Townsend for their advice and help as members of the research steering committee, and lastly to the Gulbenkian Foundation for its financial support.

Making an appeal

In practice making an appeal is the last step in a process of varying length in which the claimant seeks to reverse the decision of the local social security office. Increasing numbers of claimants are tending to appeal against such decisions; in 1965 only six per thousand appealed, by 1971 14 per thousand. However this is still only 1.5 per cent of all claims. Appellants have the right to representation, but as social security tribunals are not covered by Legal Aid they tend to be aided by either a CPAG representative, or, when CU members, by a fellow claimant[4]. The distinction which is made in this paper is between CPAG representatives who act as advocates and representatives drawn from the claimant movement itself.

The staging of the tribunal

The tribunal has to consider each appeal on its individual merit, unfettered by precedent and in theory unfettered by the DHSS policy (enshrined in the secret A Code and to some extent revealed in the Handbook) only bound by the Act itself and the statutory instruments. The hearings themselves are reasonably standardised up and down the country, not only in the manner of conducting the appeal but even the physical arrangement of the hearing. These are opened by the chairman briefly outlining the procedure, who then invites the presenting officer to put the view of the DHSS. Each member of the tribunal, together with the chairman, will have (1) the document giving the claimant's reason for appeal, (2) the local social security officer's reason for the decision and (3) a financial statement of the claimant's situation prepared by the social security office.

A typical tribunal

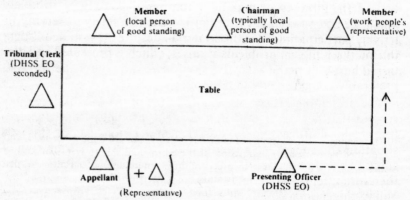

It is difficult to escape the impression even from the physical arrangement that it is the claimant appellant who is on trial, rather than the decision of the SBC[5]. The increasing professionalism of the presenting officer, the expertise of the chairman, who conducts most and often all of the questioning, tends to put the appellant — typically someone denied good education, not *au fait* with the legislation and statutory instruments — into an inarticulate and inexpert role which slides curiously into the defendant's role. Although with personal experience of social security the formal situation commonly renders the unaided claimant unable to translate experience into an effective critique of the officer's decisions. The observable tendency of presenting officers, even when placed on the same side of the conference table, to slide round to the end so that they almost parallel the position of the tribunal clerk, literally upstaging the client — reaffirms the presenting officer's identification with the tribunal and not as someone of equal status with the appellant. In this context the physical fact of having a representative almost regardless of what he or she contributes verbally is of significance for the feelings and confidence of the appellant, and therefore almost certainly for the outcome of the proceedings.

The unaided appellant

Where the claimant is unaided the tribunal, at least in terms of their sympathetic manner and questioning to get at the facts of the matter, appear to come into their own. The tribunal recreate the discussion they envisage would (or should) have taken place at the home visit or at the social security office. They look for evidence of hardship, question the state of the appellant's clothing and shoes and his family's clothing, discuss the rent level, the problem of gas, electricity and HP debts, the possibility of receiving other forms of welfare benefit, the possibility of the local authority helping with a housing problem, and so on. In this situation of the unaided appellant, the tribunal in certain situations decide to help, and question in order to find ways of doing so, essentially looking for some rationalisation which will make their decision compatible with the Act and preferably compatible with SB policy[6].

The presenting officer, sensing the drift of the questioning, may suggest that new facts are being brought into light and that therefore the local officer should look at their decision again in this new situation and suggest an adjournment. This seems to be the kind of solution satisfactory to all, the officials do not lose a decision and therefore face, the tribunal is able to demonstrate its humanity, by aiding the claimant without opposing SBC policy, and lastly, the claimant will, in all likelihood, be given an increased benefit when the case is reviewed at local level.

Yet this kind of negotiated settlement creates two distinct problems. The first concerns the problem of how the tribunal makes up its mind to regard certain claimants favourably enough to enter into this sympathetic questioning. Without doubt, although the criteria shifted subtly, and some tribunals and members within tribunals, are more liberal than others, it was easiest for the tribunals to be sympathetic to the appellant when he or she was compatible with some publicly shared stereotype of deserving poor. It was not that the tribunals were incapable of displaying their humanity to others than the classically deserving poor, but that they were much less likely to do so.[7]

The second problem created by this negotiated settlement is that appellants are left none the wiser as to their entitlements, and, as passive objects of compassion their sense of dependance and helplessness is increased rather than decreased.

The unreal world of social security

One special feature of the appeal from an unaided claimant is that the principle of taking each case on its merits serves to exclude the outer world, and to freeze the individual in some timeless situation. Where there is no external representative, the case remains at the level of the individual's difficulties and the day by day policy of the SBC. The discussion appears internal to the particular case at hand, and on those occasions when the chairman allowed the research worker to be present during the deliberations after the case, rarely were larger considerations of the overall situation in, for example, levels of unemployment, brought into the decision making situation. The discussion was instead focused on the financial circumstances, psychological make-up and cultural life-style of the appellant, and despite the terms of reference of the tribunal, it was difficult to escape the conclusion that it was these two latter which were being judged. Nor had the unaided claimant any power to shift the narrow frame of reference, often all he could do was just stubbornly reiterate "well I can't manage".

The appeal as protest

But if most appellants are unaided, even more fail to present themselves to the tribunal. In a day's hearing of perhaps a dozen cases, as few as two may actually turn up for the appeal. And, of those who do so, some are so confused and distressed that however much tact the chairman and tribunal members display in their questioning, it is almost impossible to establish the facts of the case. Those who do attend are, though not in identical ways, more deviant than those who fail. The tendency of a tribunal to look for a consensual solution, such as an adjournment provides, becomes much more apparent in the case of "heard *in absentia*" appeals. When the claimant is present the tribunal members feel they want to or should help in the light of what they have heard without opposing SBC. While some chairmen hear the presenting officer's case and then ask him to leave so that they can deliberate in private, others leave the presenting officer in and a transaction takes place more like a case conference than a tribunal hearing. On these occasions even the clerk may express a point of view: and at times we even wondered if we ought to take part as it felt almost stand-offish not to join in.

Appeals heard *in absentia* are rarely successful. Without the claimant being present to explain his difficulties in any detail means the presenting officer and the tribunal can only agree on the difficulties of helping this sort of claimant. There is, too, a measure of irritation felt by the tribunal members when no or few appellants materialise. Thus not only is the claimant handicapped by not being present in that his arguments are not heard, but also his absence seems to signify that his case and situation cannot be very serious. While some claimants do write in to explain why they cannot attend, as many are elderly, sick, disabled, or mothers with young children with no-one to leave them with, others are lodging the appeal as an expressive protest against the SBC's decision rather than treating it as an instrumental strategy to reverse it.

The aided appellant: bringing in the real world

While each of the two main forms of representation, CPAG advocate or fellow CU member, is conducted along rather different lines, both make one major difference to the event, in that they externalise it and make it public. Where in unaided and absentee hearings the discussion is internal, focusing on the claimant's situation, the Act, statutory instruments and SB policy, the representative brings in the outside world. This widening of the frame of reference in itself shifts the balance of power at the tribunal; the appellant is no longer alone physically, and his judges have become exposed to external judgment.

The representatives both from the poverty reform group and from the underclass movement stress the structural determinants of poverty; whether the antecedents are Beatrice Webb and the Minority Report, or Karl Marx and a union tradition, the common elements of this appellant's condition with others in a like situation are emphasised. While the style in which this point is driven home varies, the purpose is common. Where the middle class advocate may cite research evidence, the levels of unemployment or the range of local rents, the CU member will talk from direct experience about the length of the dole queue and the impossibility of finding alternative accommodation. The predominantly middle class character of the tribunals means that they can relate more easily to the middle class language with its impersonal courtesy of the CPAG advocates, than to what is seen as the demanding hectoring style of the unions. However, acceptability of linguistic style is not a necessary determinant of outcomes; courtesy can facilitate co-option, militancy can facilitate backlash attitudes.

Representative tribunal relations

Though both forms of representation make the appellant's case more public, the sense of concern and compassion felt by the middle class advocate linked to a structural analysis is unable to sustain the public nature of an argument. There is a tendency for a form of middle class co-option to emerge, whereby the educated and the expert enter into a compassionate complicity, where the chairman and the well-briefed middle class representative retreat into an expert's world, leaving the appellant no longer an actor in his own destiny but merely the object of the case at issue. This form of co-option is often deployed against the college educated members of the claimant unions. The strategy of mild flattery and concentration on the representative rather than on the appellant can be quite strongly felt[8]. Thus CUs, particularly where they have extensive experience of particular chairmen and are well aware of this co-option technique, seek to alert their members. "when old Rooker's most smarmy, that's when he's most dangerous and the case will go against you". Knowledge of this kind is shared between local unions; in London, unions probably have better information in this respect than most of the middle class advocates who are less locally based.

Representative and claimant relations

Not only do the unions have a continuous relationship with particular tribunals through appearing frequently before them, they also have a continuous relationship between represented and representative, roles may be reversed and both are equal members of the same organisation. Representing at an appeal is not a service carried out by an expert advocate but is part of an ongoing membership activity of CU members helping and defending one another. Thus although in actuality it happens that some CU members are better than others at representing at appeals, and among members there is sometimes a feeling that they would rather be represented by one of the "experts", there is at the same time an attempt to minimise this growth of alternative experts and to subordinate it to a practice of equality between members. Not only because of class differences between the advocate and the appellant, often skilfully exacerbated by chairmen, the advocate is essentially an alternative expert. The potential appellant applying to CPAG cannot demand representation as a right regardless of the nature of his appeal, as the CU member can and does[9]. For the CU the appellant is a person who should take an active part within the union in the planning, organising and conduct of his appeal. Deciding the conduct of an appeal is seen as a practical experience within a philosophy of self activity.

While the middle class advocate may in practice and courtesy consult the client about the strategy, the decision to support an appeal or not lies with the advocate. The advocate model is basically that of the expert who will use his skills to defend the defenceless, the training programme is mainly one of training professionals as Galahads rather than one of training people to defend themselves. (Although in practice members of a CU have used CPAG training programmes.)

How to win a rights argument

At the appeal both representatives will make a legalistic case on behalf of the appellant using one of three main lines of argumentation to change an adverse decision.

(1) The decision is not compatible with either the social security legislation or normal SB policy.

(2) The decision, while compatible with policy, is not compatible with the Act.

(3) The decision, while compatible with the main body of the legislation and with policy, ignores a situation of acute necessity and therefore entitles the tribunal and the Commission to use its discretionary powers to set these other considerations aside.

Quite a number of both advocates and the unions, while they cannot publicly reveal their knowledge at the tribunal, do in fact have the advantage of access to the secret A Codes. In view of the British pathological regard for secrecy and the severity of penalties under the Official Secrets Act, the number of activists from both main groups who are familiar with the Code is quite impressive. The Xerox machine, and the alienation of counter clerks from their work play a key role in this. Nonetheless the inconsistency of decision-making of tribunals is too profound for it to be wise to conclude that legal or even logical argument is necessarily crucial to success. Despite the efforts of lawyers to bring some sort of procedural orderliness into the SB tribunals, they remain the slum of the English tribunal system[10]. The difference between the advocates and the CU representatives then becomes less a matter of how good they are at law or logic (though these do have an important role) but the totality of the situation within the tribunal itself.

The structural analysis and the rights argumentation were intended to make the exposure of the intimate details of distress and personal relationships redundant. However in practice the social distance between the middle class advocate and the claimant appellant tends to mean that in order to gain the tribunal's sympathy for the appellant, and share the advocate's compassion, the exposure of distress is employed and the claimant is discussed as if he or she were not in the room. Claimants, in the mobilising of compassion, are thus confirmed as objects and do not become subjects in their own right.

Because there is an identity of life experience and interest between CU representative and appellant, compassion is redundant or of less importance. Poverty is an immediate and routine experience for most members of a claimant union, the humiliation and stigmatisation of the poverty situation are taken for granted — thus in an appeal when the injustice of a decision is being attacked, there is a basic comprehension of what the appellant is talking about apparently inarticulately, which releases anger rather than compassion. Put very simply the statement "I can't manage" is meaningful only to those who have some understanding of what it means not to have enough money to manage on. To anyone who has shared the experience of poverty the statement is pregnant with meaning, for most middle class people the statement appears lame and flat, with little resonance.

The role of anger

Anger is an integral part of the CU movement. It is used in a variety of ways within tribunals, the offices, at demonstrations, in cartoons and in leaflets. Anger springs from a sense of outrage and injustice and must underly any social movement; compassion may propel a social reformer but is insufficient to drive a popular movement forward[11].

Where one claimant alone is cowed by the formality of the proceedings, two or three interact and make some sort of collective appraisal as to the nature of the transactions. For example, an appeal of an unsupported mother who had been cut off because of a neighbour's hint to the SB official, was attended both by a CU representative and, as a learner, another mother. Normally shy and inarticulate she suddenly rounded on the tribunal demanding that they recognise the impossibility of this woman's situation literally cut off without a penny. Out of her own experience of scrimping and scraping in bringing up children decently, she set about this tribunal until they had to recognise that there was a problem. Occasions like this where the hitherto silent speak become a crucial part of the mythology of CUs, integrating experience and demonstrating for others how the silent and the weak can learn to defend themselves.

In another appeal where the final issue was about two vests and two pairs of knickers for a child — many other issues had been fought and won for this particular family, from getting electricity put on to forcing the local authority to doing something about their rat-infested property — the humiliation of having to argue about a pathetically small sum of money (approximately £1.60) was transferred from the claimant to the tribunal members and the presenting officer. The anger, again of the women CU members, that the official could be so mean to a child, transferred the embarrassment of discussing the precise and actual condition of a child's knickers and thus secured a significant psychological, and in due course small material, victory. .

Another form of CU appeal activity mixes anger with a sense of mockery, so that the sedate proceedings of a tribunal become a carnival. For example, where bedding and new clothing claims have been refused by the local office, as part of the appeal, evidence is brought forward. While many resourceful advocates have brought photographs, the CU style is to bring a slice of real life into the artificiality of the proceedings. The bumpy spring-broken mattresses, the worn out sheets, the children and their too small vests are brought to the appeal as evidence to challenge the social security decisions. The individuated humiliation of the home visit is turned into an offensive weapon to expose and ridicule the meanness of the social security system.

The representative becomes compere and produces exhibit after exhibit while the witnesses—whose role is audience as well as evidence givers—switch mood from laughter, to anger, to pain as the charade is played out. The moods of the tribunal members change too, shifting from amusement at the presenting officer's discomfort, to ill-concealed and sometimes open anger at the mockery. As when the silent speak, these sorts of appeals enter into the mythology as occasions when 'we showed them'! The difficulties overcome, of getting a free van to take the mattresses, the active part each played becomes a source of shared warmth and inspiration.

Material aid and the de-labelling process

Without representation the presenting officer puts forward the policy of the social security office, and the claimant his personal situation. Any conflict emerging between the presenting officer and the claimant is thus an extension of the relationship between the claimant recipient and the official donor, a relationship which is by its nature individuating, isolating and degrading. The "gift relationship" which exists in supplementary benefit is one of an exchange of public cash for personal humiliation, and where there is no representation, the transaction and the relationship are merely re-expressed at the tribunal before a larger audience. The very intimacy of the tribunal's questions, as its members seek to establish the facts, serves to degrade the claimant. Most claimants fear and detest the scrutiny of the social security officials at a home visit when their personal wardrobe is inspected and underwear examined, but at least no one other than themselves and the official witness the humiliation. Thus even more loathed are the public occasions of exposure; the local social security office with its non-private cubicles and the tribunal. For the claimant these semi-public rituals of degradation are something to be avoided not sought after. Even claimant union activists dislike going down to the social security office as their collectivity can only rarely overcome the intense individuation of the social security office procedure. Attending a tribunal unsupported by a representative or even a friend is thus for most claimants a deviant act.

The very arbitrariness of a highly discretionary system compels this excessive intimacy[12]. Because neither the tribunal nor the appellant have access to precise rules which govern the situation, both because of the logic of the situation must enter into a probing questioning into the details of material hardship, and, for some, their personal and sexual relationships. To be successful the appellant must adopt a suppliant role, like a mediaeval leper exhibiting his sores so that the tribunal is able to feel a sufficiently necessitous case exists and therefore use its substantial discretionary powers.

When the appellant is represented the rules of the game are significantly altered, in that it is played out as a public rather than a private problem, and the powerlessness of the claimant is modified. Yet crucial differences remain between the mode of operation of the middle class advocate and the union representative. Both must win appeals in order to serve the interests of the appellant. But while both need victory to legitimise themselves they need the victories for different publics. As a result the psychological style of the victory is of much greater importance to the claimant union than to the middle class advocate. The union has to use the appeal to raise an active consciousness on the part of claimants so that claimants learn to fight, securing small but useful victories while revealing the structural and impersonal nature of poverty. They turn the stigmatisation of poverty from the individual on to the rich society which condones it, and in the struggle as a group begin the slow process of de-labelling themselves. While CPAG concentrates almost exclusively on the material conditions of people's lives, the unions, because members share these conditions, are able to link material questions to self activity[13].

They neither fall into the trap of changing attitudes only, which much contemporary social and community work falls into and which has the possibly unintended effect of cooling off either individuals or whole communities to accepting unacceptable material conditions, nor do the unions embrace the narrow materialism of CPAG's approach[14]. Partly in rejection of the adjustment effect of psychotherapeutically oriented casework, the middle class advocates have tended to emphasise success in terms of cash benefits. Partly because of their own secure financial status they cannot afford to gamble as the union sharing those conditions can, on winning both cash, and affirming the appellant's subjectivity. Even the college educated activists in the unions, because they have embraced the poverty of the people they seek to mobilise, acquire a legitimacy and a strength which enables them to enter the politics of poverty, alongside the claimant, which the professional (which must include, no matter how "committed", the research worker) is in certain crucial ways excluded from.

NOTES

1. Much of the welfare rights activity in the UK can be seen to be descended from the US scene, both at the government sponsored level and also through the activities of the National Welfare Rights Organisation (NWRO). The birth of CPAG in 1965 is a key date, and its journal *Poverty* remains a central forum of discussion. See also: K. Bell, "Administrative Tribunals since Franks" *Social and Economic Administration*. Vol 4, No 4, 1970; R.J. Coleman, *Supplementary Benefits and the Administrative Review of Administrative Action* CPAG Poverty Pamphlet. No 7, 1971; M. Herman, *Administrative Justice and Supplementary Benefits*. 1972; T. Lynes, *Supplementary Benefits*. 1974.
2. The first of these studies is "Up Against the Welfare State," *Socialist Register* ed. R. Miliband and J. Saville, 1973.
3. The methodological discussion has been cut from this paper for reasons of space.
4. In practice the occasional trade-union organiser or non-CPAG social worker represented appellants. In the paper these have been treated as union representatives and advocates respectively.

5. For a brilliant account of the social significance of seating arrangements see, Paul Goodman, "Seating Arrangements, an elementary Essay in Functional Planning", *RIBA Journal.* Vol 80, No 2, 1973.

6. Herman (op cit) also notes this consensus seeking nature of tribunals, see p.51.

7. In respect of very elderly frail claimants even the CUs share something of the stereotype; on behalf of this type of claimant militant members will adopt a conciliatory approach to the local SS office, by and large successfully.

8. One elementary technique is for the chairman to look almost exclusively at the representative, ignoring his fellow tribunes and even the appellant.

9. Members are actively encouraged to appeal as the logical extension of getting their rights. On joining the member fills in a check list of needed goods and makes a request for a special needs grant immediately. In the likely circumstance of refusal this is then followed by an appeal (a technique very similar to that pioneered by NWRO in the USA).

10. CPAG has to good effect contrasted the procedures of different administrative tribunals dealing with precisely the same case. CPAG Welfare Law Reports, *Cohabitation. Supplementary Benefits and National Insurance Appeal Tribunals* (undated).

11. Turner observes that a social movement is characterised by the way that it sees the problem, as one of misfortune requiring compassion, or of injustice requiring social action. R. Turner "The Theme of Contemporary Social Movements", *British Journal of Sociology* Vol 20, No 4, 1969.

12. A point eloquently made by Jacobus Ten Broek in an American context in *The Law of the Poor*, 1966.

13. G.D.H. Cole, the social historian, even during the harsh interwar years, always fought this narrow materialistic conception of poverty, understanding that the issue was also involved with the powerlessness of the poor and their lack of freedom to make decisions concerning their own lives. He wrote, "the problem is not one of Poverty but of Slavery", quoted in C.Pateman, *Participation and Democratic Theory*. 1971.

14. While Wootton's and Sinfield's critiques of psychotherapeutically oriented casework are widely known, there has been virtually no critique of the adjustment effect of community work, such for example as reported by R. Ditton and E. Morrison in *A Community Project in Notting Dale*, 1972.

XII SUPPLEMENTARY BENEFITS AND THE PARLIAMENTARY COMMISSIONER
Martin Partington

Criticism of the Supplementary Benefits scheme in general and of Supplementary Benefits Appeal Tribunals (SBATs) in particular stems from concern about a much broader issue, namely how best to banish poverty from our society. Answers to this question, however, are far from unanimous, and criticism of SBATs may thus arise for a number of extremely varied reasons. At least four separate reasons may be identified, though they may be mingled together in practice.

(1) Some critics want to bring into question the entire credibility and value of the SB scheme, including SBATs. They have a deep rooted dissatisfaction with the whole system as a method of solving the problems of poverty and deprivation. They seek much more radical solutions to the problems of poverty.

(2) Others criticise SBATs for not being independent enough of the Commission. They are essentially complaining both that the SBATs have not used their own broad-based discretionary powers to give more money to particular claimants to cover exceptional needs;[1] and that SBATs do not, or cannot, encourage SB officials to be more generous. Often criticism of this type is a generalised complaint springing from particular cases with which the critic has been involved, as a claimant or as a welfare rights worker.

(3) A variation and extension of (2) is to urge that SBATs should be keeping under review the whole range of activities of SB officials to see that they are carrying out their duties properly. This function is certainly not performed by SBATs at present. Partly this is a reflection of the present relationship between SBATs and SB officials, which many argue is not independent enough to allow SBATs to criticise departmental action where this seems to be necessary. More substantially, the unavailability of the "A-code" makes this task impossible anyway. Nevertheless,

it may be suggested that this is an activity in which SBATs could usefully be engaged, and certainly underlies some current criticism of SBATs.[2]

(4) Yet another type of complaint of SBATs is broadly legalistic. It is based on general features of SBAT work such as the informality of the proceedings, the lack of legal aid, the lack of professional representation, no system of precedent, the absence of a higher appeal level and so on. Those who make these points, particularly lawyers, reared on a diet of the Franks Report,[3] see in SBATs severe gaps between the desirable norms suggested by that Committee and the reality of the functioning of SBATs and seek to bring SBATs up to the Franks standards.

Doubtless other brand reasons for criticising SBATs could also be identified. It is important, however, that this be attempted for only if we are clear about why we want reform, can we be clear about the actual reforms we seek to achieve.

Having spelled out four possible grounds for reform this chapter will ignore head (1). However compelling may be the arguments of those who seek a truly radical solution to the problem of poverty, I suspect that SB is nevertheless with us for some time. Heads (2) and (4) are general topics, discussed in other chapters. The remaining issue, and one largely ignored in the other chapters, is that to which this chapter is directed, namely under head (3), the methods by which general standards of administration of SB are to be controlled and, where necessary, improved.

Possibly this question might have been discussed solely as a potential function with which reformed SBATs could deal. Thus, if the personnel of SBATs were more professional[4] so that they became more independent of SB officials, if the "A-code" were to be published, if claimants' representatives became more involved in SB procedures and not just in arguing about particular decisions, SBATs might make an impact on the standards of administration of SB. But it is submitted that SBATs are not the most suitable organs for dealing with general complaints about administrative practices. Indeed, it seems more sensible to examine the work of another agency which already exists, but which, at least in the social security area, has been virtually ignored during the first eight years of its existence: the Parliamentary Commissioner for Administration (PCA).[5] I propose therefore to review what the PCA has actually been doing in the SB area and to raise some questions about what changes are needed. By so doing, the development of suitable means for improving the administration of SB may be encouraged.

Although the PCA has been operating since April 1967, this chapter is largely based on his work since 1 January 1972. The main reason for this limitation is that, from that date, the present PCA (Sir Alan Marre) decided to publish anonymised versions of all his decisions in quarterly reports. This replaced a partial selection of cases in Annual Reports which had been published by his predecessor, Sir Edmund Compton.

This chapter examines cases investigated between that date and 31 July 1975.[6] The total number of cases examined is only 24.[7] Compared with the total number of people in receipt of Supplementary Benefits and with the number of appeals to SBATs[8] this figure is extremely small. Thus, an underlying question is whether the PCA ought to be attracting more business, and if so how he might do that.

PCA's jurisdiction

The jurisdiction of the PCA is to be found in the Parliamentary Commissioner Act 1967, section 5(1):

"[The] Commissioner may investigate any action taken by or on behalf of a government department ... in the exercise of administrative functions of that department ... in any case where —

(a) a written complaint is duly made to a member of the House of Commons by a member of the public who claims to have sustained injustice in consequence of maladministration in connection with the action so taken ...."

Section 5(2) provides that the PCA shall not investigate any action in respect of which the person aggrieved has or had a right of appeal before a tribunal, subject to the proviso that

"the Commissioner may conduct an investigation... if satisfied that in the particular circumstances it is not reasonable to expect the [person aggrieved] to resort ... [to such a right]."

Section 12(1) defines "action" as including failure to act. But "maladministration"[9] and "administrative functions" are not defined.

Section 12(3) declares that

"nothing in this Act authorises or requires the Commissioner to question the merits of a decision taken without maladministration by a government department in the exercise of a discretion vested in that department ...."

It is well known that this jurisdiction is defined in a more restricted way than that found in similar institutions in other countries.[10] The limitations contained in sections 5(2) and 12(3) are particularly relevant to the SB scheme, in view of the existence of the SBATs and of the large element of discretion in the scheme. The result of these provisions is that although the PCA cannot usually question any amount awarded by SB officials to a claimant or any conditions attached to an award, which are appealable to an SBAT,[11] he will look at any other aspects of the administration of a claim for SB, including the preparation of an appeal.

Analysis of complaints

The cases investigated by the PCA reveal a wide range of problems connected with SB administration. The following analysis summarises the complaints as notified to the PCA; not all these complaints were substantiated after investigation. Full references to the cases examined are set down in the table which follows this chapter: for ease of reference in the text, each case has been assigned a code-letter which is shown in the table (thus e.g. case B denotes Case no. C528/5, reported at page 135 of House of Commons Paper 116, 1971-72).

(1) *Delay* was a common complaint which arose either in relation to the general administration of a claim (cases B, J, P, W, X and Y) or more particularly in informing the claimant about whether or not he would be prosecuted for fraud (case U). There were also cases involving delay in the setting up of an appeal (cases C, E and M).

(2) *Incorrect information or advice* was an issue in a number of cases. In case F incorrect information was given concerning the effect of a court's maintenance order. In a number of cases incorrect information about rights of appeal was involved (cases J, K, N and V). In case R, an incorrect interpretation of a paragraph in the SB handbook was given to a claimant by a Deputy Manager. A misleading advertisement relating to free optical treatment was involved in case D.

(3) *Interaction of SB with other benefits.* The complex interaction of SB with other state benefits has on occasion been the source of difficulties, misunderstandings and maladministration (which may lead in turn to allegations of rudeness and victimisation, section (4) below). Thus, in case A, medical certificates were required by two different offices which led to allegations of difficulty in obtaining SB. A more complex issue arose when a claimant argued that the requirement to register for work as a pre-condition of his receiving SB[12] should be removed since he was regarded at the Department of Employment as a person "not unemployed" and therefore was not being credited with National Insurance contributions as an unemployed worker (case S). The interaction of SB with local authority rent allowance schemes was another cause of difficulty (case X).

Confusion about the relationship between SB and certain maternity benefits seems to have been involved in case Q, in which it was finally held that a claimant who had been refused Maternity Grant had never in fact claimed SB to cover the exceptional expenses arising from the birth of a child, though she argued that she thought she had made such a claim.

(4) *Rudeness and victimisation.* General complaints about attitudes of officials have featured in a number of the PCA's investigations. In some cases (E, H and J) allegations of rudeness on the part of SB officials were made. Other complaints have alleged victimisation on the part of SB officials (cases A, H, U and Y). These may arise particularly where unannounced visits by officials are made on claimants (as in case H).

(5) *Other administrative mistakes.* In case H, a form prepared for a special welfare officer stating that a claimant was "unable to manage" and "had a severely disturbed mind" was shown by mistake to the claimant. In case L, forms were sent to a trade union official, despite a specific request by the claimant that this should not be done. In case T, the SB office failed to notify a landlord that a tenant in receipt of SB had changed his address, with the result that the property was vandalized. In two cases (G and M), the administration of the wage-stop was called into question. Incorrect information relevant to an appeal was given to an SBAT (case R).

While the range of problems is very much in line with what those who have been involved in SB cases might have expected to find, there are plenty of areas of SB administration which are not covered in these cases, which suggests that the potential of the PCA is far from fully realised. For example, there are no cases on the activities of DHSS special investigators,[13] nor are there any cases on the practice of the SBC of "superseding" decisions when appeals are lodged.[14] Again there are no cases on the administration of the "four-week rule".[15] All these are areas of possible maladministration which may come before the PCA.

Observations on the investigations of the PCA

(A) Findings of maladministration and other errors

In general, the proportion of cases in which the PCA finds that there has actually been maladministration is very low. Thus, in 1973 he found maladministration in only 88 (or 37%) of the 239 cases in which he was able to take jurisdiction and therefore investigate fully.[16] In that year, maladministration was found in 15 cases involving the DHSS.

Of the Supplementary Benefits cases examined, in only three

does the reader get the impression that the PCA was severely critical of the work of SB officials.[17] However, including the three cases just mentioned, in 23 out of the 24 cases studied (i.e. 92%) he discovered that something had gone wrong with the way the complainant's case had been handled. (For the purposes of his annual report, not all of these were classified as "maladministration".) This finding is both surprising and disturbing and emphasizes how easy it is for detailed errors and mistakes to occur. It suggests that the potential role of the PCA as a means of encouraging officials to operate to higher standards of accuracy and efficiency has not yet been fully developed.

(B)   *"Reasonable" and "unreasonable" complainants*

A second notable feature is the number of complainants who bear a very strong grudge against the SBC or the DHSS. It has already been mentioned that allegations of rudeness and victimization appear fairly frequently. A number of extracts from the PCA's reports illustrate this point.

(1)   A war pensioner complained about the DHSS on a number of counts, including administration of SB (case A). The PCA reported:

> "I feel bound to add that the constant flow of letters from the complainant does not facilitate prompt consideration of his claims. These long, repetitive and often abusive letters are in my view an inevitable cause of some delay... I appreciate that the complainant has problems and anxieties to contend with but I find his abuse of the DHSS unjustified ... "

(2)   A widower complained that a visiting officer of the SBC was rude to him when investigating an application for a grant for buying shoes (case E):

> "The complainant's account of what happened is that the [visiting] officer 'made no bones about telling me that ... the manager and assistant manager at [the local office] as well as himself ... regarded me as sponging on people who [pay income tax]' ... "

On the other hand, in the same case:

> "The officer's recollection was that retirement pension and taxes came into the conversation after the complainant had asserted that he knew his rights and was entitled to the grant...
> The officer corrected this impression: the complainant had a right to make a claim and to have it properly considered but he was entitled to receive a grant only if the Commission were satisfied that a need existed. The officer said that it was in this context that he spoke of the claimant's receiving his retirement

pension as of right while supplementary benefit was financed from taxes. He acknowledged that he spoke firmly to the complainant but denied that he spoke rudely or lost his temper . . . "

The PCA found these two accounts difficult to reconcile but noted:

"The departmental records over many years support the statement that other officers have encountered difficulty in interviewing the complainant. Many of them have reported that they have found him unreasonable and objectionable . . . I have also seen a number of the complainant's letters couched in terms which suggest to me that he is given to personal abuse of officials when he is displeased . . . In these circumstances, I do not feel able to accept the complainant's account in preference to the officer's report . . . "

(3) Another complainant alleged victimization by the SBC after investigations into overpayment of SB (case U). He had been interviewed under caution on 5 October 1971, about alleged overpayments of SB. He was advised that he might be prosecuted. It was not until 4 January 1972 that he was interviewed again, and given a strong warning that he should in future declare all his sources of income. After this, the Department considered the matter closed. The complainant and his solicitors, however, were very dissatisfied that this decision had taken so long to be reached. The SBC conceded there had been unwarranted delays. However, by this time the complainant had formed the impression that he was being victimized.

As the complainant was in arrears with his rent, arrangements were made that he would be paid the rent element of his SB only on proof that he had paid the previous week's rent. On 10 February 1972 he went to collect his rent element, but the SB officials were not satisfied that he had paid the rent. According to SB officials, he had his alsatian dog with him.

"One [official] said . . . she had looked up to find an alsatian dog with its front paws against her desk ledge some three feet from the floor, the dog began to bark and, even although she was behind glass, she was somewhat unnerved."

Another report of the incident stated that the complainant's dog had caused trouble and had been urged by the complainant to attack an official. The complainant, however, told the PCA's officers that:

"the dog was so vicious that he would not have dreamed of doing such a thing, but [sic] the dog had not barked or behaved in a hostile fashion in the office."

In the end the complainant left without his rent. He returned next day with more convincing proof that he had paid it, so was given his money. However, he regarded the initial withholding of rent as evidence of victimization. Notwithstanding this incident, the PCA found no evidence of victimization.[18]

There are a number of points to be made about these and other cases (H, J, L, Y and Z) where victimization has been alleged. In none of the cases was the allegation of victimization upheld. The PCA sees his function not only as the defender of the citizen, but, where he thinks the citizen is acting unfairly, as the defender of the Department. Hence he is quite prepared to criticise complainants for abusive letters and other actions, when he regards the complainant as having behaved unreasonably.

But even though victimization has never been proven, these cases were complex and extended over considerable periods of time. Furthermore, careful reading of the cases suggests that complainants, though admittedly sometimes difficult, are not as unreasonable as might appear from a superficial glance at the PCA's reports. For in all but one of these cases (case Z), some departmental errors were discovered; often they were major ones. In addition to the case involving the delay in informing the claimant he would not be prosecuted (case U), the Department of Employment in case L denied for six years that it had sent documents to a trade union official against the wishes of the claimant, before the PCA's investigation unearthed the truth. In case M, the wage-stop was applied for 13 months on the basis of an initially faulty calculation of a claimant's previous earnings. In such cases it is perhaps not surprising that claimants become extremely distrustful of officials. One may consider whether words of comfort or criticism offered by the PCA really satisfy complainants in such a position. It might be useful if the House of Commons' Select Committee on the PCA were to follow up such cases to see whether they reveal more substantial issues, e.g. about the training and attitudes of SB officers, than the PCA has hitherto suggested in his reports.

Again, it may be that some of the more emotional complaints are the result of the requirement that they must be in writing.[19] It is likely to be very difficult for many complainants to express themselves well in writing about what has gone wrong; they may only be able to describe this as a "feeling" of oppression and victimization because of delays, or other difficulties which are not fully understood.

These cries for help, which may look to the sophisticated eye as rather amusing or trivial, may mask a serious problem about the way cases have to be presented to the PCA. It is submitted that, as part of the debate on the desirability of training advocates before

SBATs, the use of advocates in drafting submissions to the PCA in cases of apparent maladministration should also be considered. This could help the PCA to become a more effective means of control.

One problem here is that the PCA Act 1967, section 6(2) reads:

> "Where the person by whom a complaint might have been made under . . . this Act has died or is for any reason unable to act for himself, the complaint may be made by his personal representative, or by a member of his family or other individual suitable to represent him; but except as aforesaid a complaint shall not be entertained under this Act *unless made by the person aggrieved himself.*" (my emphasis)

Another surprise, therefore, was that in two cases (B and R) representation was permitted; in neither case was there any evidence that the person aggrieved was unable to act. The Office of the PCA has confirmed that, "as a matter of practice", complaints by organisations or individuals (e.g. solicitors) on the authority of the person aggrieved are readily accepted, even though the apparently restrictive conditions set down in section 6(2) (i.e. death or inability to act) have not been fulfilled. This is desirable as a matter of policy. But surely the law should be changed to accommodate this policy, so that we all may know that welfare rights workers and others can take up cases on behalf of "persons aggrieved".

(C) *Effectiveness of PCA in altering departmental practices*

Although many of the cases investigated reveal only minor errors, a number raised wider issues and his reports have noted that administrative practices or other procedures relating to SB are to be altered. The question here is how effectively these alterations in procedure are carried out.

In case N, the complainant, a disabled war pensioner, had SB awarded to him in 1969; but it was not until 1971 that it was discovered he was in receipt of a war disablement pension. Thus he had been overpaid SB by £185.60. Now under the 1966 Act, section 26(1), the SBC have power to recover payments made to any person who "whether fraudulently or otherwise" has misrepresented or failed to disclose any material fact. By section 26(2) questions relating to what are recoverable amounts are to be referred to an SBAT and its decisions are conclusive.

According to the PCA, the former position under the National Assistance Act 1948 was that there could be a reference to a local tribunal solely on the question of the amount which could be recovered. He went on:

> "The additional right of reference on the question of whether

there had been misrepresentation or failure to disclose a material fact ... was introduced by the [1966] Act ... [Due] to an oversight, this change in the law was not reflected in the Department's instructions to their local offices, who continued to follow the procedure which had been applied under the National Assistance Act. It was because of this that people in the complainant's position were told of their right only of reference on the question of the amount which could be recovered."

Following the PCA's investigation, local offices were given new instructions and the relevant forms were reprinted. In the case, the tribunal found that the payment of war pension was discovered as a result of some enquiries made in June 1971 and that if these enquiries had been made earlier (e.g. in September 1969 when SB was first claimed) no overpayment would have resulted. The tribunal considered that remission of some or all of the amount was proper. The Department pointed out that the tribunal had found that the complainant had failed to disclose this income and considered it unreasonable that they should bear the whole onus of discerning where income may not have been disclosed by a claimant. But nevertheless the Department waived £155.35 of the overpayment (refusing to refund to the complainant £30.25 already repaid to the SBC).[21]

This case has been discussed fully because of its potential value as a precedent for welfare rights workers.[22] It emphasises that if the DHSS are in some respect at fault, this can be relevant for an SBAT when deciding whether any overpayments can be waived or not.[23]

More important, for the present discussion, are the changes in office procedures. One might have hoped that the technical problem revealed by the PCA would have been cured. However in a later case it was discovered that another SB office was still using the same old form (case V). It is clearly important that all offices should be made aware of the decisions of the PCA. Again, the Select Committee may be able to help here.

Finally, it is slightly disturbing that the PCA did not refer in his later report (on case V) to the earlier report (on case N). It might have been expected that in criticising the Department he would have wished to draw their attention to the fact that this issue had already been discussed once.

Another example of a broader administrative issue criticised by the PCA was where, in a small integrated office (dealing with SB and National Insurance claims under a single manager) liaison broke down. The PCA noted that new instructions to encourage liaison were drawn up as a result of this case (case B). This is one of the few cases which have subsequently been discussed by the Select

Committee.[24] There Dame Mildred Riddelsdell on behalf of the DHSS remarked:

"We have to strike a balance between piling too much into the circulars sent to the clerks and not telling them enough, but as a result of this case a reminder was sent to our local offices about exchanging information between the SB and insurance sides ..."

As the result of another case, the Department arranged to review its arrangements for advertising free optical treatment (case D). As things stood at the time, a patient might become committed to expenditure (because he had received the optical treatment) before knowing whether he would get SB to cover the cost. Whether any changes in the advertisements have in fact resulted from this case is not known.

It is clear, therefore, that the PCA can reveal general administrative problems which ought to be publicized throughout the Department. The extent to which this is successfully done is at present largely a matter of speculation. It may be necessary for further steps to be taken to make the PCA's decisions known in the relevant offices.

(D) *The PCA's understanding of supplementary benefits*

The final question to be examined is how far the PCA really understands issues raised by the system of SB. In so far as he has wide responsibilities for controlling maladministration in the Civil Service as a whole, he cannot become involved in every detailed issue. Further, he must be very dependent on the information from each Department as to what ought to happen in individual cases. One may guess that his workload (and that of his staff) is not yet sufficiently heavy for individual investigators constantly to be assigned to the same area of work; it is not known whether he would regard this as a desirable work pattern anyway. However, a welfare rights expert, looking at some of his reports, might feel that he has not in some cases really understood the significance of the case.

Take, for example, the case of the smallholder who suffered a nine month delay while his SB was assessed (case B). A difficulty here was that the claimant was self-employed; therefore assessing his income was a more than usually difficult task. One of the significant findings by the PCA, which he did not criticise, was that:

"It appears ... that the local office took the view that, although the claimant might not be actually working full-time on his land, he was nevertheless running his smallholding work in business on his own account. The local office felt that it would be establishing a precedent to accept that, because a smallholder did not undertake manual work on the land, or, during bad weather, was prevented from working on the land, he should be subsidised by SB . . . "

Commenting on this, the PCA notes that the SBC were "wary of establishing a precedent", without apparently being aware that one of the alleged virtues of SB is the flexibility that only a precedent-free, individualised system of justice can provide and that the SBC's "wariness" was therefore a failure to respond to one of the main (alleged) advantages of the SB scheme.[25]

In a wage-stop case (case G), a former salesman became unemployed in September 1969. In July 1970 a sub-committee of one of the now defunct Social Security Local Advisory Committees interviewed him and thought that a wage-stop should be applied. The DHSS implemented this decision, but it was removed on appeal to an SBAT in September 1970. However in November 1970, after a general increase in SB rates, he was paid no more and was subjected to a wage-stop of 90p. He was not told of this decision. A further increase in the level of SB in September 1971 was not passed on to the complainant, so his wage-stop was then £2.25 a week. In October 1971, he queried this. On 21 October 1971 he was informed that the Department of Employment had re-classified his occupation as a clerk. This was the first he had heard of this decision.

It is clear from these and other facts that administrative errors had occurred, which were duly criticised by the PCA. But there is no reference in his decision to the procedures that ought to be adopted in wage-stop cases and are set out in the SB Handbook: an important feature of these procedures is that the wage-stop should not be applied without prior discussion with the claimant of his earnings.

In another case involving the wage-stop, the PCA again does not refer to the SB Handbook, though it would seem that the SBC decided the complainant's "normal earnings" without any discussion with him (case M).

If therefore the PCA does not always report on SB cases in ways a welfare rights expert might hope, nevertheless a number of his reports do contain useful general statements on SB policy, e.g.

"The Department tell me that the instructions to their local offices provide that a notice informing a claimant of right of appeal shall be sent with *all* payments." (Case J) (My emphasis)

In case M, a number of appeals by a claimant were to be heard by an SBAT on 13 March 1972. On that date he put in another appeal which the DHSS decided to process so that this appeal could be heard with the rest. The PCA notes that the DHSS:

> "agree it was wrong to process and present this appeal to the tribunal on the day it was received, contrary to normal procedure, since it gave the complainant no opportunity to study the documents ... "[27]

One feature of the PCA's investigatory powers is that, by virtue of the PCA Act 1967, section 11(3), he has access to the "A" and "AX" codes. If welfare rights workers were to become involved in taking issues to the PCA, this might well be a method of finding out some of the rulings and procedures which are at present secret.

Conclusion

This chapter has examined whether the PCA is capable of imposing an element of quality control on the ways in which the SB scheme works. He has some jurisdictional advantages which give him much greater potential than SBATs in this regard.[28]

(a) He (and his officers) can gain access to DHSS offices and to all case papers.
(b) He can also study the secret "A" and "AX" codes.
(c) He has power to take up complaints not only about technical issues of administration, but can also ask whether a discretionary rule, made by the SBC, is so unfair or bad as to amount to maladministration.[29]

Given these factors, there is room for guarded optimism that he could develop into a valuable adjunct to the protection of the individual against the SBC and its officialdom.

However, despite the fact that in the cases which have come before him he has been able to discover that little things are going wrong all the time, and that occasionally major blunders occur, the PCA's caseload is at present extremely small. Unless the number of SB cases increases dramatically, he and his staff will not be able to get a broad view of this area of administration. They will be unlikely to see the welfare implications of the cases that do come before them; nor will they understand the frustrations caused to claimants by SB administration which lead them to complain of victimization and rudeness. Again, the effect of the PCA on the Department as a whole will remain extremely limited.

Even if the PCA and his staff develop their own knowledge of problems in this area, their effectiveness will be muted if there is no system of following up the results of conclusions he has reached. In this regard, the Select Committee of the House of Commons needs to examine in more detail the impact which the PCA is making at local office level.

NOTES

1. See chapters 5 and 6 above

2. Professor John Griffith, who kindly commented on a draft of this paper, regards it as "bizarre" that anyone should ever have thought that SBATs could have an effective role in controlling SB officials. However personal experience suggests that some SBATs do, from time to time, take SB officials to task for their handling of particular cases and that this *could* become a recognised function of SBATs.

3. See chapter 3 above.

4. Cf. W.E. Cavenagh and G.N. Hawker, "Laymen on Administrative Tribunals", *Public Administration*, 52, 1974, p.211.

5. The already extensive literature on the British PCA includes H. Street, *Justice in the Welfare State*, 2nd edn., 1975; K.C. Wheare, *Maladministration and its Remedies*, 1973; F. Stacey, *The British Ombudsman*, 1971; G. Marshall, "Maladministration", [1973] *Public Law* 32; and, most recently, R. Gregory and P. Hutchesson, *The Parliamentary Ombudsman*, 1975.

6. It will be seen from the table of case-references that one or two cases from 1971 are included.

7. Three SB cases are dealt with in the selection of decisions published in H.C. 49 (1974-75) but these and any subsequent decisions are not covered by the present survey.

8. *Social Security Statistics 1973* reveal that in the year ending Nov. 1973, there were 3,897,000 successful claims, 1,852,000 of which resulted in regular weekly payments (Table 34.05); there were 24,485 appeals (Table 34.20).

9. See, though, article by Marshall cited in note 5 above.

10. See e.g., D.C. Rowat (ed.) *The Ombudsman*, 1968, esp. part 1.

11. 1966 Act, s.18.

12. 1966 Act, s.11; Handbook, 1974, para. 7.

13. Cf. Ruth Lister, *As Man and Wife?*, CPAG Poverty Research Series No. 2, esp. ch.3.

14. R.J. Coleman, *Supplementary Benefits and the Administrative Review of Administrative Action*, CPAG Poverty Pamphlet No.7, 1971.

15. See now though, Case C331/T reported in H.C. 49/1974-75.

16. See H.C. 106/1973-74, Annual Report for 1973, pp. 4-5. He found maladministration in the same proportion of cases in 1974 (H.C. 126/1974-75).

17. See cases B (para. 28); R (para. 25) and U (para. 26). The PCA is personally responsible for drafting all decisions in cases fully investigated by his officers. His style is such that it is not always clear whether he is censuring the Department or not. It would be extremely desirable if the PCA could adopt a method of making this clearer, e.g. by ending the case report with the words "maladministration found" or "not found".

18. The PCA's account of this whole story is not, with respect, as clear as it might be.

19. See PCA Act 1967, s.5, above.

20. Other Ombudsmen, of course, go even further. For example the Swedish Ombudsman can investigate issues on his own initiative without any complaint at all. See Rowat *op.cit.* p. 29. And on the practice of the PCA, see Gregory and Hutchesson, *The Parliamentary Ombudsman*, pp. 222-3.

21. Case N, paras. 6-8.

22. On appeals under s.26(2) of the 1966 Act, the 1972 edition of the SB Handbook, para. 232, merely stated: "Appeal Tribunals can also consider . . . whether or not benefit has been overpaid." In the 1974 edition, this has been altered to read (para. 240) ". . .whether, as a result of misrepresentation or failure to disclose a material fact, benefit has been overpaid", a correct statement of the statutory position, as revealed in the PCA's report on Case N.

23. See also Case V, which reveals and discusses the circumstances in which the DHSS may use their discretion not to enforce complete recovery of overpayments.

24. 2nd Report from the Select Committee on the PCA, 1971-72 (H.C. 334). paras. 215-219.

25. Compare R.M. Titmuss, "Welfare 'Rights', Law and Discretion", *Political Quarterly*,42,1971, p.113.

26. 1974 edition, paras. 77-84.

27. Lawyers may see in this incident a breathtaking breach of the rules of natural justice, a point not taken by the PCA. To his credit the tribunal chairman decided not to hear this appeal.

28. For many of the following points I am indebted to comments made by Tony Lynes.

29. This practice was first suggested to the first PCA by the Select Committee on the PCA, 2nd Report, 1967-68, paras. 15-17 (H.C. 350). An example of a potential rule reviewable under this head might be that relating to the allowances for repairs and insurance for owner-occupiers on SB. It could be argued that these should be reviewed much more frequently than they are at present and that the failure of the SBC to do this might amount to maladministration.

TABLE: Location of Cases in Reports of the PCA

The cases referred to are to be found in the PCA's reports, full references to which are set out below. For ease of reference, each case has been given a code letter. This table also gives details of the periods covered by each of the PCA's reports discussed.

Code Letter	Case No.	Page No.	Report: House of Commons Paper No:	Period covered by Report
A	C401/S	116	H.C.116/1971-1972	1971 (and some cases in 1972)
B	C528/S	135		
C	C145/B	42	H.C.490/1971-1972	Jan. 1 1972 - 31 July 1972 (except cases in H.C.116 above)
D	C224/B	109		
E	C519/B	120		
F	C6/G	85	H.C. 18/1972-1973	1/8/72 - 31/10/72
G	C167/G	29	H.C.178/1972-1973	1/11/72 - 31/1/73
H	C127/G	91		
J	C249/G	111		
K	C275/G	116		
L	C146/G	22	H.C.290/1972-1973	1/2/73 - 30/4/73
M	C204/G	31		
N	C289/G	93		
P	C434/G	111		
Q	C370/G	91	H.C.406/1972-1973	1/5/73 - 31/7/73
R	C408/G	98		
S	C542/G	84	H.C. 42/1973-1974	1/8/73 - 31/10/73
T	C567/G	88		
U	C 40/T	51	H.C. 2/1974	1/11/73 - 31/1/74
V	C234/T	78	H.C.170/1974	1/2/74 - 30/4/74
W	C270/T	82		
X	C361/T	21	H.C.281/1974	1/5/74 - 31/7/74
Y	C381/T	99		
Z	C498/T	109		

XIII SUPPLEMENTARY BENEFIT APPEAL TRIBUNALS: AN URGENT CASE FOR REFORM
Ruth Lister

Awareness is growing of the need for the reform of the supplementary benefit appeal tribunal system. Although other chapters consider many aspects of the present functioning of the tribunals, I would like to preface my suggestions for reform with a summary of what my research in London suggests to be their main shortcomings. The research was based on intensive interviews with 63 of the chairmen and members serving on the seven London tribunals, observation of each of these tribunals, and the experience of the CPAG Citizens' Rights Office and local branches of CPAG throughout the country:

Present shortcomings

Criteria for judging the tribunals' performance were provided by the Franks Committee: the trinity of openness, fairness, and impartiality. The Committee interpreted these three conditions as follows: "openness appears to us to require the publicity of proceedings and knowledge of the essential reasoning underlying the decisions; fairness to require the adoption of a clear procedure which enables parties to know their rights, to present their case fully, and to know the case they have to meet; and impartiality to require the freedom of tribunals from the influence, real or apparent, of Departments concerned with the subject matter of their decisions".[2]

The central conclusion from my research was that these three essential conditions, and in particular, fairness and impartiality, are not being adequately met in the supplementary benefit tribunals sitting in the London area. The even lower rates of successful appeals and the experiences of those representing claimants suggests that the situation is as bad, if not worse, in the rest of the country.

In what ways do the tribunals fail to meet these three conditions? First with respect to openness, a major problem is the non-attendance of appellants. This has a very damaging effect on their chances of success. A number of factors are probably involved, including the failure of the appeal papers to stress the importance of attending; the absence of help or advice with the appeal before and at the hearing, and the long distances many appellants have to travel, particularly since the number of tribunals in Britain was reduced during 1971 from 151 to 120.

The other shortcoming relates to what Franks termed "knowledge of the essential reasoning underlying the decisions". It would require telepathic powers to understand the reasoning behind the majority of written decisions which the Child Poverty Actions Group has seen. It is a rare statement of reasons that actually explains on what grounds a decision was arrived at, and this is still the case despite a letter from the Council on Tribunals on the subject sent to all tribunal chairmen at the end of 1972.[3] It is also significant that greater care appears to be taken by tribunals in justifying a decision to the Commission than to the appellant.

Second, regarding fairness, we find that there is no "clear procedure which enables parties to know their rights and to present their case fully". The regulations leave the chairmen considerable discretion as to how to run the hearings.[4] Informality is presented as the supreme virtue of the hearings. But while it may be very desirable to preserve an informal atmosphere, observations and the comments of some tribunal members and of those who have appeared before the tribunals suggests that the principle of informality can reign at the expense of fairness. Appellants are not always able to present their case fully, and are on occasion interrupted by the tribunal with questions of doubtful relevance to the case. The treatment of evidence by the tribunals also leaves much to be desired. Decisions by the Commission to withdraw benefit completely tend to be confirmed on the basis of totally inadequate evidence, including hearsay evidence, while, on the other hand, complaints have been made by Child Poverty Action Group members acting as representatives that documentary evidence produced by them has not been accepted.

The dangers of too great an emphasis on informality were recognised long ago by the Franks Committee, which was "convinced that the attempt which has been made to secure informality in the general run of tribunals has in some instances been at the expense of an orderly procedure. Informality without rules of procedure may be positively inimical to right adjudication, since the proceedings may well assume an unordered character which makes it difficult, if not impossible, for the tribunal properly to sift the facts and weigh the evidence".[5]

Relevant to the third aspect of the fairness of the proceedings referred to .by Franks, that appellants should know the case they have to meet, is the question of representation. Only a minority of appellants is represented, and of those who are, it is usually by a friend or relative. Statistics produced by the DHSS show a clear relationship between representation and success.[6] This can largely be accounted for by the fact that the majority of appellants, unversed in social security law and policy and in the techniques of presenting a case, are in no position to present an effective counter-argument against the full-time presenting officer for the Commission. Yet few tribunal members appear to regard this imbalance as a problem. Lack of help and advice with the actual drafting of the appeal statement can also place the appellant at a considerable disadvantage.

The appellant's greatest disadvantage, however, lies in the fact that some tribunals are failing to fulfil their primary role, namely that of providing an independent adjudicating body. To quote the Franks Committee once more: "When Parliament sets up a tribunal to decide cases, the adjudication is placed outside the Department concerned. The members of the tribunal are neutral and impartial in relation to the policy of the Minister, except insofar as that policy is contained in the rules which the tribunal has been set up to apply".[7] This is not a description of the reality of supplementary benefit tribunals at the present time. Many of those sitting on the tribunals are not making independent and impartial decisions. They are functioning merely as appendages of the Supplementary Benefits Commission.

The tribunals' failure to make impartial decisions stems largely from the ignorance of many members of the provisions of the legislation and of the wide discretionary powers given to them by it. Neither the chairmen nor the members are given any training. As a consequence, the social security law is regarded as largely irrelevant and decisions tend to be made on the merits of the appellant rather than of the appellant's case. This means that the values and attitudes of the members (who are far from representative of the groups appearing before them) assume crucial importance. These attitudes in many cases are reminiscent of those enshrined in the Poor Law. Appellants, and thus appeals, are categorised according to whether they are "deserving" or "undeserving", creating a distinct bias against certain groups of appellants.

But the problem of the tribunals' impartiality is even more serious than that. The view which many members have of the tribunal as a kind of case committee taking a further look at the facts obscures the basic conflict between the interests of the appellant and of the Commission. Many tribunals see their role as trying to give a bit extra to a "deserving" case and, as one tribunal member comp-plained, they "tend to start from the premise that the Commission must be right". Because of this, and because of their own ignorance of the law, they tend to rely heavily on the Commission's presenting officer and on the clerk to the tribunal as impartial sources of information and advice. But the advice that both the presenting officer and clerk give, as employees of the Commission, tends to be based not on the law itself, but on the Commission's interpretation of the law as codified in its internal rules of policy. Many members do not realise that these rules are not binding on the tribunal; some, moreover, do not even understand the distinction between the law and Supplementary Benefits Commission policy. Even where the distinction is understood, there is a marked reluctance to be seen to be challenging the Commission's official policy.

Proposals for reform

The task of the reformer is clear: to create the conditions of open-ness, fairness and impartiality (and in particular the last two), essential to a tribunal system's proper functioning. Less clear, of course, is the best means of achieving these ends. There would appear to be three main courses open to the reformer. The first, advocated in a recent Fabian pamphlet, would be to scrap the tribu-nals altogether and replace them and the national insurance tribu-nals with a "social court".[8] The second would be to amalgamate the national insurance and supplementary benefit tribunal systems within the existing national insurance tribunal framework. The third would be radical reform of the existing supplementary benefit tribunal system.

The proposals for a social court are, in my opinion, miscon-ceived. The advantages claimed for it could equally be achieved by radical reform of the tribunal system, and it throws away those advantages that a tribunal system does have, such as easy accessibil-ity. Even if the dangers of undue legalism recognised by the authors of the pamphlet can, as they suggest, be avoided by the setting up of judicial training schools, they seriously underestimate the deterrent effect a court could have on potential appellants. The percentage of claimants who make an appeal is already low, and to introduce the courts into the system is likely to reduce it still further

The amalgamation of the national insurance and supplementary benefit tribunals *within* the framework of the tribunal system would seem to be a much more satisfactory means of dealing with the problem. This possibility is considered in chapter 14 and so I do not intend to discuss it here, except to say that most of the proposals for reform outlined below would still be necessary if the two tribunal systems were to be amalgamated.

The proposals for reform of the existing system can be divided into three categories: dealing with the membership: the tribunal hearings; and the general structure and organisation of the appeals system.

The membership

(1) *Appointments*

One of the threats to the tribunals' independence is the selection procedure, which still leaves control largely in the hands of the DHSS. It was recommended by the Franks Committee that the responsibility for the appointment of chairmen and members to tribunals should be withdrawn completely from the Minister of the relevant Department and be placed with the Lord Chancellor's Office and Council on Tribunals respectively. It is time that this recommendation was implemented with the modification that responsibility for the appointment of members should also rest with the Lord Chancellor.

A transfer of responsibility for appointments is, however, unlikely to make much tangible difference unless it is accompanied by a determined effort to widen the scope of the membership to make it more representative of the groups appealing. In terms of sex, age and social class, the London tribunals are unrepresentative of the local community and even more so of the groups appearing before them. A positive attempt, in particular, needs to be made to involve claimants and ex-claimants who would bring to the tribunal first hand understanding of the problems faced by claimants. One possibility put forward by Geoffrey Hawker would be to advertise nal vacancies and appoint an independent selection board.[9] Another would be to give a statutory right to certain groups, such as trade unions, immigrant organisations, and claimants' unions, to submit nominees, thus widening the present procedure by which local trades' councils nominate the workpeople's representatives.

(2) *Chairmen*

Supplementary benefit tribunals are virtually alone in not having adopted the recommendation of the Franks Committee that all chairmen should be legally qualified. Only six per cent of all supplementary benefit tribunal chairmen have any legal training. Should it be made obligatory for all chairmen to be legally qualified? In my pamphlet, *Justice for the Claimant,* I adopted the current conventional wisdom and recommended that they should be. On reflection, I have become less certain of the advisability of such a proposal. The main arguments that have been put forward in favour of legally qualified chairmen are, on the face of it, strong. As well as a better understanding of the substantive law, the main advantages attributed to a legally qualified chairman are his knowledge of the principles of fair procedure, and ability to conduct the proceedings in an orderly manner. He is, it is argued, likely to be more skilled in drawing out relevant facts, in evaluating the quality of evidence, and also in helping unrepresented appellants. He would also be better equipped to give adequate reasons for the tribunal's decisions. A further advantage, particularly in the context of supplementary benefit tribunals, is that he would understand the distinction between law and policy and would not have to depend upon the clerk to the tribunal for advice on the law.

The two main arguments that have been put forward against legally qualified chairmen are that they would make the tribunals too legalistic and that this would increase still further the dominance of the chairmen over the members. A practical problem is that of attracting sufficient lawyers of calibre to do the job. The main reason given by the chairmen and members I interviewed for their opposition to the idea of legally qualified chairmen was that the appeals are social rather than legal problems, requiring a common-sense approach to get to the facts; legal training was seen as being unnecessary and irrelevant. This last argument is based upon a sharp distinction between law and fact which is not tenable, for the relevance of different facts is in part a function of the law. Nor would I support the view that legal training is irrelevant. But I believe there is some substance in the first two arguments against legally qualified chairmen and that the answer might be not to rule out lay chairmen altogether, but to give them adequate training in procedure and the relevant law so that they are able to fulfil their functions in a judicial manner. The experience which CPAG has of other types of tribunals suggests that a legally qualified chairman does not automatically guarantee the appellant a fair hearing. Some lay chairmen have proved themselves to be capable of running the tribunals fairly, and it would be a waste to lose their services. What is essential is that the chairmen should be properly trained and that much greater care and thought should be put into the appointing of the chairmen. Essential, too, is some form of accountability, a question which will be looked at when the reform of the structure of the appeals system is discussed.

(3) Training

Training is crucial not only for chairmen, but for members also. Great emphasis has been placed by the Franks Committee and others on the importance of the quality of the personnel of tribunals, and of their having an expert knowledge of their subject. Few have this expert knowledge before their appointment, and the view that it can be gained merely through sitting on the tribunals is not supported by the evidence. My research in London found no relationship between length of time on the tribunal and knowledge of the law. Of twenty members and chairmen who had sat for more than the average three years, only seven showed signs of having a reasonably good grasp of the Act and two of the four who had sat for ten years or more appeared to be totally ignorant of their powers within the law.

Training was one reform supported by a clear majority of the tribunal members I interviewed. The most popular form suggested was a short course of lectures and discussions, possibly combined with a correspondence course. Any training course would need to cover the principles of fair procedure and information about the administration of supplementary benefits, but should concentrate mainly on the legislation, and the tribunal's powers within it. It should also include some information about the social and economic conditions of claimants. The training would have to be carried out by an independent body for otherwise the members would simply be trained in Commission policy. This should present no problem if certain of the structural reforms recommended below were carried out.

A further factor contributing to the tribunals' present ignorance is the fact that they do not have access to the relevant sections of the confidential codes in which Commission policy is set out in detail. Both tribunal members and appellants should be able to see the rules on which the Commission's decisions are based, though on the explicit understanding that the tribunal is in no way bound by them.

The hearings

(1) Rules of procedure

The training of chairmen in the rules of fair procedure should do much to improve the conduct of the hearings, but necessary also is the establishment by statutory instrument of basic rules of procedure. This would help to ensure that proper standards are maintained throughout the country. Appellants should be provided with the rules, set out in simple language, prior to the hearings, so that they are better equipped to cope at the tribunal. This proposal is unlikely to be popular with those who sit on the tribunals. Apart from the minority who were highly critical of the present arrangements, the majority I interviewed felt that a more precise formulation of the rules of procedure would harm the character of the tribunal, making it too formal and rigid. But this is to confuse atmosphere and procedure, and as the Franks Committee observed, "the object to be aimed at in most tribunals is the combination of a formal procedure with an informal atmosphere".[11] The Committee itself was in favour of a definite order of events laid down within the framework of the requirements of natural justice. It considered that this would promote the clarity and regularity necessary for a fair hearing. As well as laying down a definite order of events, a set of rules of procedure should establish the following:

> (a) the right of both sides to state their initial case without interruption;
> (b) the degree of proof required of the Commission in specific types of cases — this is particularly important where the appeal is against a decision to withdraw benefit completely;
> (c) the absolute right to call witnesses and present documentary evidence;
> (d) the relative weight of hearsay and first-hand evidence and the inadmissibility of anonymous allegations;
> (e) the exclusion of all interested parties from the deliberation — this is to prevent observers from the DHSS sitting in on the deliberations, which has happened under the present rules, although it should not have done;[12]
> (f) the duty to furnish a clear, typewritten record of the proceedings as is done in National Insurance tribunals;
> (g) the form in which the reasons for the tribunal's decision are to be set out. This should be a statement which relates to the relevant statutes the facts and arguments presented;
> (h) the rights of appellants who do not attend the hearings.

(2) *Representation*

Much has been written recently about the need to extend legal aid to tribunals. The Lord Chancellor's Advisory Committee on Legal Aid has finally recommended that legal aid should be available to those appearing before tribunals and this recommendation is to be welcomed. But it would be a serious mistake to assume that to implement the recommendation will itself ensure that all appellants have access to adequate representation. Legal aid is only the first step, and if it is to have any real impact, the legal profession must respond to the challenge and broaden its horizons. Nor should tribunal representation become the sole province of lawyers; the challenge must also be accepted by others in the field, such as social workers and Citizens' Advice Bureaux. Thought must be given to how the problem can best be tackled comprehensively on a national basis; the aim should be that no appellant who wants it is denied suitable representation, legal or lay, because of their financial or geographical situation. Furthermore, what is involved is not only representation at the actual hearing, but advice and help at the stage of drafting the appeal. A duty should be placed on local social security offices to inform all appellants of the availability of any such service provided in their areas. In fact it is high time that there was implemented the recommendation contained in the Beveridge Report that "there should be in every local Security office an Advice Bureau to which every person in doubt or difficulty can be referred, and which will be able to tell him, not only about the official provisions for social security, but about all the other organisations — official, semi-official and voluntary, central or local — which may be able to help him in his difficulty."[13]

The organisation and structure of the appeals system

(1)   A presidential system

An important aspect of the general structure of a national appeals system is the provision made for supervision and co-ordination. Other than the general overview maintained by the Council on Tribunals, there is no such provision for supplementary benefit tribunals. The tribunals sit in isolation and lack any information on the practices of other tribunals. The Council on Tribunals has neither the power nor the resources to play an effective role,[14] and the responsibility of the DHSS for the organisation of the tribunals places yet another strain on their independence. Even if the role of the Council on Tribunals were strengthened, the breadth of its responsibility would be too wide for it to provide the kind of structure needed to overcome the present isolation of the supplementary benefit tribunals. Just over half of the busiest tribunals (e.g. industrial tribunals and rent assessment committees) have adopted a presidential system and there does not appear to be any *a priori* reason why supplementary benefit tribunals should not follow suit.

With an adequate staff the president's role could include the organisation of the hearings and the co-ordination of meetings for chairmen and members; the circulation of selected decisions and, particularly important, the supervision of training. He or she could also feed information back to the DHSS from the tribunals. The great advantage of such a system would be a better co-ordinated and more consistent approach to their task from the tribunals. Together with the next proposal, the presidential system would do much to establish the independence of the tribunals from the Department.

(2) The clerk

One of the most urgent questions facing the supplementary benefit appeals system is the role of the clerk. It is not a new problem; it was the subject of much of the Franks Committee's questioning of witnesses and has been raised by many people since. Yet no attempt has been made to resolve the issue. It was clear from my research that the clerks play a crucial role as a source of information and advice, and it is not unknown for them to intervene when they feel that the tribunal is on the wrong lines. Their influence can be particularly strong at the deliberation stage when the interested parties have left the room, and I myself have observed a clerk virtually taking the role of advocate for the Commission so that the tribunal's final decision was considerably less generous than the members had originally contemplated. Clearly this is a very grave encroachment on the tribunal's independence. The proper training of the tribunal chairmen and members should do much to reduce the tribunals' reliance on the clerks for advice, but the issue of the clerk's role must still be tackled.

Proposals for the solution of the problem have been along two main lines. The first, favoured by the Morris and Franks Committees,[15] is that the clerk's role should be severely circumscribed and that he should not be present at the tribunal's deliberation unless sent for to advise on a specific point. This would follow the practice adopted in the magistrate's courts. But so long as the clerk is an employee of the DHSS, there is a danger in his being able to give any advice at all. Thus a more satisfactory solution would be to remove responsibility for the clerk's appointment from the DHSS altogether, and to establish an independent corps of clerks under the Lord Chancellor's office. This alternative was rejected by the Franks Committee, though its attractions were recognised, mainly on the grounds that it would provide inadequate career prospects. But, as Wraith and Hutchesson have argued, this drawback should be overcome if the corps were to cover all tribunals and also the courts, the clerks being trained accordingly.[16]

(3) *The right of further appeal*

Apart from the betting levy and independent schools tribunals, appellants to supplementary benefit tribunals are alone in having no further right of appeal. Not only is there no second appellate body, but also they were excluded from Section 9 of the Tribunals and Inquiries Act 1958, which provided an appeal from other tribunals to the High Court on a point of law. The only option available to the dissatisfied appellant is the highly complex and lengthy process of applying for a prerogative order from the High Court, to quash the original decision.[17] There is no justification for this, and it should be a matter of utmost priority to establish a second-tier appeal body staffed by senior lawyers as in the National Insurance system, though preferably with a wider range of legal experience than the National Insurance Commissioners. Access to the second-tier body could be unrestricted or could be conditional on an initial decision by that body as to whether the decision involved a question of law rather than of fact. Or it could also include questions of fact where the original tribunal was not unanimous in its decision.

The advantages of a second-tier body are threefold. First, in view of the serious doubts thrown on the ability of the tribunals, as at presently constituted, to make truly independent decisions, it is imperative that the dissatisfied appellant should have the right to take the case further without either expense or difficulty. Secondly, if it is accepted that there are some decisions that involve points of principle affecting all similarly placed claimants, and that these claimants should be treated consistently, then there is a need for a qualified body that can make decisions which will be binding on all lower tribunals and on the Commission. Finally, as argued by Jonathan Stein, "as a method of control the appellate body can imbue the tribunals of first instance with a greater sense of accountability".[18] The knowledge that their decisions may be scrutinised by a higher body could concentrate marvellously the minds of the tribunal on the need to give a reasoned decision based on the facts presented as they relate to the law.

Supplementary benefit tribunals have for too long been the poor relation of the tribunal system. Yet they play a crucial role in the administration of justice for poor people; their decisions affect an appellant's very livelihood. It is thus inconceivable that they can continue to be run in the amateurish way that they are at present. Reform is essential if the claimant's right to a fair and impartial means of appeal against the Commission's decisions is not to remain a hollow one.

NOTES

1. *Justice for the Claimant.* CPAG Poverty research series 4, 1974.

2. Report of the Committee on Administrative Tribunals and Enquiries 1957, Cmnd. 218. para. 42: chapter 3 above.

3. Report of Council on Tribunals for 1972-73, App. B.

4. SB (Appeal Tribunal) Rules 1971, S.I. 680, rule 11(10).

5. Franks Report, para. 64.

6. Chapter 10 above. table 4.

7. Franks Report, para. 25.

8. Fulbrook, Brooke and Archer, *Tribunals: a Social Court?* Fabian Tract 427, 1973.

9. G. Hawker. "Problems of Public Service", *New Society*, 4 Oct. 1973.

10. Page 64.

11. Franks Report, para. 64.

12. Report of Council on Tribunals for 1973-74, para. 79.

13. Social Insurance and Allied Services, Cmd. 6404, 1942, para. 397.

14. In the experience of CPAG, the Council on Tribunals is unable even to deal efficiently with individual complaints: Ruth Lister, *Council Inaction.* CPAG Report, 1975.

15. Report of the Committee on Procedure and Evidence for the Determination of Claims for Unemployment Insurance Benefit, 1929, Cmd. 3415, p. 36; Franks Report, para. 61.

16. R.E. Wraith and P.G. Hutchesson, *Administrative Tribunals,* 1973, chap. 11.

17. See Appendix B.

18. J. Stein, *Protecting the Right to Supplementary Benefit* (unpublished paper).

XIV APPEAL STRUCTURES OF THE FUTURE
Harry Calvert

This chapter first concerns itself with the function of the supplementary benefit (SB) scheme and the place of an appeals structure in it, in particular its contribution to the process of getting good decisions made. It then considers the implications of the foregoing and the aptness of some existing structures. Finally it outlines proposals for a system of integrated social security tribunals.

The place of an appeals structure within the supplementary benefit scheme

I take the function of the SB scheme to be to ensure the provision of a culturally-determined minimum level of income for persons still in need after all other sources of income (earnings, private wealth, national insurance entitlement) have been taken into account. It may be noted in passing that the Act of 1966, like its predecessors, thrusts upon the SBC the duty to "exercise its functions in such a manner as shall best promote the welfare of the persons assisted ..." and that some commentators have taken the view that the Commission's function is thus wider than simple income maintenance.[1] Such a wider function might well affect the criteria of good decision-making within the scheme. I am here, however, taking the narrower and more generally accepted view, that the SB authorities[2] are concerned simply to ascertain income entitlement by reference to need.

An appeals structure is not a necessary part of the implementation of a governmental scheme, even though the implementation may involve making large grants of public money to one individual and denying such funds to another, as witness industrial development schemes. It is, however, a common feature of such schemes. When it appears, it appears as part of a larger mechanism concerned with the making of decisions. Of course, "good" decisions are wanted. No doubt, getting the "right" decisions made, legally and, in a narrow sense, morally, is the most important consideration here, but it is not the only one.

"Right" decisions

The law does not always function efficiently as a means of attaining the policy objectives pursued by government. A comprehensive scheme of "right" decision-making ought, therefore, to include some mechanism for ensuring justice where the law fails. This is one reason for the establishment of a Social Security Commission, for which I argue below.

In the vast majority of cases, however, getting the "right" decisions made is a matter of administering the law. This does not mean that questions of value have no relevance, as will be seen. All legal concepts are in some degree open and administration needs to have regard to prevailing principles of social philosophy. I shall return to this in a moment. The first thing that is required, however, is the skilled delimitation of the boundaries prescribed by law within which alone a proper decision can be made. This calls for a thorough and sound working knowledge of SB law. This is not so much a matter of being able to rehearse any given provision on cue as of two other things. The first is having a sufficiently sound knowledge of the relevant law to sense that a particular matter has significance; the second is having the ability to discover, by using legal tools which require a familiarity with a sometimes odd terminology, what that significance is.

At present, there can be few people who possess all these skills. Few lawyers will possess them because the services of the legal profession are much too little called upon for practitioners to have developed a sound knowledge of a somewhat idiosyncratic body of law. Few administrators will possess them because some SB matters have a legal significance outside SB law and few administrators possess the necessary general legal skills. This is not, of course, to say that such skills could not be acquired by formal or perhaps even self-education.

These skills are not all. Their deployment will define the area within which a proper determination must fall, but they will never render the process of decision-making automatic. Though in most cases the creative element will be slight and insignificant, it will always be there, and this is so whether one is talking of determinations "as of right" or exercises of discretion. The differences between these two creatures are much less than is often supposed. The popular view is that matters of "right" involve no choice whereas matters of discretion involve complete freedom of choice for the decision-maker. This is quite wrong. Take, as a matter relating to "rights", the standard task of calculating resources. We all know that "earnings" are brought in under Schedule 2, para. 23 of the 1966 Act. Suppose a claimant, a part-time cleaner, is paid £3 p.w. but her employer has always driven her to work and back and "given" her 50p on Friday. Does the value of the ride, or the 50p or both, rank as earnings? In the present state of SB law, the only possible answers to these questions are that they either "ought" or "ought not" so to rank. Even characterisation as "earnings" of any actual £3 in any given week is a creative act. At the end of the day, there has to be a decision as to whether to subsume the actual concrete facts of the given case under the abstract concepts of which the rule is necessarily constructed—shall this "thing" be treated as belonging to this "class"?

By way of contrast, take section 7 of the 1966 Act: "Where it appears to the Commission reasonable in all the circumstances they may determine that benefit shall be paid to a person by way of a single payment to meet an exceptional need."

Uncertain though its scope may be, one thing is clear about the discretionary power thus created. It is not absolute. The Attorney-General would successfully challenge in a court the award of ENPs of £1 million to the spouse of each member of the Commission. More realistically, an unsuccessful claimant might hopefully contest the rejection of his claim if he could establish that it had been rejected, in spite of the Commission's thinking it reasonable in all the circumstances, for irrelevant reasons such as his colour, or his having no fixed address.

Of course, there is still plenty of room for creative decisions. The scope of section 7 is very much broader than in the case of the "earnings" example above. But the task of decision-making in both cases is the same in kind, even if it differs markedly in degree. The differences in degree are not, furthermore, quite what at first blush they seem. One reason why the "earnings" question seems so narrow in scope is that increasingly detailed "sub-rules" have confined it. The SB scheme would not be radically different if it provided simply that "Every person in Great Britain ... whose resources are insufficient to meet his requirements shall be entitled ... to benefit" (section 4(1)), eschewing all the subsequent elaboration in the 1966 Act. Equally, everyone knows (as indeed the Handbook confirms) that increasingly detailed "sub-rules" do in fact confine the exercise of the section 7 discretion. It is not simply a matter of whether the claimant has an "exceptional need". In practice, the question may well be whether a pair of sand shoes can be ranked as a second pair of shoes for purposes of the SBC's clothing tariff, a question remarkably similar in kind to the question whether the 50p given to the cleaner can be ranked as "earnings".

I am not saying that the two instances are identical. The "earnings" example involves rules laid down by or under an Act of Parliament, unchangeable except by duly authorised amendment; the ENP example involves "rules" which are not, strictly speaking, law at all, but changeable simply by the Commission itself. The legal rules must be observed; the Commission can ignore its rules. In a matter of right, to ignore the rules because the individual case requires it is impermissible; in a matter of discretion, to observe the departmental rules without considering the individual case is equally impermissible. What I am saying is that there is more to administering the law than just applying rules; that in the case of both questions of right and matters of discretion, right decision-making involves making choices in a manner, hopefully, consonant with the policy of the scheme; and that for this reason the making of right decisions in the area of SB is not as different from making right decisions in other areas as is sometimes thought. The corollary is that both in SB and in these other areas, right decision-making requires an understanding of the policy of the scheme in question and a sense of the importance of furthering policy objectives to the extent that the opportunity to do so presents itself in the course of decision-making.

In one other way, prevailing principles of social philosophy may bear upon the process of making SB decisions. As procedural precepts for ensuring good decision-making, it is widely felt that the decision-maker should be free from the sort of personal interest in the matter which might render his judgment upon it partial; and it is also felt that to make decisions without hearing both sides of the argument is no guarantee of fairness. So far as the substance of the decision is concerned, it is a corollary of the widely-accepted notion of distributive justice that like cases should be treated alike. To some extent, these precepts are reflected in general principles of law governing the making of decisions — the principles of "natural justice" should be observed; discretion ought not to be exercised capriciously or arbitrarily. The recent trend in case-law towards generalisation of hitherto specific procedural injunctions into the general requirement of "fairness" fortifies the need to have decisions made by mechanisms responsive both to the requirements of the law and to the influences of prevailing notions of justice.

Personal factors

Acquiring a sufficient familiarity with SB law and policy requires fairly high intelligence and considerable application. I am doubtful if an adequate standard of ability is attainable if it is treated as a spare-time activity, as is the case at present with chairmen and wingmen of SBATs though not, of course, in the case of SBC administrators. Furthermore, I believe that if the administration of SB law improved in the way I would like to see it improve, it would become even more intellectually demanding and even more difficult to administer properly on a part-time basis.

Certain qualities of character seem to be needed. To a large extent, responsible administration is a function of the procedural factors considered below. Apart from this, however, the quality of administration will improve if (a) the decision-maker senses the need to get it right because, in the vast majority of cases, only he can get it right and (b) he is given some personal incentive to get it right. (a) is not the case at present with "front-line" SBC administrators, a significant proportion of whose decisions are overturned on review or appeal; it is, of course, the case with SBATs, since the controlling jurisdiction of the High Court is hardly ever invoked. (b) is to some extent present in the case of SBC administrators who function within the existing Civil Service career structure; it is almost totally absent in the case of SBATs.

It is desirable that decision-makers should be impartial and judicial, i.e. lack any personal interest in the matter and be accustomed to basing decisions on an evaluation of all the relevant considerations. SBC officers are not necessarily partial but they are at constant risk of being partial. There can be conflicting policies on particular matters and the "official" policy is not necessarily the "right" one; yet there will be a tendency for the SBC officer to toe the official line. Tribunals, on the other hand, are not in theory susceptible to the same influences. So far as being judicial is concerned, the problem is one of forming the right intellectual habits. "Over-the-counter" administration may be regarded as unlikely to do this. Tribunal activity may develop it, the more readily if service is full-time than if it is spare-time.

Procedural factors

The concern here is with the process of decision-making in the broadest sense, and with features which might render it more efficient.

(a) *The process of decision-making.* In this context, the importance of rules of substantive law is often underestimated. Rules, whether formal and legal, or informal and persuasive only, are one of the best guarantees that substantial justice shall be done, that distributive justice shall be attained and that the decision-maker does not lose the confidence and respect of his clientele unjustifiably.

With some hesitation, I suggest that the function of legal rules should be confined to defining policy. At the outset, I defined the function of the SB scheme as "to ensure the provision of a culturally-determined minimum level of income for persons still in need ...". In fact, SB policy is a good bit more complex than this, since there is a potential conflict between this and other policies. So, provision otherwise is supposed to be made for the under-16s, hence the limitation of benefit to persons of 16 or over.[3] Family integrity is supposed to be preserved, hence the aggregation of resources and requirements of married couples and cohabitees.[4] We would rather people went in need than that they should be idle, hence the wage stop and the trade disputes disqualification.[5] People should be rewarded for extreme bravery in defending the realm, hence the disregard as resources of sums payable to holders of the Victoria Cross or George Cross.[6] It appears presently to be the view that there should be Parliamentary control over the measurement of income needs, hence the scale rates.[7]

Within the area thus delimited, the sole concern is to provide benefits according to need. Rules are useful here; they can facilitate the process of decision-making in commonly recurring types of case and go a long way towards dispensing distributive justice. The decision-maker can appeal to them to rebut a charge of prejudice or partiality. At the same time, no two cases are exactly alike and no rule can anticipate all the problems. The need, therefore, is for rules which can be ignored for "good" reason; and the criterion here is whether or not the application of the rule fosters or hinders the implementation of policy. There should be two sources of such rules: (1) a Social Security Code under the supervision of a Social Security Commission; (2) precedents. Precedents would be a secondary source in the sense that the Code should deal with more commonly recurring situations and would, accordingly, from time to time absorb doctrine developed in precedents, altered if and as necessary by the Commission.

In overseeing the Code, the Commission would not merely refer to the doctrine developed in precedents. It would itself take the initiative, both developing the Code in the light of existing policy, and adjusting it to the demands of policy-changes effected by legislation proper. The Code would have a status comparable to that of the Highway Code and the Code of Practice instituted under the Industrial Relations Act 1971 and now functioning under the Trade Union and Labour Relations Act 1974. Although the legislation governing these two codes is not identical[8] the effect expressly provided for the former (i.e. a failure to observe the Code creates a presumption of liability) appears to be being accorded to the latter. A Social Security Code ought to operate similarly. One satisfying its requirements for benefit ought, prima facie, to receive it, but might be refused it for "good" reason, i.e. because to grant it in the given case would not further the policy. Thus, the Code might provide that monthly travel grants for prisoners' wives not otherwise provided for should be paid; but payment might be refused in a particular case were it established that the true reason for applying was to visit someone else. Similarly, one failing to satisfy its requirements (e.g. through already having two pairs of shoes) would be prima facie disentitled, but would get benefit on proof of needing more by reason of a medical condition affecting the feet.

Precedent should function in a similar manner. It is an institution which is to some extent abused by lawyers and to some extent misunderstood by critics. It is abused by lawyers insofar as they assume that any two cases are identical in all respects; insofar as they ignore differences without argument as to whether they are significant or not; and insofar as they are too reluctant to justify the abandonment of a precedent in the face of a change of policy. It is misunderstood by critics insofar as they assume that these are vices inherent in precedent.

Quite apart from making for openness of decisions (which I consider below) a system of precedents is a valuable adjunct to decision-making in a number of ways. First of all, it tends to make for distributive justice, to ensure that like cases are treated alike. Secondly, it makes for the appearance of distributive justice. Thirdly, it is an efficient method of approaching decision-making; to make each decision anew is, theoretically, to consider anew the relevance of each fact, to search anew for the relevant law and to formulate afresh each relevant argument. A good precedent will contain a catalogue of all such points and be a valuable starting-point for what should always be done anew — making the decision.

This amounts to advocating that decisions should be based on more rules and precedents than are presently published. How different would this be from the present position? There are, we are told, vast quantities of rules (e.g. in the "A" Code etc.) that are not presently published. There are even precedents — whenever an SBAT recognises "one of those cases" before it, it is classifying according to a system of mental precedent and being guided towards a decision by it. The trouble is that the process is taking place without the intellectual rigour which ensures that precedent discharges its proper function. A mass of published rules and precedents is not, however, bad in itself. Quite the contrary; provided that they are rendered easily accessible, they are a good thing. They become bad only at the point at which they are so massive, complex or ill-organised that they are, in effect, inaccessible. They are not bad, it must be emphasised, on the ground that the administration of SB must be discretionary and not controlled by rules; precedents are not alternatives to discretion — they are guides to its proper exercise.

(b) *The context of decision-making.* It is implicit, in suggesting that decisions should be made according to rules, that those rules should be published. The Social Security Code should be readily accessible to the public. Precedents should be equally available. These are simply particular aspects of openness which, with fairness, constitute the essential features that should accompany decision-making.

The great value of openness consists in the discipline which it imposes upon the process of decision-making. If the hearing is in public, the tribunal is under pressure to ensure that it is conducted properly. If reasons must be published, the tribunal is encouraged to base its decisions upon good reasons which will survive scrutiny. In neither respect is the existing law satisfactory. SBAT hearings are still held in private. The only scrutiny as of right is that of members of the Council on Tribunals; they are few in number, usually busy and have not yet established the right to sit-in on the making of the determination.[9] In the year 1972-3, the whole Council and its Scottish Committee mustered only 25 visits, hardly a rigorous control spread over thousands of tribunals and tens of thousands of sittings.[10]

Franks acknowledged the need for publicity of proceedings but excepted the then National Assistance Appeal Tribunals from that general principle, the issues to be determined involving "the disclosure of intimate personal or financial circumstances." The fear was that "if any or all of these appeals were to be heard in public many applicants might be deterred from appealing or even from applying for assistance."[11] This was, I think, questionable at the time and is even more so now. It was questionable at the time first because it assumed that there was or would be a significant number of persons not deterred by disclosing intimate personal or financial information to SBC officers and tribunal personnel, who would be deterred if the circle of persons informed were widened at all. It was questionable at the time also because any claimant runs the risk of having that information fully disclosed before a magistrates' court under sections 29-33 of the 1966 Act (nor will the Divisional Court spare a claimant in the unlikely event of an eventual application to them).

Similar information can also be relevant in national insurance cases, yet privacy is not insisted upon. It was questionable also because the appropriate way to protect the appellant's interest (the only avowed justification) is surely to give him a right to have the proceedings conducted in private, not to impose an absolute bar preventing a public hearing even when he wants one.

It is even more questionable now that, as may reasonably be speculated, the degree of shame attaching to poverty is diminishing. There is a need to avoid deterring claims and appeals simply for fear of publicity; but it is surely a need which would be adequately met by providing a tick box on the appeal form and by the chairman informing the appellant of his right to privacy at the start of each hearing.

So far as publishing reasons for decisions is concerned, the reforms of 1971 have not turned out as satisfactorily as one might hope.[12] SBATs have tended to state reasons in such general and imprecise terms as to fail to enable an unsuccessful appellant to understand the precise cause of failure of his appeal. It must be emphasised that a statement of reasons of this type would almost certainly not satisfy the requirements of the law on the matter which are that the reasons must be proper, adequate and such as to deal with the substantial points raised.[13] In the absence of any controlling mechanism other than the Divisional Court, application to which is highly unlikely, it must be left to the Council on Tribunals to improve the practice[14] yet the same problem has been very speedily and effectively cured in the case of Attendance Allowance Boards by a controlling central second-tier tribunal, the National Insurance Commissioners.

The other desirable feature of the context of decision-making is fairness. Fairness to Franks required "the adoption of a clear procedure which enables the parties to know their rights, to present their case fully and to know the case which they have to meet."[15] Those requirements are as valid today as they ever were. But they pose problems. One of the relevant criteria is that the system must not be such as to impose intolerably high personal costs on parties involved in it. In particular, pursuing one's appeal must not be such an awesome process as to deter the claimant. One has therefore to seek to reconcile clarity with informality of procedure. If the demands of clarity and informality are clearly understood, there is no problem. The fact is, however, that they have been misunderstood and the efficiency of SBAT decision-making has suffered accordingly. Clarity requires merely that the issues should be joined in order that the debate can be relevant and in a manner easily comprehensible by all the parties. This is the function of formal pleadings in ordinary litigation before the courts; and such pleadings are, of course, somewhat complex and ritualistic. The function is, however, a highly desirable one, even if the formality is not, and there has been a tendency to sacrifice clarity for informality in SB appeals. The result (and this is based entirely on my own limited observation) is that one still today sometimes finds a tribunal which tackles the work in such a sloppy, ill-ordered fashion that it is extremely difficult to get to and stay on the point. Sometimes the eventual decision is made without adequate consideration of that point (although the stated reasons may indicate otherwise); sometimes it is made on another point not raised until the hearing. It is, of course, entirely proper for the tribunal to take up a relevant point which only emerges at the hearing but in such a case the appellant ought not to suffer from lack of notice of it and an adjournment might be the proper course.

The points at issue should emerge from the pre-hearing procedures. The SBC officer does usually attempt to isolate the crucial points; the average unrepresented claimant cannot be expected to do so — for him it is a matter of asserting a real need rather than debating a fine point. The role of the SBC officer is, however, confined in a number of crucial ways and he cannot be expected to do full justice by a claimant's case.

Informality requires simply that ritual, ceremony, authoritarianism and anything else which might make the experience of appealing a harrowing one for the appellant should be avoided insofar as it is not necessary to the efficient conduct of the hearing. The appellant must be allowed his say yet it is quite probable, if unrepresented, that he may not get near the relevant point at all. Informality does not require that he be granted the liberty to stray from or stay away from the point indefinitely. It requires that the chairman should guide him gently towards it rather than bullying him.

Apart from the general questions of openness and fairness, one other aspect of procedures should be considered — fact-finding. The point is again made hesitantly, since it is based upon limited personal experience, but there is cause for some unease about the manner in which SBATs set about the business of finding facts, whether favourable or unfavourable towards an appellant. Thus there are proper and improper uses of an appellant's claims history. In an ENP case, for example, I would like to have a provisional determination made solely on the basis of evidence as to existing need and only then to have reference to the claims history for deciding whether provision has already been made or resources deliberately abandoned. Premature reference to the claims history is too prone to go to character and offer scope for prejudice. Or take the cases of undisclosed earnings or cohabitation. Evidence here may consist of an investigating officer's report of what neighbours say they have observed. The danger is not that the investigating officer is fabricating the neighbour's evidence, or even that he may have misunderstood or exaggerated it. It is that the neighbour may himself have got it wrong, perhaps quite genuinely, and there is no opportunity for having his evidence tested. It is often said, and rightly, that it is ridiculous to exclude all hearsay evidence when some of it might have probative value. It follows, or at least appears to, that the proper response to hearsay evidence is to take care over the weight to be attached to it. That no doubt is a good precept for a perfect world. Ours unfortunately does not qualify; mere mortals may tell themselves that little weight should be attached to two or three separate items of evidence and yet be compelled to the conclusion they apparently support. Industrial Tribunals adopt a realistic approach here. Pragmatically, they decline to entertain heresay evidence of a dubious kind but admit it of a more reliable kind, e.g. a doctor's letter stating that X had a compound fracture and could not walk for nine weeks. So far as the oath is concerned, I think the cons outweigh the pros. So far as exchanging brief summaries of evidence beforehand are concerned, I think the pros outweigh the cons.

The need for appeals

It follows from the above that there should be some provision for taking a second look at some cases. It would involve too great an input of scarce resources to ensure that good decisions were made in all cases first time off. We can only afford a fairly unsafe system of decision-making at the lowest level. This level should operate as a filter. We shall need some mechanism to take a second look at some cases; and it must be a mechanism which ensures a tolerably high standard of decision-making. If it is to be adequately accessible to appellants it must function in their locality. If the volume of work were slight, one might conceive of a peripatetic body. The annual level of appeals even before the existing SBATs, however, makes this out of the question. It does not follow that the exact pattern of the existing local SBATs should be retained. For a number of reasons stated below, I think they should not. But it does mean that a considerable number of separate "benches" are required. The significance of this is that if other of the interests listed above (e.g. consistency of decisions; a published body of precedents) are to be adequately served, a second-tier appeal body is required, one, though only one, of whose functions will be to ensure that local variations in the administration of a nationwide scheme are not perpetuated irrationally. There is an apparent lack of distributive justice when travel grants for prisoners' dependants are issued liberally in one area and not at all in another.

At present, we have two different procedures for taking a second look at front-line decisions, (a) appeal proper and (b) review, the first essentially a judicial· procedure, the second essentially an administrative one. The system of appeals proper presently lacks a second, central, co-ordinating tier. The administrative review structure, however, does not; it is presently organised at local, regional and central levels. The existing SB structures are not, however, the only ones available.

Other existing structures

For various reasons, none of our existing courts of law is suitable as the second-tier appeal body. The administration itself, which by review may supervise the making of decisions, can never attain the appearance of impartiality necessary for deciding appeals — it will always, in fact, be partial. If we are to build onto existing structures, it is to tribunals, particularly those for national insurance, that we must look, both because their present concern is with other interlocking parts of the social security system and because they already handle some supplementary benefit matters.

At the apex of the national insurance structure of tribunals, the National Insurance Commissioners are among the few lawyers with the capacity to undertake the skilled administration of supplementary benefits law. Their working expertise is presently confined to the limited and complementary range of national insurance, industrial injuries and family allowances law; but supplementary benefits and FIS law could easily be added. The techniques and policy are, after all, very similar. So far as the legally qualified chairmen of the NILTs are concerned, one would take the same view if they were full-time but, like chairmen of SBATs, they are not. It is my impression that the part-time role is at present the chief vice of NILTs. The law is complex; the sources are voluminous; it is not the sort of expertise which is readily mustered during hours off from a busy practice. It would be even worse were the load substantially increased by the addition of SB and FIS work. Nevertheless, I do not think this to be an insuperable obstacle. It is time, I believe, to depart from part-time adjudication in both SB and NI tribunals. Full-time appointees, like the Commissioners, could master the range.

Members of the national insurance tribunals are already well-versed in stating reasoned decisions and working a system of precedent. The NILTs and, to a lesser and understandable extent the Commissioners, do their work expeditiously and economically. Their procedures are apt for the purpose — reasonably straightforward, simple and informal in the best sense. In this respect, they are to my mind slightly superior to the SBATs of which I have experience.

As long ago as the Franks Report in 1957, we were urged to rationalise and simplify the tribunal structure. This has been well done in the case, for example, of the Industrial Tribunals, which exercise a fairly wide-ranging jurisdiction. It is odd that the trend in social security should seem to be towards diversification. It has hardly been successful; Attendance Allowance Boards when confronted by questions of law, have clearly lacked the necessary minimum of legal expertise. The Council on Tribunals argued unavailingly but to my mind rightly against proliferation. It is therefore with no great hope of success that I advocate the integration of all the social security tribunals into a single structure. This is justified by the advantages of scale. It is also a course rendered attractive by the deficiencies of the existing SBAT system.

What is wrong with SBATs?

First of all, I think there is a great deal right with them. In my experience, the work is discharged expeditiously and, by and large, sympathetically. If the surroundings are often insalubrious and dingy, that is our fault for not spending more on them, not the tribunals' fault. They are, I am suggesting, too inexpensive. Some chairmen are impressive; others are not so. Yet for some reason, the performance of chairmen in SBATs is often less capable than in NILTs. This manifests itself in a number of ways:

1. Occasionally, appellants are browbeaten. This may be understandable on some occasions, as when a representative is gratuitously insulting or irrelevantly hostile.

2. Clerks tend to assume a more dominant role in SBATs than in NILTs. To some extent I think this is because the latter have a slightly more judicial tradition.

3. More important than either of the above, SBATs are sometimes too informal. This may seem an odd complaint, but without going to the length of arguing for formal pleadings and a rigid procedure, it remains true that a better-structured procedure would be preferable to what sometimes happens now. I once found it impossible, and have frequently found it difficult, to join the relevant issue before an SBAT. The "impossible" case occurred some years ago,

though after the 1966 Act. The claimant had been refused benefit of any kind (vouchers included) as having "no fixed address". He had, in fact, been sleeping rough when the claim was made and appeal heard. I tried in vain before the tribunal to point out that there was nothing in the Act or regulations about having to have a fixed address and that the claimant did in fact satisfy all the relevant conditions, and was thus entitled to benefit, but I never got a "yea" or a "nay" to these points. The presenting officer simply said he had no fixed address; the chairman asked me if I disagreed with that; I said "no, but ..." and was interrupted. That seemed to conclude the matter. I sought to press the point, with interruptions, but at the end of the day, the tribunal's impatience with my inability to understand that they didn't award benefit to claimants of no fixed address was barely concealed. They eventually gave that as their reason for refusing benefit but issued vouchers! In a recent case, I had the greatest difficulty in convincing a tribunal that the statutory discretion to have regard to otherwise disregarded resources of the claimant[16] did not entitle them to take into account the total incomes of adult children still living with the family, as not being a resource of the claimant at all.

It may be that I am a bad advocate, yet NILTs seem to understand me well enough. I rather think the explanation lies elsewhere. I believe that many of the above vices are attributable to history — to the time when the poor law guardians really were agents for the dispensation of state charity. That tradition has, I believe, lived on through the national assistance tribunals and still pervades SBATs today; not consciously in the minds of the members, but in the traditional way in which the task is approached. SBATs do not yet live out in practice the fact that some benefit is a right, and that even in the case of discretionary awards there are legal limits to the range of matters which can be taken into consideration.

There is, I believe, another reason why SBATs behave as they sometimes do. They are, by comparison with NILTs, virtually uncontrolled. In part this is simply a corollary of the fact that many of their decisions are discretionary — a man can arrive capriciously at a decision which he could (though not necessarily would) have arrived at properly. An appellate body may of course decline to substitute its own discretion for that of the lower tribunal. But in the case of SBATs, there is no appellate body at all. I could in my "no fixed address" case have gone to the Divisional Court, but that is hardly a realistic course for a claimant who is sleeping rough. SBATs have no readily accessible Commissioners brooding over them. They do not have the discipline of a written body of doctrine derived from the decisions of other SBATs to guide them as the

NILTs have Commissioners' Decisions. The SBC officer at least has the Commission's Codes. Strictly speaking, SBATs cannot even have regard to these. SBATs sit in camera. The conditions for palm-tree justice are almost all present and it is remarkable that the justice actually dispensed does not approximate to that variety a good deal more frequently than is in fact the case.

I do not believe that these vices can easily be removed just by tinkering about with SBATs as they are at present. The imposition of a superior co-ordinating and controlling tribunal, the parallel of the National Insurance Commissioners, and the introduction of other practices prevailing in the National Insurance tribunals — sitting in public the rule, circulation of a body of case-law — would go some way towards abating the evils which attend SBATs. But a complete break with the past would be a more convincing way of tackling the problem. Since the integration of social security tribunals would be advantageous in other ways, that is the course which should be taken.

An integrated tribunal structure

I therefore propose that SBATs and NILTs should be integrated and that above them there should be a second, co-ordinating and controlling central tier, the equivalent of the present National Insurance Commissioners. One reason for this is what I have called the advantages of scale. A second is the fact that NILTs as well as SBATs could be improved upon and that therefore the new structure should be different in some respects from both.

I have mentioned above some of the existing defects in the NILT system. The quality of decision-making on a part-time basis would be impaired still further in a part-time tribunal handling the extended range of matters. In both NILTs and SBATs, though to a greater extent in the latter, the role of the clerk is less than wholly satisfactory — a fact attributed by commentators to the departmental career structure to which he belongs, even though he occupies for the time being an office which is part of the adjudicatory system; a fact, also, which may be fortified by the fact that he is the only full-time career man associated with the tribunal. Complaints about tribunal premises are in part referable to the fact that permanent suitable premises are not justified because of the infrequency of sittings. They arguments would have less force if SBATs and NILTs were integrated and if the number of centres were reduced as a consequence of establishing a full-time system.

Many of these defects have at their root problems of staffing. It is impossible, it is said, to get good, permanent clerks because a good enough person will not want to end his days there. Similar arguments are heard about insurance officers — adequate service (and it needs to be and often is very good) can be secured only by viewing the duties as a step up in the civil service cursus honorum. Similarly, we have to make do with a larger number of part-time chairmen, both of SBATs and NILTs, because men of a sufficient calibre are said not to be forthcoming on any other basis. We can and should get over this. Before proposing the method, I wish to mention two other defects of the present system which are relevant.

The first is a simple matter. The qualification for National Insurance Commissioner is that the person appointed must be a barrister (or in Scotland an advocate) of ten years' standing. This is not satisfactory. First, it is not a guarantee that the man appointed will be of the right mettle. Although I am impressed by the calibre of most of the Commissioners with whose work I am familiar, it remains possible for a man without experience of or sympathy with the social security system to be appointed directly to the highest appeal tribunal. A good man will adapt speedily and render good service. However, the office may be treated as a convenient way of "pensioning off" a politician past the peak of his profession. The second reason for believing this to be unsatisfactory is the more important. It excludes utterly others who might be excellent in the job. The largest class of these is NILT chairmen, usually solicitors, some of whom have built up extensive experience over many years in their tribunals. Thus, one who has done only a limited amount of legal work over ten years may be appointed; one who has actually adjudicated with great success in social security claims for twenty is disqualified.

The second matter is more complex. It relates to the vexed questions of representation before tribunals, the legal aid and advice system and the nature of tribunals. In brief, I believe that the need for advice for claimants in connection with social security appeals is much more extensive than is commonly appreciated. It arises from the very complexity of the social security system and the fact that no chairman can be expected to keep absolutely on top of the work. At the same time, I believe that the £25 scheme for legal advice under the 1972 Act is in theory not perfect and in practice even less so. In theory, it is not perfect because the inexpertise of the legal profession in social security law renders their services uneconomic. In practice, the scheme is just not getting off the ground — it has been available for some time now but claimants are not using it.

I am even more strongly against legal aid for tribunal representation. I believe that there is a need for representation in some cases to improve the fact-finding which is done by tribunals and sometimes to provide legal argument. But again I feel that our private legal profession is ill-suited to the work. In part, the explanations are the same as for legal advice — the services of the legal profession tend to be less expert and more costly than we should afford; and there is some truth in the common objection that the first thing an advocate does is to ask for an adjournment. In part, they are due to the fact that the role of the tribunal differs in important respects from that of the forum in which the profession usually works. Courts of law are usually the scene for an adversarial contest and the judge plays a passive role. The client has hired his man, and his man owes him a good fight. The emphasis in a tribunal should differ markedly; the bench is more like a board of inquiry — the chairman should play a more active role seeking to investigate for himself and his wingmen. The representative's role should be a subordinate one — that of assisting the tribunal in its conduct of the investigation, in particular by ensuring that it pursues all matters in the interest of the claimant. Professional advocates, accustomed to the courtly role, do not seem to find it easy to slip into the new one.

These considerations prompt me to suggest that we need a fresh start to the question of representation of claimants before tribunals and that the suggestions from the Lord Chancellor's committee are not what we want.[17] In a sense, we are getting a fresh start from bodies such as CPAG and claimants' unions but such representation is often unsatisfactory, particularly in the case of the latter bodies. The vices in the present staffing practices for tribunals, and the grossly inadequate methods of providing legal services for claimants prompt me to suggest that one of the greatest single contributions that could be made towards the improvement of appeal mechanisms in the future is the creation of a totally new career structure within the sphere of social security adjudication. This is a radical step to propose and I anticipate that it will not be received with any warmth by most people presently involved with social security tribunals and that it will mostly be received with hostility by such members of the legal profession as hear about it. It is a strange fact but true that lawyers are very good at finding reasons against anyone else tackling legal work, even though they themselves do not undertake it. Social security work accounts for a miniscule proportion of the income of most practitioners. Very few tackle the work at all; those who do are usually providing a public service which is, so far as their own financial services are concerned, uneconomic. Yet some catastrophe will befall us if anyone else is allowed to do it!

This attitude has some justification but not much. Its justification lies in the fact that lawyers can point to some occasions in the past when they have taken a stand for the individual in circumstances in which others might have feared to do so. One suspects, however, that significant motivation may lurk, not so much in a dog-in-the-manger attitude, as in a real sense of insecurity deriving from the fear that the wedge will be driven inexorably in until a state-run national legal service finally erodes their monopoly. To my mind, a decision should be made about a national legal service on its own merits and quite independently of the present, strictly confined proposals. But, realising that my proposals may encounter the combined weight of the professional legal bodies and their parliamentary confreres, I still believe them to be worth consideration.

The extent of integration

I am proposing a merger of the adjudicative sides of Supplementary Benefits and National Insurance, Industrial Injuries, and Family Allowance matters. I would ultimately like to see a merger of the administrative sides also. This latter is a very much more complex problem but is justified by past, present and future factors. Despite the creation of the DHSS, Supplementary Benefit is still in effect independently administered — only the ultimate responsibility (and that a narrow one) resides in the Secretary of State, e.g. in relation to appointment of members of the SBC. His responsibility in respect of the other social security services is much broader.

At present, the two sides of social security are closely integrated in their social function. It is desirable that this should be reflected in their administrative organisation. We should start thinking now about separating the present DHSS functions in relation to contribution, classification and insurability on the one hand and to benefit on the other. It is this latter function that seems ripe for unification with the present SBC functions in a new Social Security Commission.

I am not here concerned with administrative merger except in respect of three functions:

(1) I have suggested above that amongst the functions of a Social Security Commission should be the promulgation and servicing of a Code with a legal status similar to that of the Highway Code. Quite apart from the enormous task of establishing a Social Security Commission, the preparation of a comprehensive Social Security Code would itself be a task of great complexity. Transitionally, in anticipation of the establishment of a Commission, the SBC and DHSS should prepare preliminary codes dealing with the two sides of social security according to the present distribution of functions between them.

(2) I have also suggested above that the Commission should have an "equity" jurisdiction; i.e. that it should dispose of the

occasional case (and with a Code and proper tribunals, such cases ought to be very rare) where the legal, as opposed to Code, rules actually prevent decisions in accordance with the real policy by front-line decision-makers and tribunals. This is a function which would be discharged by a proper "ombudsman" and its discharge may result from a review of the functioning of the office of Parliamentary Commissioner. Pending either this event or the establishment of a Commission (both of which might reasonably be speculated to be remote) some provision could be made administratively; it is simply a matter of seeking to ensure that the SBC and DHSS use existing powers to that end.

(3)   There will continue to be a need for front-line decisions, whatever body is charged with the overall supervision of the social security system. In the interim, this function will no doubt continue to be discharged by existing DHSS and SBC officers whose initial role would not greatly change when they entered the service of a Social Security Commission. Although the initial role would not change, however, their position would be considerably altered by the need for a totally new career structure in the adjudicative service, to which I now turn.

The adjudicative service

Social security tribunals (SSTs) should now be recognised for what in fact they are. For 90% of the people 90% of the time, tribunals are *the* courts and social security tribunals are the most important courts. There are things called the courts of justice where leviathans such as ICI, the GLC and the occasional well-to-do eccentric with unusual sexual proclivities may sometimes disport themselves, greatly to the benefit of a quaint, outmoded and, in many respects, noble profession. There are other courts where we may be called upon to account for our delinquent behaviour. But when it comes to realising our rights, most of us will never come nearer to these courts than the pages of our daily papers.

SSTs should become a self-contained adjudicative service directly under the control of the Lord Chancellor's Department. I say self-contained; by this I mean that the service should contain its own final appeal tribunal, though without prejudice to the ultimate controlling jurisdiction of the High Court if this is felt to be desirable as an ultimate constitutional safeguard. Although there would be other parallel, adjudicative services, (e.g. Industrial Tribunals), the value of expertise in popular tribunals is such, and the inadequacies of courts of general jurisdiction are so glaring, that I see no place either for a general administrative court or an administrative division of the High Court. As an actual working model, the National Insurance Commissioners seem to offer more than the above-mentioned and as yet untried devices.

For reasons stated above, the SSTs would need to be organised in two tiers, the lower tier functioning in the locality, the upper tier entertaining appeals from local tribunals and publishing decisions in selected cases as precedents. The upper tier would be staffed by full-timers, as are the NI Commissioners at present. In the lower tier, I would retain the same personnel as at present — chairman, wingmen, clerk — though the present differences between the SBAT panels and the NILT panels[18] would need to be resolved. It is however necessary, if a sufficient quality of decision-making is to be obtained, that some other changes should be made, thus:

(1)   Chairmen should be properly trained and experienced. I do not think it essential that they should have jumped through the hoops of the Bar or the Law Society. But they should have developed expert knowledge in social security law and experience in decision-making.

(2)   Chairmen should be full-time appointees. This is to some extent a function of obtaining and maintaining a sufficient expertise. It is also desirable in order to avoid the tendency for tribunal work to be treated as a spare-time occupation to which the chairman will not necessarily be able to give his best. Wingmen could remain part-time.

(3)   Clerks should be an established part of the adjudicative service. Their loyalties should lie and should be seen to lie with the tribunal rather than with one of the parties to appeals. Chairmen should be seniors and full-timers in the same service as clerks.

(4)   The adjudicative service should contain its own advice and advocacy staff. They should be readily available for consultation near the front-line and an unsuccessful claimant, when notified of the rejection of his claim, should also be notified of the whereabouts of the advice staff and of his right to consult them free of charge. It should be the policy of the advice staff that they will act for an unsuccessful claimant wherever he contests the findings of fact on which the rejection of his claim has been based or where the view of the law taken by the front-line decision-maker is at all questionable. There is a danger that such a service might become or seem to be too bureaucratic and therefore the present right of advocacy for other representatives must be continued. The risk that a case rejected by the advice service might subsequently succeed would be salutary. It would

not be the only factor conducing towards a proper discharge of duties for reasons which follow.

Many of the vices of the existing systems of adjudication (clerks owing "allegiance" to the SBC or DHSS; chairmen being part-time etc.) are attributable to the lack of a proper career-structure in social security adjudication. If the SST service were to contain Commissioners who could be drawn from ranks wider than those of barristers of 10 years' standing (and similarly chairmen of Medical Appeal Tribunals); full-time local chairmen; an advice and advocacy service; and clerks, a proper career-structure would become possible.

The long-term structure

I envisage the following steps in the career structure, as shown in the diagram on the following page.

1. Clerk
2. Advisor; senior clerk
3. Senior advisor
4. Local chairman; chief advocate
5. Medical Appeal Tribunal (MAT) chairman
6. Commissioner
7. Chief Commissioner

There could be either direct entry at the clerk level after a period of suitable training; or entry by transfer from the SBC or DHSS after a shorter period of training. Clerks would initially serve for a period under another clerk before being appointed to their own tribunals. After a period of service as a full-fledged clerk, clerks would qualify for promotion to senior clerk, serving MATs and Commissioners; or, after a period of service plus further training, clerks would qualify for promotion to advisor and thence, after further service, to senior advisor. Both advisors and senior advisors could work as advocates. Advisors, however, would handle initial inquiries and take suitable cases; senior advisors would, in addition to the more difficult advocacy work, function as chief advocates before local tribunals and MATs and appeal appropriate cases before the Commissioners. Local chairmen and the chief advocates (who would appear before the Commissioners and who would head the advice and advocacy branch) would be chosen from amongst the ranks of senior advisors but there should also be direct entry at the level of local chairmen from suitably qualified outsiders such as barristers and solicitors. Similarly, MAT chairmen (who would have to travel on circuit within regions) and Commissioners would be drawn from the ranks of local chairmen and suitably qualified outsiders. MAT chairmen would, of course, qualify for appointment as Commissioners. The Chief Commissioner, who would head the entire service, would be appointed from the Commissioners. Entry after the initial stage (as clerks) i.e. at local chairman, MAT chairman or Commissioner level, should be exceptional. Mere experience as a barrister or solicitor ought not to suffice.

A POSSIBLE CAREER STRUCTURE FOR A
SOCIAL SECURITY ADJUDICATION SERVICE

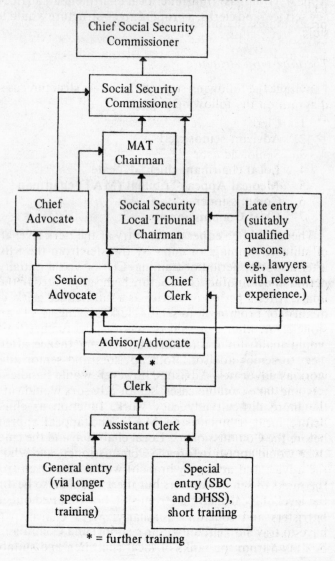

* = further training

Transitional arrangements

If Commissioners are going to take on what is presently SB work, their ranks will need to be swelled immediately. There is no reason why the ranks of the better SBAT and NILT chairmen should not be drawn on for this purpose, as well as appointing via the existing channels. Similarly, fewer local chairmen and MAT chairmen will be needed. Existing personnel might satisfy all or some of the need. Any shortfall would need to be made good by recruitment from the legal professions. Pending the establishment of suitable training programmes, the ranks of clerks, senior clerks, advisors and senior advisors would be filled from amongst the existing personnel of the SBC and DHSS. There is at present a half-hidden wealth of talent here. A great deal of review work, requiring a fairly sophisticated knowledge of social security law, is presently handled within the SBC and the Department. Much of it is not, properly-speaking, review work at all, but rather appeal work. To the extent that it proved impossible to solve the transitional problem from this source, there is a case for making much greater use of the £25 scheme under the Legal Advice and Assistance Act 1972 and for a strictly temporary extension of legal aid to SST work.

Conclusion

I am sensitive of the dangers which many may feel would attend the establishment of an adjudicative service which would be largely severed from the existing branches of the legal profession. Even if their existing training and experience equip lawyers singularly inadequately for social security work, nevertheless there may be something in their tradition of independence which is of great value to the claimant. The obverse of this is that a state-run and financed adjudicative and advice service will inevitably become bureaucratised and that an attempt to establish such a service would yield yet another "we and they" situation. These are real risks, but my judgement is that, given the will, the evils could be avoided. Experience in United Kingdom law schools today (and, I trust, in other places) teaches one that there is no dearth of talented people who are socially conscious and who would bring to the job a genuine desire to serve. The problem is one of tapping these sources.

NOTES

1. See M. Penelope Hall, *The Social Services of Modern England*, 6th edn., p. 54.
2. Strangely the duty in s.3(1) of the 1966 Act is not thrust expressly upon SBATs, but presumably it is imported by s.18(3) which authorises the SBAT

on an appeal to substitute for the SBC's decision any decision which the SBC could have made.
3.   1966 Act. s.4(1).
4.   S.4(2) and Sched. 2, para. 3.
5.   Sched. 2, para 5(2); s.10 and Social Security Act 1971.
6.   Sched. 2, para. 20(c).
7.   Sched. 2, paras. 9 and 10.
8.   Road Traffic Act 1960, s.74; Trade Union and Labour Relations Act 1974, sched. 1, para. 3.
9.   See SB (Appeal Tribunal) Rules, 1971, S.I. 680, r.11.
10. Report of Council on Tribunals for 1972-3, para. 7.
11. Franks Report, Cmnd. 218, 1957, paras. 41 and 180.
12. SB (Appeal Tribunal) Rules 1971, r.12.
13. *Re Poyser and Mills' Arbitration* [1963] 1 All E.R. 612; and see Commissioner's Decision R(A) 1/72 dealing with the statement of reasons under the Attendance Allowance Regulations 1971, S.I. 621, reg.14(2).
14. Report of Council on Tribunals for 1972-3, paras. 70-72 and Appendix B.
15. Franks Report, para. 41.
16. 1966 Act, Sched. 2, para. 6.
17. Comments of the Lord Chancellor's Advisory Committee on the 24th Report of the Law Society on Legal Aid and Advice, Nov. 1974 (H.C. 20).
18. Cf. 1966 Act, sched. 3, para. 3(1) and National Insurance Act 1965, s. 77.

XV CONCLUSION
Michael Adler and Anthony Bradley

Previous chapters have sought to explain the historical development of tribunals in the supplementary benefits scheme; to examine
the concepts of discretion and entitlement in the scheme; to consider the present functioning and operation of the tribunals; and to
suggest some possible reforms. We believe that there is ample evidence in this volume and elsewhere for the view that the system of
SBATs is not functioning as well as it should. Of course this does
not mean that SBATs are a complete failure, nor that many SBATs
do not handle some cases well, nor that all claimants before SBATs
come away dissatisfied. But at present there is more criticism of
SBATs than of any other tribunal in Britain. Inevitably, whatever
precise role they may serve in the supplementary benefits scheme, it
is *as tribunals* that they will be judged, particularly by researchers
and experienced representatives of claimants who have experience
of other tribunals in action.

Since the Franks Report in 1957, the place of tribunals in the
machinery of justice in Britain has been clarified. But this does not
mean that there are absolute standards of procedure or court-like
behaviour to which tribunals must conform. The effectiveness of a
class of tribunals cannot be judged in isolation from the scheme of
administration with which it is associated. Thus SBATs must also
be judged *as part of the social security system*. They would not be
functioning effectively if in attitude or behaviour they were running
contrary to the objectives which underlie the supplementary benefits scheme. It is one of the principal arguments in this concluding
chapter that the place of tribunals within the supplementary benefits scheme has never been made clear, by contrast with, say, the
function of tribunals within the national insurance scheme where
the purpose of the tribunals is to ensure that the statutes and
regulations which affect the insured person are correctly applied to
his circumstances.

In the absence of any clear delineation of the function of SBATs, we believe that their present structure can be understood only by reference to the previous history of adjudication of disputes about means-tested income assistance in Britain (chapters 1 and 2). Apart from a superficial examination by the Franks Committee, available evidence suggests that their structure has not been publicly re-examined since it was first settled in 1934.

Not even the growth of the welfare rights movement in Britain has brought about an official re-examination of these tribunals. Yet the 1966 Act itself gave ample support to this movement by establishing for the first time a statutory right to means-tested benefit. In establishing this right, the Government of the day was probably most concerned with the problems of old people, many of whom were reluctant to claim national assistance because of the poor law associations which that scheme held for them. But the new statutory right was not restricted to the elderly. Although the 1966 Act was intended to end the sharp distinction between contributory and means-tested benefit, very little administrative integration has in fact taken place, and no attempt was made to integrate the contributory and means-tested tribunal structures. Yet the nature and quality of "entitlement" largely depend on the procedures by which rights may be enforced and appeals taken against official decisions.[1]

The continued existence of two sharply contrasted tribunal structures has resulted in the perpetuation of a number of discrepancies. For example, as the Fisher Committee on the Abuse of Social Security Benefits pointed out, the national insurance and supplementary benefit systems each contain a cohabitation rule. Since these two systems of administration are matched by two different schemes of adjudication, the situation may arise, if a widow is in receipt both of widow's benefit and of supplementary benefit, where two different outcomes result from the same facts.[2] And the law at present provides no way of resolving the conflict.

Whether as a direct result of the welfare rights movement, or as a result of the realisation that the contributory and means-tested schemes are complementary to each other, it is increasingly recognised that the supplementary benefits scheme is part of the law and is not merely a matter for administrative discretion. Thus in the Family Division of the English High Court, in *Reiterbund* v. *Reiterbund*,[3] the late Sir Morris Finer declared that supplementary benefits have become part of family law with which all legal practitioners must be familiar: "The whole emphasis of the present law and its administration is to insist that supplementary benefits are the subject of rights and entitlement, and that no shame attaches to the receipt of them". And in a very recent series of High Court decisions, the work of SBATs has come under judicial review.[4]

A further pressure towards legalisation of the supplementary benefit system derives from the increasingly forthright demands of the recipients of benefit which can be attributed to the welfare rights movement. Through the Child Poverty Action Group and other pressure groups, community action projects, neighbourhood law centres, claimants' unions, self-help organisations which meet the needs of particular groups such as the disabled or one-parent families, trade unions who take up claims to benefit for strikers' dependants and through numerous other organisations, the civic and legal competence of the citizen[5] is supported in his or her dealings with the SBC. The citizen is encouraged to appeal to law; this, in Nonet's analysis, is to hold authority accountable to rules and to found demands upon reasons derived from rules. According to Nonet, "an important aspect of legal competence is the capacity for independent criticism of authority on the basis of reason and the law".[6] Thus the citizen and the organisations which support him contribute to the process of legalisation in a welfare agency by seeking authoritative justification of official decisions, by requesting that decisions be based on rules and principles which will bear public scrutiny and discussion, and on rules rather than policies. The concepts of right and entitlement seek to diminish official reliance on unpublished policies which the public has played no part in formulating.

In this situation, a claimant's dissatisfaction may be based on the substance of the rule which has been applied in his case or on the treatment he has received from DHSS officials, but in either case he will be inclined to pursue rights of appeal open to him. Although the particular cause of dissatisfaction may not be a matter which the tribunal can remedy, discontent may readily widen to include the legitimacy of the appeal procedure itself.

The present structure of SB appeals appears to assume that a claimant's affairs are so private that he or she will not discuss them with another. But this is increasingly unrealistic because of the group activities already mentioned. As rights organisations acquire wider experience and a larger clientele, they may assist a claimant in his appeal not merely to help him but also to obtain an authoritative determination of the position of others similarly placed. If the determination is favourable to the claimant, the organisation will seek to secure the same result for other claimants in the same situation. If it is unfavourable, the organisation may seek to alter the ruling by political pressure or to get round it by seeking to establish distinguishing or exceptional circumstances in later cases. (For that matter, the Government responds in a somewhat similar way, as the subsequent history of the *Simper* case shows).[7] Yet SBATs sit in private; their decisions are not published and have no effect as precedent. Although they must in law give reasons for decisions, the reasons are often perfunctory and uninformative.

A classic illustration of the conflict inherent in such a situation was provided by the case of the prisoner's wife taken up by CPAG in 1968. Prison rules allowed a monthly visit from the wife to the prison. The internal rules of the SBC at that time allowed her a travel warrant only once every two months. The appeal to a tribunal for a monthly warrant succeeded but the success did not directly benefit other prisoners' wives: unless the SBC had brought its rules into line with Home Office policy, every other prisoner's wife would have had to appeal to her own local tribunal in the hope of the same success, but with no certainty that her tribunal would also be disposed to depart from SBC policy.

Another example is the uncertainty of the position regarding extra heating costs (discussed by Henry Hodge in chapter 5). When a claimant can show on an appeal that his actual heating costs are significantly greater than those allowed by the SBC's own rules, the tribunal may at its discretion allow the actual costs to be paid, confirm the SBC's allowance or award an intermediate figure. At present, there is no machinery for securing that this discretion is exercised in a reasonably consistent manner by different tribunals.

Discretion exercised in such circumstances can lead only to arbitrary decisions. How can variation between the attitudes of different tribunals not cause relative injustice?

While certain types of appeal (e.g. for clothing grants or extra heating) may come in sufficient number for each tribunal to develop its own policies, other appeals, e.g. from prisoners' wives, are unlikely to come before the same tribunal often enough for a body of experience to be developed. In the absence of direct procedures for helping to secure consistency, indirect means operate — through the control which the Department exercises in the appointment of chairmen and members, the overt influence of the presenting officer as spokesman for the SBC's policies and the covert influence of the clerk, who will be more familiar with SBC's policies from the inside than are the chairman and members. It is not surprising, as Steve Burkeman records in chapter 7, that attempts are being made in some cities for this indirect influence to be countered by claimants' organisations seeking to awaken Trades Council members on the tribunals to the use which they could make of their position to assist claimants.

A strong and reasoned justification can be given, as it was by Richard Wilding in chapter 4, for the administrative use made of the Commission's discretionary powers. It seems that the SBC is actively developing the welfare context of its operations.[8] But what in all this is the role of the appeal tribunals?

The evidence contained in previous chapters suggests that the rationale of SBATs as they presently operate could perhaps be expressed in the following way. SBATs act as an informal safety-valve for claimants who are dissatisfied with the way their claims for benefit have been decided by officials. When the citizen does not accept the civil servant's decision, he may have his claim considered by three members of the public sitting as a local tribunal. Their function is to ensure:

(1) that the decision made falls broadly within the scope of the Act and regulations;
(3) that the claimant has the opportunity of a personal hearing to bring forward evidence of hardship; and
(4) that the final decision can reasonably be supported in terms of the tribunal's perception of social justice within the supplementary benefits scheme.

Where the Commission's decision is confirmed, the tribunal's seal of approval may make the decision more acceptable to the claimant and thereby help to assure him that every possible consideration has been given to his case.

However, the available evidence also suggests both that the tribunals fail to perform even this somewhat minimal role at all satisfactorily, and that this minimal function is no longer adequate.

In addition to the limited protection that SBATs offer to the aggrieved claimant, it must not be forgotten that the very existence of the tribunals also serves to protect civil servants and the Department from the full weight of public criticism that might otherwise fall upon them, and to protect Ministers from having to justify decisions on individual claims in Parliament. An acute observer of the Unemployment Assistance Board in the 1930s wrote, "Formally the Appeal Tribunals might be justified as a protection to the individual applicant for assistance, as a guarantee that his case had been adequately considered and that he had not had to rely solely on the decision of a local official of the central Government. But the Unemployment Assistance Board well appreciated that these tribunals were *even more a protection to themselves* (i.e. to the Board)".[9] In our view, the value to the Government of being able to turn political criticism aside with a reference to the right of appeal to an independent tribunal far outweighs the price that would have to be paid if appeal tribunals made full and independent use of the powers which in law belong to them. Because of their important political function, it ought to be in the Government's interest to ensure that they function effectively.

Responsibility for the tribunals

One problem that makes reform of tribunals more difficult than reform of most pieces of administrative machinery springs from a false understanding of judicial independence. The Government is not responsible for the decisions of courts and tribunals, but it is responsible for the structure of the machinery of justice. If SBATs are not functioning satisfactorily because of structural weaknesses in the system, there is nothing in the much-stressed impartiality or independence of the tribunals to absolve the DHSS from responsibility for taking steps to improve the position. This constitutional responsibility of the Department is sometimes obscured by the existence of other bodies or agencies which could be thought to have some responsibility. However, responsibility of the SBC itself (as distinct from the DHSS) does not include the tribunals. The Council on Tribunals may be some kind of watch-dog over the functioning of existing tribunals[10] but it has no executive powers, is starved of resources and is reluctant to intrude into matters of departmental policy. The Lord Chancellor's Department has some general interest in the working of tribunals in England and Wales, but is again unable to match the resources and expertise of the DHSS. The Parliamentary Commissioner for Administration is not able to investigate the procedures or decisions of tribunals. In the British system of government, while occasionally MPs may debate the functioning of tribunals,[11] they are kept at arms' length from taking legislative initiatives in departmental affairs. The civil courts are able to intervene when a manifestly unlawful decision is made by a tribunal but apart from this have no responsibility for tribunals. It is with the Department of Health and Social Security that responsibility for reform lies.

Principles underlying a reformed tribunal system

If the tribunals were seen by all concerned to be functioning satisfactorily, it would not matter that their role had not been defined. As it is, we believe that the role of the tribunals needs to be clarified in order that their working may be improved. We suggest that a tribunal ought to ensure:

(1) that the decision which it makes is a correct application of the Act and regulations to the facts of the claimant's case as established before it;

(2) that, unless there are circumstances which make it inappropriate, the decision is a proper application of the Commission's established policy;

(3) that the claimant not only has the legal right of a personal hearing and of being represented, but also is enabled through the provision of adequate advice and assistance to have his case presented fully to the tribunal; and

(4) that, where the personal circumstances of the claimant justify departure from Commission policy, the tribunal should be able to exercise a residual discretion to alleviate financial hardship, guided by the tribunal's perception of social justice.

The effect of these principles should be to enable SBATs to dispense a standard of justice no lower than that prevailing in national insurance tribunals. They are also consistent with the 1966 Act and the principles upon which it is based.

Possible approaches to reform

Four possible approaches may be suggested.

(1) By administrative means, improvements could be made to the system so that the present tribunals worked somewhat better. Attempts could be made to secure better calibre chairmen and members, to provide some form of training and arrange conferences, to give different instructions to clerks, to extend the publication of SBC policies and so on. This appears to have been the cautious response of the DHSS to recent criticisms. But there are severe limits to what this approach can achieve and it is doubtful whether the speed of the response matches the seriousness of the criticisms.

(2) By a combination of legislative and administrative means, to take steps to improve the structure of tribunals within the Supplementary Benefit scheme e.g. by the creation of a second-tier tribunal, by providing an appeal on points of law to the courts, by introducing new statutory requirements for the appointment of chairmen and members. By this approach (which is advocated by Ruth Lister in chapter 13) the position of tribunals within the SB scheme would be improved: but the nature of the SB scheme would not be affected and reform would do nothing to integrate SB tribunals with other social security tribunals.

(3) By a broader use of legislative means, the functioning of social security tribunals as a whole could be reviewed with the aim of creating an integrated system of tribunals for all social security purposes, headed by a national appellate tribunal (as advocated by Harry Calvert in chapter 14). This approach would with

advantage run counter to what seems to have been the preference of DHSS for proliferating rather than integrating tribunals, but it would be a massive operation to carry through. A
lesser and easier variant would be to transfer SB appeals to the
National Insurance Local Tribunals and the National
Insurance Commissioners (as proposed in chapter 9). This
course has much to commend it but is not without possible
disadvantages.

(4) Any of the foregoing approaches could be accompanied by a different but no less urgent inquiry, namely to reconsider the role
of supplementary benefits within the whole scheme of social security. Is too much at present being asked of the SB scheme? If
so, ways should be devised of reducing the numbers dependent
on means-tested benefits e.g. by improving the benefit rates and
coverage of the National Insurance scheme, by establishing
new, non-contributory, non means-tested benefits (for the disabled or for one-parent families) or by adopting schemes for tax-
credits or negative income tax. Additionally, or alternatively,
the SBC could be stripped of its discretionary powers, and
responsibility for awarding ECAs and ENPs could be vested in
the social service departments of local authorities.

Of these various approaches, we believe that approach (1), even if
pursued more energetically than it appears to be at present, would
be inadequate. Approach (4) raises broad issues of social policy
which do not turn essentially on the tribunal question. While we do
not wish to reject (3), it would go beyond the scope of this chapter to
examine in detail all its implications for the social security system.
We therefore conclude this chapter by examining some essential
issues that would arise if approach (2) were adopted, while leaving
open the possibility of transferring SB appeals to a modified
national insurance adjudication system.

Reform of the supplementary benefit tribunals

We now summarise the reforms which we believe would be necessary to give effect to the principles outlined above.

1. At present SBATs are administered and serviced by officials of
    the DHSS. This responsibility should be transferred to a differ-
    ent agency to strengthen both the real and apparent indepen-
    dence of the tribunals from departmental control. The new
    agency might be called the Social Security Tribunals Service if
    similar responsibility for other tribunals were also transferred
    to it from DHSS.
2. Responsibility for appointments to SBATs should be placed on
    the new Service. The composition of the tribunals should be

reformed. The same method of appointment should be adopted for all members and there should be no separate appointment of chairmen. All members, including those who serve as chairmen at tribunal hearings, should be treated alike in such matters as the payment of fees and expenses. Nominations for membership of local panels should be invited from a wide range of national and local organisations, including e.g. community groups and one-parent family groups, as well as Trades Councils. Local panels should contain a stronger professional element than at present (law and social work are the relevant professions) and also be more widely representative; thus panels should contain an equal number of men and women. For the purpose of hearing appeals, tribunals should consist of three panel members, and should designate their own chairman. All tribunals which did not include a legal member should have access to an independent legal assessor.

3. The Social Security Tribunals Service should be responsible for ensuring that adequate training for all members of local panels was provided, by arrangement with selected universities, polytechnics and colleges of further education.

4. The Social Security Tribunals Service would be responsible for recruiting, appointing and training the tribunal clerks, whose entire responsibility would be to the tribunals to which they are allotted. Serving members of DHSS would be eligible for transfer to the Service.

5. Since the re-constituted tribunals would be functioning on a local basis then, even with opportunities for training and regular meetings of local panels, some mechanism for securing reasonable consistency and the observance of minimum procedural standards would be needed. There should be a further right of appeal to a national tribunal which would sit when required at regional centres. A difficult question is whether the further right of appeal should be unrestricted or restricted. Various restrictions are possible: e.g.

    (a) by requiring leave for appeal to be given, either by the local tribunal itself or by the national tribunal;

    (b) by confining appeals to points of law (including statutory interpretation, matters of procedure, evidence and burden of proof);

    (c) by allowing appeals only in certain types of case (e.g. cohabitation, repayment of over-paid benefit); or

    (d) by excluding appeals in certain types of case (e.g. exceptional needs payments).

The difficulty with any restriction is that the claimant would almost certainly be unable to understand for himself whether or not he could appeal further. Particularly important would be the treatment of issues of discretion. An appeal would certainly be appropriate against the improper exercise of discretion (e.g. failure to take account of all relevant considerations) but not necessarily against every discretionary decision. Possibly the right approach would be to allow a full right of appeal, with the national tribunal having the power to discourage appeals which were simply against the merits of a discretionary decision unless some additional evidence or other factor justifying intervention could be stated in the form of appeal. We believe it should be possible for the SBC to appeal against the decision of a local tribunal (although we do not expect that the Commission would do so except for very strong reasons) but we suggest that this should be subject to suitable arrangements for the interim payment of urgently needed benefit which had been awarded by the local tribunal, as at present in the National Insurance scheme.[12]

6. The national tribunal would give authoritative guidance to local tribunals on matters of law and it therefore should include senior lawyers. But there is a case, even at this level, for including the contribution which those with special knowledge relevant to problems of poverty can make to adjudication.

7. Selected decisions of the national tribunal would be published. They would serve a double purpose: (a) to give binding directions to local tribunals on matters of law and procedure, and (b) to give guidance to local tribunals in the exercise of discretion.

8. From the national tribunal, there should be a further right of appeal on matters of law, preferably to the Court of Appeal in England and to the Inner House of the Court of Session in Scotland, or alternatively to a nominated judge of each court.

9. An essential accompaniment to the new system of tribunals would be to increase the provision of advice and assistance to claimants in connection with possible appeals. We doubt whether the extension of the statutory legal aid scheme to include representation at tribunals would be sufficient to meet this need.

Relationship between legal rules, administrative policies and discretion

Reform of the tribunal structure would make it necessary to re-examine and to clarify the present relationship between statutory rules, SBC policies and the discretion of tribunals. We summarise the present position before making proposals for reform.

At present, the provisions of the 1966 Act and of regulations made under that Act, as interpreted by the courts, are binding on the SBC and on tribunals. The Act received Parliamentary approval; the regulations have received indirect Parliamentary approval since they are required to be laid before Parliament. But the SBC's own publications, like the Supplementary Benefit Handbook, do not have legal force. While they may be used by claimants at an appeal to support their arguments, they do not bind tribunals or the SBC. While these publications could be the subject of Parliamentary discussion, they do not need Parliamentary approval. In addition, there are the internal administrative codes (e.g. the A Code) intended solely for use by officials of the SBC, which are unpublished and secret. Not even MPs are allowed to see the Codes. In view of their secret nature, it would be wrong of any tribunal ever to rely on them even at the request of a claimant who had somehow managed to see a copy. Yet the exercise of discretion in local offices is controlled and directed by the detailed rules which these codes contain.

We believe that the SBC should publish the detailed policy rules on which the exercise of discretion is based. This would subject these policy rules to the possibility of democratic scrutiny and open discussion. This does not mean that the SBC should publish its internal rules on administrative procedure and office management which at present may also be included in departmental codes. Nor does publication mean that the policy rules need be put into legalistic wording, nor that the grid of rules should become so fine a mesh that no scope for discretion remained. In particular, it would need to be made explicit that individual circumstances might arise which would justify an outcome different from that indicated by the general rule. These various purposes would be served by the publication of a Supplementary Benefit Code. In discretionary matters, a tribunal could legitimately express decisions in the following forms:

(1) "This case falls within the general policy laid down in the Code and we are not satisfied that a different result would be justified by the following personal circumstances or special factors which were submitted by the claimant: ..." (Appeal disallowed.)

(2) "Although the SBC considered that there were in this case the following special circumstances which justified treatment less favourable to the claimant than that contemplated by the Code, we consider that the case properly falls within the general policy in the Code and benefit is therefore awarded." (Appeal allowed.)

(3) "Although the SBC considered that this case fell within a provision.in the Code according to which benefit should be withheld, we consider that by reason of the following facts personal to the claimant, it would be right to pay benefit here." (Appeal allowed.)

It would be essential for the local tribunal to specify in each case the special circumstances alluded to. It would be for the national tribunal to give guidance to local tribunals on the nature of the personal circumstances which would justify different treatment from that envisaged in the Code.

Local tribunals would thus be able to rely on the following published sources, each carrying appropriate authority: (a) Acts of Parliament; (b) statutory regulations; (c) the Supplementary Benefit Code; (d) selected decisions of the national tribunal; and also (e) decisions of the superior courts on appeal from the national tribunal.

The SBC would continue to maintain its own internal instructions for administrative purposes only but the scope of these would be very much less extensive than the present A-code and their non-publication would cease to be a matter of controversy. Sources (a) to (c) above would be subject to Parliamentary discussion and where necessary to Parliamentary approval. The SBC would be required to follow decisions of the national tribunal and of the courts, until steps had been taken to amend the Acts, regulations or Code, as the case might be.

The result would be a structure for the exercise of discretion which we believe would conform with the principles outlined above and increase public knowledge of the process of decision-making. There is no reason why the structure should produce excessive rigidity or legalism, or force officials to disregard established human need.[13]

NOTES

1   Cf. Lynes, *Penguin Guide to SB*, 1974, pp 23-26.
2   Fisher Report. Cmnd. 5228, 1973, chap. 13.
3   [1974] 2 All E.R. 455.
4   *Simper's* case [1974] Q.B. 543, *Moore's* case [1975] 2 All E.R. 807, *Taylor's* case [1975] 2 All E.R. 790, *Clarke's* case, *The Times*, 31 July 1975.
5   For a discussion of this concept, see P. Nonet, *Administrative Justice*, 1969, chap. 4.
6   Nonet, p. 84.
7   For discussion of the Government's response to the *Simper* case, see Christopher Smith, "Discretion or Rule of Thumb?", *New Law Journal*, 22 Mar. 1973, p. 267 and "Discretion or Legislation", *New Law Journal*, 7 Mar, 1974, p. 219.

8   Olive Stevenson, *Claimant or Client?*, 1973.

9   John D. Millett, *The Unemployment Assistance Board*, 1940, p. 250 (italics supplied); and chapter 2 above.

10   A distinctly leisurely watch-dog, on the evidence of Ruth Lister, *Council Inaction*, CPAG Report, June 1975.

11   See the brief debate on SBATs. 26 Feb. 1975, H. C. Deb., cols. 662-72.

12   National Insurance Act 1965, s.81 and NI (General Benefit) Regulations 1970, S.I. 1981, regulation 13.

13   In October 1975, when this book had reached an advanced stage of publication, the DHSS published a *Review of Main Findings, Conclusions and Recommendations* of a research study on SBATs carried out by Professor Kathleen Bell, of the University of Newcastle upon Tyne. Although her recommendations differ from ours in many detailed respects, we agree with her view that there is "an unanswerable case for a comprehensive review as a matter of urgency" (page 20). We believe, however, that proposals for reform need to include a consideration of a number of issues which were clearly outside the scope of her research, for example the legislative and administrative structure of the SB scheme, and which we have sought to discuss in this book.

APPENDIX A

*Number of Appeals heard by SBATs, NILTs and
the National Insurance Commissioners 1960–1973*

Year	National Assistance/ Supplementary Benefit Appeal Tribunals	National Insurance Local Tribunals	National Insurance Commissioners
1960	7,757	41,139	2,775
1961	14,922	39,731	2,421
1962	10,043	42,561	2,368
1963	9,998	42,435	2,562
1964	9,735	37,447	2,626
1965	9,582	37,601	2,665
1966	12,335	36,409	2,500
1967	15,265	38,590	2,336
1968	19,905	36,514	2,510
1969	22,437	34,812	2,459
1970	28,717	35,641	2,576
1971	29,648	29,334	2,261
1972	36,051	35,903	2,189
1973	26,002	29,477	2,039

Note 1 : The figures are drawn from the annual reports of the Council on
Tribunals. In the case of supplementary benefit appeals, very
considerable disparities exist between these figures and those
contained in the annual reports of the DHSS and more recently
in *Social Security Statistics*. No complete explanation for these
disparities is available.

Note 2 : From 1967 SBAT totals include a small number of appeals under
section 6, Selective Employment Payments Act 1966.

Note 3 : From 1971 SBAT totals include appeals under the Family Income
Supplements Act 1970 : in 1971 there was 1,753 FIS appeals; in
1972, 2,309; and in 1973, 1,515.

Note 4 : The National Insurance figures include industrial injuries appeals
and in the case of the National Insurance Commissioners also
appeals from medical appeal tribunals on points of law.

APPENDIX B

Judicial review of tribunal decisions

Social security legislation since 1945 has applied throughout Great Britain. But because the background of common law differs between England (and Wales) and Scotland, this explanatory note deals with the two jurisdictions separately. For a fuller account reference may be made to R.E. Wraith and P.G. Hutchesson, *Administrative Tribunals*, 1973, App. I.

English Law

At common law, every tribunal with a limited jurisdiction is subject to control by the High Court on the following grounds.

A.   If the tribunal exceeds its jurisdiction (e.g. by making an order beyond its statutory powers).

B.   If it acts contrary to natural justice i.e. if its decision is biased, or if a party has been denied a fair hearing (e.g. by the tribunal receiving evidence behind the back of the claimant).

C.   If it fails to perform its statutory duty (e.g. if it fails to give reasons, where this is a statutory requirement).

D.   If it wrongly fails to exercise its jurisdiction (e.g. by refusing to consider an appeal properly brought before it).

E.   If it commits an error of law, either by wrongly applying a rule of common law (e.g. as to the existence of a contract of letting) or by wrongly interpreting a statutory provision. The concept of error of law is elastic: it may include failure to take into account all relevant considerations; taking into account irrelevant considerations (e.g. the colour of a claimant's hair); making a decision which there is no evidence to support (e.g. refusing on mere suspicion to accept a claimant's account which is supported by evidence); and making a decision which on the evidence available no reasonable tribunal could make. But it is not an error of law to make a decision which there is some evidence to support, nor to exercise discretion in a manner which a claimant may consider unduly severe.

Thus judicial review at common law is essentially based on rules of jurisdiction, natural justice and matters of law. The scope of review is much narrower than a full right of appeal on the facts or on the merits of a case, which permits a complete rehearing (e.g. the appeal which lies from national insurance local tribunals to the National Insurance Commissioners).

The remedies which at common law enable the High Court to

exercise its supervision of tribunals are the prerogative orders:

(1) Certiorari, which has two main purposes: (i) to quash decisions which are in excess of jurisdiction or in breach of natural justice; (ii) to quash decisions for "error of law on the face of the record" i.e. for errors of law which are disclosed on the face of the decision or on documents incorporated with the decision (e.g. the Presenting Officer's written submissions, if these are expressly confirmed by the tribunal).

(2) Mandamus, to enforce the performance of a public duty owed to the applicant.

(3) Prohibition, to bar a tribunal from considering a case which manifestly lies beyond its jurisdiction.

These remedies are granted by the Queen's Bench Divisional Court in London.

The 1948 Act provided in section 14(4) that decisions of an appeal tribunal were "conclusive for all purposes". One aim of this section was probably to protect National Assistance Tribunal (NAT) decisions from judicial review at common law. Its precise effect would have been difficult to determine but the High Court was never asked to interpret the clause. If the clause simply meant, "There shall be no appeal to the High Court from an NAT", the clause was unnecessary, since appeal to the High Court from a tribunal exists only where statute provides for it. If, at the other extreme, it meant, "All the common law powers of the High Court to supervise NATs are totally excluded", it would have had the draconian effect of making each NAT complete master of its own jurisdiction, thus enabling the NAT to disregard key provisions of the 1948 Act or the rules of natural justice. Judicial interpretation of similar clauses in other Acts has fluctuated between these two extremes, but it is now settled that a "conclusive for all purposes" clause does not prevent judicial review of a tribunal's decision on grounds of jurisdiction or natural justice i.e. Categories A to D above. Its effect on Category E (error of law) is more problematic: in the past it has usually been considered that an error of law does not in itself cause a tribunal to exceed its jurisdiction, but an important House of Lords decision (*Anisminic Ltd.* v. *Foreign Compensation Commission* [1969] 2 A.C. 147) appears to have established that whenever a tribunal commits an error of law, it thereby exceeds its jurisdiction. Reading back this view of the Anisminic decision into the 1948 Act, section 14(4) would now seem to have had no prejudicial effect on the scope of review.

In the National Insurance Act 1965 (formerly 1946), there is no clause which seeks to make decisions of the National Insurance Commissioners conclusive, but section 75(1) seeks to give finality to

Commissioners' decisions. It is now settled that a finality clause simply means that there is no further right of appeal to the High Court (*R.* v. *Medical Appeal Tribunal, ex parte Gilmore* [1957] 1 Q.B. 574). As the Commissioners habitually give full reasons for their decisions, it is possible by use of certiorari for error of law to seek review in the High Court of the correctness in law of the Commissioners' decisions. Where tribunals such as the SBATs do not habitually give full reasons, the practical scope of certiorari in this respect may be very restricted as it may be difficult to establish what process of legal reasoning (if any) was in fact applied by the tribunal. Since there is a legal duty on SBATs to give reasons for their decisions (S.B. (Appeal Tribunal) Rules 1971, rule 12), it is in law possible by mandamus to enforce the duty to give adequate reasons before seeking certiorari for error of law. But this complex process would involve two successive applications to the High Court. An added practical difficulty is that a tribunal might respond to the mandamus by presenting carefully drafted reasons which were not in the tribunal's mind when it first made the decision, but which might be proof against further judicial review.

· The Franks Committee recommended that in principle there should be an appeal on law to the High Court against all tribunal decisions and this was in general adopted (Tribunals and Inquiries Act 1958, section 9). Where a statutory right of appeal on law is available, many matters which could otherwise be raised by certiorari can be raised on the appeal. Indeed the scope of an appeal on law includes some matters which could not be raised by certiorari (see para. 107 of the Franks Report). Obviously an appeal on law is more convenient.

The Franks Committee recommended, however, that no appeal on law should lie from NATs and the National Insurance Commissioners, and that review of these tribunals should be exercised by certiorari. As stated above, for most purposes certiorari for error of law has been a convenient enough way of seeking review of Commissioners' decisions. The style of these decisions, written by expert lawyers of high standing, naturally is suited to judicial consideration—indeed it could well be argued that Commissioners' decisions should not be reviewed by the Divisional Court but by the more senior Court of Appeal. By contrast the decisions of NATs/ SBATs were and are likely to be scrappy and incomplete, and so obviously lacking in legal style that the Divisional Court might be tempted to say, "what more could a body of laymen administering rough and ready justice be expected to do?" The Simper decision (*R. v. Greater Birmingham Appeal Tribunal, ex parte Simper* [1974] Q.B. 543), was important because the Divisional Court was

not willing to accept such a lax standard. Subsequent judicial decisions have fluctuated in this respect (e.g. *Taylor's* case, [1975] 2 All
E.R. 790 and *Moore's* case [1975] 2 All E.R. 807.)

The Franks Committee's recommendations on these matters
were accepted. No appeal on law from either Commissioners or
NATs were provided by the Tribunals and Inquiries Act 1958. The
1958 Act (section 11(1)) also reinstated certiorari and mandamus to
remove any surviving doubts that "conclusive" and "finality"
clauses had excluded them. From time to time, Commissioners'
decisions have been reviewed by the courts, including the House of
Lords. But only since the 1966 Act, and in a recent handful of
instances, have SBAT decisions been taken into the High Court.
The paradox therefore is that Commissioners' decisions have
received greater judicial scrutiny than the tribunals which badly
need legal guidance.

The effect of the 1966 Act was to put SBATs in broadly the same
position as NATs had been. The imposition in the 1971 Appeal Tribunal Rules of a general duty to give reasons for decisions was poten-
tially of great significance, although the full potential has not yet
been realised. The only complicating factor in the 1966 Act was the
inclusion of a fresh "conclusive" clause in section 18(3): as this was
enacted after the Tribunals and Inquiries Act 1958, section 11 of the
1958 Act could have no effect against the 1966 Act. Thus the 1966
Act revived earlier doubts about the effect of the "conclusive"
clause. In practice, however, the SBC have wisely not sought to protect SBAT decisions behind the "conclusive" clause where jurisdictional issues have been in dispute.

Scotland

Social security tribunals are British institutions, but in Scottish
cases they are subject to the supervisory jurisdiction of the Court of
Session in Edinburgh. What precisely would make a social security
case "Scottish" for this purpose has not been authoritatively settled.
(The fact that appeals from National Insurance local tribunals in
North-East England are often heard by National Insurance Commissioners sitting in Edinburgh would not be sufficient to bring
these appeals within the jurisdiction of the Court of Session). In
principle, the supervisory jurisdiction exercised at common law
over tribunals by the Court of Session is the same as in English law,
at least so far as excess of jurisdiction and natural justice are concerned (Categories A to D above). The essential difference between
English and Scots law is not one of legal principle but of remedy.

The prerogative orders do not exist in Scots law. Instead the Scottish system relies on the ancient remedies of reduction, interdict and declarator and a statutory equivalent to mandamus (Section 91, Court of Session Act 1868). This difference in remedies explains why section 11 of the Tribunals and Inquiries Act 1958 made separate but parallel provision for Scotland.

The main cause of uncertainty in Scots law is the scope of review for error of law. There is no direct equivalent in Scotland to certiorari for error of law on the face of the record. By an action of reduction, it is possible to deal with some clear cases of legal error, especially where these may affect jurisdiction, but there are probably errors of law which in England can be attacked by certiorari but which in Scotland could not be attacked by an action for reduction. Since 1948 there appears to have been no instance where a Scottish decision of the National Insurance Commissioners has been subjected to review in the Court of Session for error of law. But reduction is available against a tribunal's decision where there has been an excess of jurisdiction or a breach of natural justice. The Franks Committee were ill-informed about Scots law, suggesting that the English High Court would have jurisdiction to review Scottish decisions of social security tribunals. But the Committee added (para. 110) that if necessary a Scottish equivalent to certiorari for error of law on the face of the decision should be introduced by legislation. No such legislation has been introduced. The anomaly remains that a claimant for social security in Scotland does not have the same rights to pursue his claim into the superior civil courts as in England.

Conclusions

Both the English and Scottish Law Commissions are engaged on a study of remedies in administrative law, and each may separately propose a new "petition for review" which would replace the prerogative orders in England and, for certain purposes, the Scottish equivalents. In the present context, the simplest reform needed both in England and Scotland would be to provide an appeal on points of law to the civil courts from both national insurance and supplementary benefit tribunals. It would, however, be absurd to provide for an appeal on points of law to the High Court and the Court of Session direct from SBATs as presently constituted, that is from wholly lay tribunals unable to articulate the legal issues relevant to a decision. The question of an appeal to the civil courts on a point of law, while important, is secondary to the urgent need to establish an efficient structure for supplementary benefit appeals within the social security scheme.

Note The Tribunals and Inquiries Act 1971, has replaced the Tribunals and Inquiries Act 1958, without any change in the law. Sections 9 and 11 of the 1958 Act are now sections 13 and 14 of the 1971 Act.

Anthony Bradley

THE CONTRIBUTORS

Michael Adler   is Lecturer in Social Administration at the University of Edinburgh.

Anthony Bradley   is Professor of Constitutional Law at the University of Edinburgh.

Steve Burkeman   works in the City of Liverpool's Area Management Unit; he was previously Director of CHECK Rights Centre, Liverpool. He has contributed to this book in his personal capacity.

Elizabeth Burns   works in the Citizens' Rights Office, Edinburgh.

Harry Calvert   is Professor of Law at University College, Cardiff; he was previously Professor of Law at the University of Newcastle upon Tyne and is the author of *Social Security Law*.

Ross Flockhart   is Director of the Scottish Council of Social Service.

Henry Hodge   is Deputy Director and Solicitor of CPAG; he has published numerous articles on aspects of welfare law.

Rosemary Johnson is Lecturer in Sociology at the University of Edinburgh.

Norman Lewis   is Lecturer in Law at the University of Hull and is the author of "Supplementary Benefit Appeal Tribunals", published in *Public Law,* 1973.

Ruth Lister   is Assistant Director and Research Officer, CPAG, and has written numerous pamphlets and articles, including *Justice for the Claimant*.

Tony Lynes   is a part-time adviser to the Secretary of State for the Social Services; he was formerly the first Secretary of CPAG and is author of *The Penguin Guide to Supplementary Benefits*. He has contributed to this book in his personal capacity.

Coral Milton is a sociologist who was previously a Research Associate in the Legal Advice Research Unit of the Nuffield Foundation.

Martin Partington is Lecturer in Law at the London School of Economics.

Hilary Rose is Professor of Applied Social Studies at the University of Bradford; she was previously a Lecturer in Social Administration at the London School of Economics.

Richard Wilding is an Under-Secretary in the Civil Service Department; he was previously an Assistant Secretary in the Supplementary Benefits Division of DHSS.